STRATEGIC ADVANTAGE

STRATEGIC ADVANTAGE

Challengers, Competitors, and Threats to America's Future

BRUCE BERKOWITZ

In cooperation with the
Center for Peace and Security Studies
Edmund D. Walsh School of Foreign Service
Georgetown University

Georgetown University Press
Washington, D.C.

Georgetown University Press
Washington, D.C.
Georgetown University Press, Washington, D.C. www.press.georgetown.edu
©2008 by Georgetown University Press. All rights reserved. No part of this book may be reproduced or utilized in any form or by any means, electronic or mechanical, including photocopying and recording, or by any information storage and retrieval system, without permission in writing from the publisher.

Library of Congress Cataloging-in-Publication Data

Berkowitz, Bruce D., 1956–
    Strategic advantage : challengers, competitors, and threats to America's future /
Bruce Berkowitz.
      p.   cm.
    Includes bibliographical references and index.
    ISBN 978-1-58901-222-6 (alk. paper)
    1. National security—United States.   I. Title.
UA23.B419   2008
355'.033073—dc22

                                2008005136

15 14 13 12 11 10 09 08   9 8 7 6 5 4 3 2
First printing

Printed in the United States of America

Figure 2.1 is a reproduction of the original engraving from Gale, *The Making of the Modern World*, first edition. © Gale, a part of Cengage Learning, Inc. Reproduced by permission. www.cengage.com/permissions.

All statements of fact, opinion, or analysis expressed are those of the author and do not reflect the official positions of the CIA or any other U.S. Government agency. Nothing in the contents should be construed as asserting or implying U.S. Government authentification of information or Agency endorsement of the author's views. This material has been reviewed by the CIA to prevent the disclosure of classified information.

To T. G.

CONTENTS

vii

ACKNOWLEDGMENTS

I am glad to have the opportunity to thank several people for their ideas, comments, and support as I wrote this book: Rachel Abrams, James Adams, Thomas Behling, Bruce Bueno de Mesquita, Anthony Downs, Joseph Engelbrecht Jr., Randall Fort, Adam Garfinkle, Grant Hammond, Gregory Ip, John Lehman, Tod Lindberg, Andrew Marshall, Christopher Mellon, Linda Millis, Steven Mufson, John Playfair, G. Bingham Powell, Tim Roemer, Henry Rowen, Kori Schake, Rex Swensen, and Charles Wolf. Funding for this project was provided by the Hoover Institution at Stanford University, whose support was much appreciated. Thanks are also due to Kelley, and, once again, Bob.

STRATEGIC
ADVANTAGE

Challenges

THIS BOOK is intended to help readers better understand the national security issues facing the United States today and offer the general outline of a strategy for dealing with them. National security policy—both making it and debating it—is harder today because the issues that are involved are more numerous and varied. The problem of the day can change at a moment's notice. Yesterday, it might have been proliferation; today, terrorism; tomorrow, hostile regional powers. Threats are also more likely to be intertwined—proliferators use the same networks as narco-traffickers, narco-traffickers support terrorists, and terrorists align themselves with regional powers.

Yet, as worrisome as these immediate concerns may be, the long-term challenges are even harder to deal with, and the stakes are higher. Whereas the main Cold War threat—the Soviet Union—was brittle, most of the potential adversaries and challengers America now faces are resilient. In at least one dimension where the Soviets were weak (economic efficiency, public morale, or leadership), the new threats are strong. They are going to be with us for a long time.

As a result, we need to reconsider how we think about national security. The most important task for U.S. national security today is simply to retain the *strategic advantage*. This term, from the world of military doc-trine, refers to the overall ability of a nation to control, or at least influ-ence, the course of events.[1] When you hold the strategic advantage, situations unfold in your favor, and each round ends so that you are in an advantageous position for the next. When you do not hold the strategic advantage, they do not.

As national goals go, "keeping the strategic advantage" may not have the idealistic ring of "making the world safe for democracy" and does not sound as decisively macho as "maintaining American hegemony." But keeping the strategic advantage is critical, because it is essential for just about everything else America hopes to achieve—promoting freedom, protecting the homeland, defending its values, preserving peace, and so on.

The Changing Threat

If one needs proof of this new, dynamic environment, consider the recent record. A search of the media during the past fifteen years suggests that there were at least a dozen or so events that were considered at one time or another the most pressing national security problem facing the United States—and thus the organizing concept for U.S. national secur-ity. What is most interesting is how varied and different the issues were, and how many different sets of players they involved—and how each was replaced in turn by a different issue and a cast of characters that seemed, at least for the moment, even more pressing. They included, roughly in chronological order,

- regional conflicts—like Desert Storm—involving the threat of war between conventional armies;
- stabilizing "failed states" like Somalia, where government broke down in toto;
- staying economically competitive with Japan;

- integrating Russia into the international community after the fall of communism and controlling the nuclear weapons it inherited from the Soviet Union;
- dealing with "rogue states," unruly nations like North Korea that engage in trafficking and proliferation as a matter of national policy;
- combating international crime, like the scandal involving the Bank of Credit and Commerce International, or imports of illegal drugs;
- strengthening international institutions for trade as countries in Asia, Eastern Europe, and Latin America adopted market economies;
- responding to ethnic conflicts and civil wars triggered by the reemergence of culture as a political force in the "clash of civilizations";
- providing relief to millions of people affected by natural catastrophes like earthquakes, tsunamis, typhoons, droughts, and the spread of HIV/AIDS and malaria;
- combating terrorism driven by sectarian or religious extremism;
- grassroots activism on a global scale, ranging from the campaign to ban land mines to antiglobalization hoodlums and environmentalist crazies;
- border security and illegal immigration;
- the worldwide ripple effects of currency fluctuations and the collapse of confidence in complex financial securities; and
- for at least one fleeting moment, the safety of toys imported from China.

There is some overlap in this list, and one might want to group some of the events differently or add others. The important point, however, is that when you look at these problems and how they evolved during the past fifteen years, you do *not* see a single lesson or organizing principle on which to base U.S. strategy.

Another way to see the dynamic nature of today's national security challenges is to consider the annual threat briefing the U.S. intelligence community has given Congress during the past decade. These briefings are essentially a snapshot of what U.S. officials worry most about. If one briefing is a snapshot, then several put together back to back provide a movie, showing how views have evolved.[2]

Figure 1 summarizes these assessments for every other year between 1996 and 2006. It shows when a particular threat first appeared, its rise and fall in the rankings, and in some cases how it fell off the chart completely. So, in 1995, when the public briefing first became a regular affair, the threat at the very top of the list was North Korea. This likely reflected the crisis that had occurred the preceding year, when Pyongyang seemed determined to develop nuclear weapons, Bill Clinton's administration seemed ready to use military action to prevent this, and the affair was defused by an agreement brokered by Jimmy Carter.

Russia and China ranked high as threats in the early years, but by the end of the decade they sometimes did not even make the list. Proliferation has always been high in the listings, although the particular countries of greatest concern have varied. Terrorism made its first appearance in 1998, rose to first place after the September 11, 2001, terrorist attacks, and remains there today. The Balkans appeared and disappeared in the middle to late 1990s. A few of the entries today seem quaint and overstated. Catastrophic threats to information systems like an "electronic Pearl Harbor" and the "Y2K problem" entered the list in 1998 but disappeared after 2001. (Apparently, after people saw an airliner crash into a Manhattan skyscraper, the possible loss of their Quicken files seemed a lot less urgent.) Iraq first appeared in the briefing as a regional threat in 1997 and was still high on the list a decade later—though, of course, the Iraqi problem in the early years (suspected weapons of mass destruction) was very different from the later one (an insurgency and internationalized civil war).

All this is why the United States needs agility. It not only must be able to refocus its resources repeatedly; it needs to do this faster than an adversary can focus its own resources.

Adversaries with Staying Power

The evidence of the need for endurance is a bit more subtle, but it is there if you look for it. For example, back in the Cold War, the U.S.

Summary of U.S. Intelligence Threat Assessments, 1995–2007

1995	1997	1999	2001	2003	2005	2007

• North Korea
• Russian political and military developments
	• Continuing transformation of Russia and China
	• State threats to regional stability
	• North Korea
	  • Iran
	  • Iraq
	• Transnational issues:
	  • Proliferation
	  • Drug trafficking
	  • Crime
	  • Information system threats
	• Regional hotspots:
	  • Middle East
	  • South Asia
	  • Bosnia
	  • Aegean
	• States and regions with large-scale misery
	  • Ethnic and civil conflict
	  • Refugees
	  • Disease and starvation
		• Transnational issues
		  • Proliferation
		  • Terrorism
		  • Drug trafficking
		  • Information warfare threats and Y2K
		• Russia and China
		• Regional troublemakers
		  • Iraq
		  • North Korea
		  • India/Pakistan
		  • Balkans
		  • Aegean
		  • Haiti
		  • Africa
			• Transnational issues
			  • Terrorism
			  • Proliferation
			  • Information warfare threats and space
			  • Narcotics
			• Regional issues
			  • Israel/Palestine
			  • Iraq
			  • Iran
			  • North Korea
			  • China
			  • Russia
			  • Central Asia
			  • South Asia
				• Terrorism
				• Iraq
				• Proliferation threats:
				  • Iraq
				  • North Korea
				  • Libya
				  • Iran
				  • India/Pakistan
				• Transnational threats:
				  • Impact of Globalization
				  • Latin American populism
				  • HIV/AIDS
				• Other hotspots
				  • Sub-Saharan Africa
				  • Latin America
					• Terrorism
					• Afghanistan
					• Iraq
					• Proliferation
					• Libya
					• North Korea
					• Iran
					• China
					• Russia
					• Potential areas for instability
					  • Middle East
					  • Africa
					  • Latin America
					  • Southeast Asia
						• Global Jihadists
						• Iraq
						• Afghanistan
						• Proliferation
						  • Iran
						  • North Korea
						• Political instability in all areas of the world that affect our interests
						• Globalization and emerging powers
						• Transnational challenges
						  • Energy
						  • Drug trafficking
						  • Possible pandemics

Note: The lines connecting the items above show how an issue rose or fell in its ranking over successive briefings.
Sources: See the text notes.

Embassy in Moscow occasionally sent an end-of-the-year cable back to Washington, hoping to break up the usual routine. It was not an analysis of the latest ups and downs among the Kremlin leadership or an assessment of the latest missile trucked through Red Square in the October Revolution parade. Rather, it was a collection of the latest jokes making the rounds in Moscow. (One sample: "General Secretary Leonid Brezhnev takes a day off to show his mother his city mansion. Later in the afternoon he drives her in his limousine out to his country dacha. That evening they are served a sumptuous dinner. After the servants clear the table, Brezhnev leans back in his chair and boasts, 'Well, Mama, what do you think? Has your son not done well?' His mother nods, and says she is impressed. But then she leans toward him and whispers with concern, 'But Lenya, what if the Bolsheviks come back?'")

These jokes—and the fact that the embassy passed them along— reflected an important underlying truth: Americans knew, at least at some gut level, that despite the Soviet Union's enormous military power, it was, in the larger picture, fundamentally weak. Its economy was hopelessly inefficient. Its citizens had lost faith in their leaders. Its political elite was jaded and cynical.

In fact, we not only believed the Soviets were hollow. We were counting on it. Our grand strategy—containment—was based on that assumption. George Kennan first articulated the idea in his 1946 "long telegram" and his article "The Sources of Soviet Conduct" the following year.[3] American leaders thought that if we could counter the Soviets each time they tried to expand their influence and control, eventually the fault lines within the Soviet Union would cause it to collapse or morph it into something less threatening.

Compare that to today. One rarely hears humor about al-Qaeda, nuclear proliferation, North Korea, the ex-KGB officers who currently run Russia, or the theocratic government of Iran. This is because we understand, at least intuitively, that we are dealing with threats today that are fundamentally different from the one we faced in the Cold War, and no one is prepared to joke about it. Whereas the Soviet Union was brittle, these new threats are resilient. In at least one dimension in which the Soviet Union was fatally weak, each of our current adversaries is remarkably strong. Consider the following three differences and their implications.

Morale and Public Support: The Case of Al-Qaeda

Soviet citizens hated their government so much that the regime had to wall them in to keep them from fleeing. Warsaw Pact "allies" saw the Soviet Union as an occupying power. Except in some corners of academia and the flakier extremes of the political left, Marxist-Leninist ideology had lost any cachet it ever enjoyed by the 1970s or so. Kremlin leaders were old, pampered, faceless apparatchiks, caricatures their people feared, loathed, and laughed at.

Now compare that with al-Qaeda today. Its members are so devoted they are willing to fly aircraft into buildings. They detonate backpack bombs in subways (Madrid, London) and resort hotels (Bali, Casablanca). Young Muslims travel thousands of miles to join the organization. Islamicist websites enjoy huge audiences worldwide, and Osama bin Laden is a revered figure in much of the Muslim world. You can argue that these terrorists are evil, but you do have to admit that they are highly committed.

This is because militant Islamicism, wherever it exists, is a grassroots movement whose members eagerly volunteer, partly because their immediate culture encourages them, and partly because their society provides few alternatives. During the past half century a baby boom in the Middle East and South Asia has produced hundreds of thousands of young Muslim males. Many are alienated and disillusioned because the corrupt, restrictive regimes under which they live do not offer them sufficient opportunities to earn a living or vent political steam. The result is a pool of potential recruits with time on their hands and worries about their future. It is a potent social and economic mix that is sweeping across the Eastern Hemisphere and spilling over into the slums of Europe, where the problem is further complicated by the fact that so many European countries do not want to assimilate Muslims, or do not know how.

Terrorists do not join al-Qaeda because they spend too much time watching al-Jazeera. Rather, al-Jazeera and the scores of Internet sites that lionize bin Laden simply reflect their audiences' existing perspectives. America can launch the slickest public relations campaign to win the hearts and minds of Muslim twentysomethings. But in the real world, an Under Secretary of State for Public Diplomacy and Public Affairs like Karen Hughes has no more chance of convincing these young men to abandon extremism than an al-Qaeda leader like Ayman al-Zawahiri has of convincing an American kid living in Cleveland to cancel his subscription to *Maxim*. It is built into the current culture.

During the Cold War, U.S. military planners assumed that many non-Russian members of the Soviet Army would not fight (or at least not enthusiastically) and that some of the so-called Warsaw Pact allies—Poland, Hungary, Czechoslovakia—might even change sides.[4] By the 1980s the idea of exploiting the fault lines of the Soviet empire was taken for granted.[5] Émigrés and defectors were an important source of intelligence, as were "walk-ins," Soviet bloc officials who offered to provide intelligence on their own initiative. Today, in contrast, if a known al-Qaeda operative were to approach a U.S. official with a briefcase, the American's immediate instinct would likely be to take cover. The entire dynamic is different.

These features give al-Qaeda and similar groups remarkable resilience. In December 2001 al-Qaeda seemed on the ropes. But after lying low for a while, it transformed itself. Today it is a largely virtual organization, even more networked than before. The new al-Qaeda has a minimal, concealed central command and distributes its operations worldwide among cells in Iraq, East and North Africa, Southeast Asia—and Europe. Its websites offer texts, memoirs, magazines, and even video documentaries with high production values.[6]

Economic Efficiency: The Case of China

Now consider China. Like al-Qaeda, it also has a lot more staying power than America's old Soviet opponents, but its strength is in a different dimension—economic. The Soviet Union failed largely because of its cumbersome, inefficient, centrally planned economy. Because the Soviet economy was devoid of incentives and full of discouragement, by the 1980s, the Soviet gross domestic product was flat, and America then twisted the knife by accelerating the arms race. The stalling Soviet economy was a working assumption of U.S. officials as early as 1977, when the Central Intelligence Agency's Directorate of Intelligence reported that "the Soviet economy faces serious strains in the decade ahead. . . . Reduced growth, as is foreshadowed over the next decade, will make pursuit of [the Soviet Union's] objectives much more difficult, and pose hard choices for the leadership."[7]

This was also the view of top U.S. officials. It was built into the Carter administration's Presidential Directive 18, which defined U.S. national strategy. This directive said that, "though successfully acquiring military power matching the United States, the Soviet Union continues to face major internal economic and national difficulties, and externally it has few genuinely committed allies."[8] The Reagan administration took the idea a step further. When Reagan addressed the British Parliament in June 1982, he said that "it is the Soviet Union that runs against the tide of history by denying human freedom and human dignity to its citizens. It also is in deep economic difficulty. The rate of growth in the national product has been steadily declining since the fifties and is less than half of what it was then." The logical path, then, was to leave "Marxist-Leninism on the ash-heap of history."[9]

Now compare that situation with China today. Mao Zedong's heirs may keep his portrait over Tiananmen Square, but they are not foolish enough to follow his economic notions. After Deng Xiaoping defeated the Gang of Four in the late 1970s, China adopted free market reforms. Its economy has expanded at double-digit annual rates ever since.

Yet not only is America unlikely to stress the Chinese economy into oblivion; we do not *want* China to implode like the Soviet Union. The political chaos throughout the Pacific Rim would be unfathomable, the refugee problem would be enormous, and the shelves of Wal-Mart would be empty.

Indeed, the Chinese and American economies are so thoroughly intertwined that it is hard to even consider China a "threat," at least in the conventional sense of the word. The total annual trade between the two countries currently is more than $385 billion, up from $4.9 billion in 1980, when China had just begun adopting market reforms. Today China is our second-largest trading partner (after Canada), our fourth-largest market for exports, and our second-largest source of imports. The *People's Daily* reports that U.S. investments in China total more than $48 billion, distributed in 45,000 projects. The U.S. Treasury reports that China, in turn, holds about $600 billion of the federal debt.[10]

So where U.S. Cold War policy may have been predicated on the Soviet Union imploding, today our national policy is implicitly predicated on *preventing* that from happening in China. Despite its overall strength, several Chinese weaknesses could lead to political crises, which, in turn, would cause major problems for the United States: labor unrest, conflict between the cities and the countryside, a shortage of workers fifteen or twenty years from now resulting from China's population control policies, competition over natural resources from India or Japan—or simply a slowdown in economic growth. China will face more competition from the next tier of modernizing countries, like Vietnam. Already the rate of foreign investment in China has begun to taper off; the rate of foreign investment in China actually dropped in 2006 for the first time since 1990.

Yet the most important factor that defines the relationship between the United States and China is that the leaders of the two countries have exactly the opposite assessment of the same set of facts. U.S. leaders are betting that Chinese citizens will get a taste of economic freedom and demand political freedom to go with it. Americans are also betting that the next generation of Chinese leaders will be compelled to grant these freedoms if they hope to maintain the growth and stability that is necessary for the regime to survive.[11]

Chinese leaders, however, are betting exactly the opposite. They are wagering that they can balance economic freedoms with political controls indefinitely. A comment by Premier Wen Jiabao (second in the

Chinese hierarchy, behind President Hu Jintao) in a February 2007 *People's Daily* editorial made the views of the leadership clear. "We are still far away from advancing out of the primary stages of socialism," Wen wrote, using a euphemism from Marxist theory to say that China had not progressed far enough for the Communist Party to relinquish control. Some officials and writers had speculated that faster reform was needed to defuse the unrest that might accompany the growing disparities in income accompanying China's rapid development.[12] Wen was heading off any debate and made the position of the government clear by saying, "We must stick with the basic development guideline of that stage for 100 years"—referring to the stage that precedes democracy, meaning, in effect, that the Chinese leadership did not anticipate major political reforms for at least another century.

History is likely on America's side. The record shows that countries that modernize usually become democratic. The conditions necessary for modernization (education, freedom of communication, decentralization of decision making) eventually create an environment favorable for democracy.

For now, however, Chinese economic growth means that China has more political clout, more economic influence, and more money to spend on its armed forces. Its defense budget has grown at about the same rate as its gross domestic product. Also, some recent developments are troubling, like its test of an antisatellite weapon in January 2007 and its purchases of modern submarines and fighter aircraft from Russia. These actions suggest that Chinese military planners aim to develop the capability to compete with the United States, at least in their region.[13] But the most important aspect of Chinese economic growth, political influence, and military power is so obvious that it is usually is overlooked: *They are going to be with us for the indefinite future.* Unlike the Soviet threat, there is no logical, conceptual endpoint to the Chinese challenge.

Leadership Sophistication: The Case of Russia

Finally, consider the current regime in Russia. The old Soviet leaders were the best advertisement for containment a Western leader could want. They openly supported revolution abroad. If you happened to forget about their military power, they would obligingly truck their tanks and missiles through Red Square in a May Day parade. And if you were not sure exactly what those tanks and missiles were for, they would stage a military exercise rehearsing an invasion of Western Europe. With the gulag, the ubiquitous secret police, single-ticket elections, and state censorship on everything from political speech to telephone books, the Soviet Union was a villain out of Central Casting. Such a ham-handed adversary made it easier for Western leaders to rally the popular support containment required.

Alas, the strongmen who govern Russia today not only dress better than the old Soviet apparatchiks; they are also smarter and subtler. Little wonder; of the thousand or so top officials in Russia today, about a quarter served in the KGB or its successors—and that is just what their official biographies say. Read between the lines and look for gaps in employment and suspicious assignments, and some experts will say the figure is closer to three-quarters.[14] In essence, a good portion of today's Russian leadership is a semiclandestine network of the most sophisticated, ambitious, well-connected, and ruthless members of the old regime. From their statements, they appear to believe that if the Soviet Union was a failure in any respect, it was mainly in tactics, possibly in strategy, but not in principle. The result of this heritage and mindset: a new, improved autocrat.

Thanks to alcohol, tobacco, and social stress, the average life expectancy for a Russian male today is just fifty-eight years, about ten to fifteen years less than his counterparts in the United States and Western Europe.[15] But Russians blame Mikhail Gorbachev for the Soviet collapse itself, and they link the economic troubles of the early 1990s to privatization, which they blame on oligarchs who profited from the process. The past ten years are seen as a period of recovery and reassertion of national greatness, and that is credited to Vladimir Putin. The skies of downtown Moscow today are filled with construction cranes, the streets are filled with Mercedes-Benz cars, and the traffic gridlock resembles Washington's.

Russian leaders counter their opponents at home in ways that demonstrate just how much more sophisticated they are than the old Soviet leaders. The Soviets jailed dissidents; today's Russian leaders jail oligarchs (who just happen to be the most likely source of an effective opposition). When Putin took control of appointing Russian regional leaders in 2005, he denied having done so, arguing that he only changed the procedures; you had to read the fine print to understand that the new procedures effectively gave the federal executive veto power over appointments.[16] When Russian leaders cracked down on foreign organizations that promoted democracy or monitored freedom, they did not simply ban them. Rather, they enacted a mandatory registration process that achieved the same purpose.[17]

Where the Soviets tried to control the entire economy (killing it in the process), Russia's new elites just corner key market sectors, like oil and gas, using legal maneuvers to seize companies, and then they manage their acquisitions through crony networks. Rather than rebuilding the Soviet-era, state-controlled broadcast media, Russian authorities use legal maneuvers to take effective control of the largest commercial news organizations and strong-arm tactics to intimidate individual journalists.

Russian leaders today have a defter touch, but they are perfectly willing to get tough if they think they need to. Regime opponents do seem to have a way of disappearing, sometimes via mysterious illnesses and conveniently timed accidents. Eleven journalists were murdered between 2002 and 2007; none of the cases were solved.[18] It is a velvet glove / iron fist approach that Tony Soprano would admire.

With oil and gas in cooperative hands, the Russian government can use them to assist Russian foreign policy, and especially in keeping former Soviet states in line. They can sell energy at favorable prices to win friends and withhold supplies to exert control. Russian leaders are so adept at using carrots, sticks, and leashes that they not only maintain control; they even stand for election—and win. Putin was reelected by 71 percent of the voters in 2004, and he likely could have gotten an exemption to constitutional term limits had he wanted to run in 2008.

You can see similar trends elsewhere. Despots learn from each other's mistakes and become more sophisticated all the time. Even the dictators today who do not risk elections, like North Korea's Kim Jong Il and

Libya's Muammar Qadaffi, seem cagier than those of the past. They know when to turn up the heat (and win concessions), as when North Korea launched a half dozen missiles and exploded a nuclear weapon in 2006. They also know when to turn down the heat (and win concessions), as in 2005, when Libya surrendered its nuclear weapons program.

The overall trend is clear. Today America faces adversaries that are more resilient and more adaptable than the Soviet Union ever was.

Two Challenges

Since the Soviet Union collapsed fifteen years ago, scholars and pundits have been looking for a single, integrating organizing concept, like the Cold War–era doctrine of containment, to explain the course of world events and provide a road map for U.S. policy. But if there is any lesson from the recent past, it is that *there is no single organizing concept, and there is not going to be one.* And *that* is exactly what we need to prepare for. America is destined to encounter and confront a continuing stream of varied problems, each requiring a different approach than the one that came before, and many presenting choices that are entirely at odds with each other. National security will, for the foreseeable future, be something that we constantly have to *manage*, adapting as necessary, attending to the urgent threat while maintaining the sense of proportion that ensures us options and the means to stay in the competition for as long as necessary—which is to say indefinitely.

So the task is to design a grand strategy that can deal with this complexity, and build the organization that can carry it out. There are two challenges for the United States. First, *how do we prepare ourselves for an environment where threats can arise and change nature suddenly, and often from unexpected quarters?* This is the immediate, near-term problem and includes such threats as proliferation, terrorism, and flare-ups in regions like the Levant, the Persian Gulf, the Taiwan Strait, and the Korean Demilitarized Zone. It also includes other emergencies, like the potential for political instability as a result of a disaster or a sudden pandemic, which might not seem to involve an adversary but are fast-breaking and require fast action.

The second challenge: *How do we keep up with our geopolitical competitors and retain the political, economic, and cultural influence we have enjoyed for the past century?* This is the long-term problem we face, extending thirty, forty, or fifty years into the future. It has even larger stakes—namely, the fate of nations and the world order. Our success will decide whether the United States can keep its predominant role in the world and set the agenda for world events.

To deal with these two general challenges, U.S. national security policy and organizations need two general qualities. The first is *agility*. In a world where threats can emerge suddenly and change form quickly, we have to be at least as agile as the competition.

The second quality is *endurance*, so we are able to keep our power and influence for as long as necessary—which currently seems likely indefinitely. Endurance, in turn, has two components: *pacing*, so that we do not expend so much of our wealth, manpower, and attention on one problem that we are ill prepared for others; and *growth*, which depends on productivity and promoting the innovation and entrepreneurship that will allow us to keep up with our competitors.

Just as there is no single geopolitical concept explaining the challenges the world presents today, there is also no single solution that will deal with all of them effectively. So forget what you have heard proposed—American hegemony, world community, a bigger military, a stronger UN, closing the borders, expanding free trade, or promoting democracy. None offers a comprehensive fix to all the different national security problems America faces today. Indeed, there are more choices to make than solutions to be found, and national security policy today is something that we need to constantly adapt and adjust, even as we keep an eye on our ideals and long-range goals.

Next, we look at some of the big trends in politics, economics, technology, and society as a whole that are shaping the threats we face today. Then we consider some specific threats and what we must do to deal with them.

CHAPTER ONE

Trends

TODAY'S national security environment is defined by about a half dozen big trends in technology, military affairs, the economy, politics, culture, and demographics that we need to be aware of:

- The information revolution continues to affect just about everything. New technology keeps improving the ability of people to organize for politics, business, mutual inspiration, crime, and war.
- World demographics is changing. Most European populations are getting older and shrinking. Most Asian, African, and Latin American populations are younger and growing bigger. Among industrial nations, the United States is an exception; its population is growing, thanks mainly to immigration, both legal and illegal. These demographic trends are shaping global politics today and will continue to do so.
- Despite globalization, traditional cultures are reasserting themselves. The incentives to remain true to one's tribe remain powerful in most of the world. Ironically, at a time when technology is making it easier to organize on a world scale, the same technology is making it possible for smaller groups to organize more effectively and in a

dispersed fashion. The net result: The traditional nation-state has lost some of the advantages it enjoyed throughout most of the nineteenth and twentieth centuries, allowing older forms of geopolitical organization to make a comeback.

- No one argues that anything other than capitalism and free trade is the most efficient way to organize an economy. Though many people in the world do not believe either is fair, even they accept—if only implicitly, by their behavior—that capitalism and free trade work better than any other approach, best explaining how economic decisions are really made.

With these trends in mind, let us look at them more closely and consider how they are shaping the threats America faces.

Technology Trends

Technology—information technology (IT) in particular—is a good place to start. It is not solely responsible for all the threats and challenges we face, but it does seem interlaced with almost everything that we have to worry about. This is because, even fifty years since the microprocessor was invented, few other things in our lives are changing so much and so fast as information technology.

At the most basic level, the engine driving all this technological change is still Moore's Law. In 1965 Gordon Moore, then an engineer at Fairchild Semiconductor and later one of the cofounders of Intel, observed that the number of switching elements one could design into a microprocessor grew exponentially over time as manufacturing technology improved, and this increased the computing power of the chip at a parallel rate.[1] Experience has borne this out, and Moore's Law continues to chug along, as Figure 1.1 shows. The computing power of the most advanced microprocessor has continued to double about every eighteen to twenty-four months (IT mavens debate the exact rate, but the important thing is that the rate is exponential and continuing).

FIGURE 1.1
Moore's Law

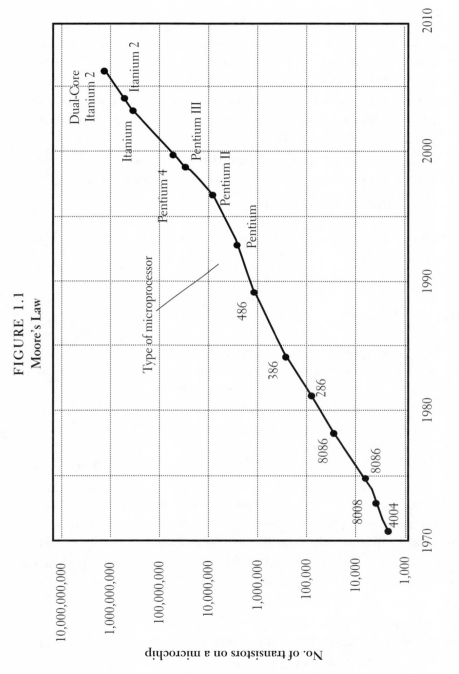

No. of transistors on a microchip

Year

Source: Intel.

Computer memory has followed a similar path: exponentially increasing capability for a given cost, space, or weight. In 1956 a hard disk drive with 5 megabytes of memory cost $50,000, or about $10,000 per megabyte, and had the volume and weight of a kitchen refrigerator. As of 2005, one could buy a 250-gigabyte (250,000-megabyte) hard drive for $250, and it weighed less than a pound. Or, to put it another way, one could buy an MP3 player with two thousand times as much capacity as that refrigerator-sized device, and it was small enough and light enough to clip onto the lapel of your jacket.

The cost of moving data also continues to drop. Thanks to satellites, fiber optics, and cellphones and WiFi, the Internet can be almost everywhere. Connectivity got an unintended boost when major fiber optics and satellite operators like Global Crossing and Iridium went bankrupt, allowing other companies to buy the infrastructure at bargain prices and offer lower rates.

In fact, telecommunications technology is so cheap and ubiquitous that the units used to measure it just a few years ago, like registered Internet domains, are irrelevant. Surveys say that there were about 600 million active Internet users worldwide as of 2005, yet even that understates what is going on, because the term "active Internet user" is itself becoming meaningless. Today almost anyone who uses an electronic communications device is, as often as not, "on the Net." (VoIP, or voice-over Internet protocol—meaning a telephone connected to the Net—is one example.) The technology is built in, interconnected, and inescapable.[2]

Surveys say that only a few people are IT "omnivores," plugged in to the latest gizmo or hooked on the newest gadgets. But this misses the point. The technology revolution is affecting nearly everyone. As IT gets more powerful and cheaper, it filters down into everyday devices and affects more users in more ways. Electronic devices unaffordable ten years ago are now available over the counter, off the rack, and almost everywhere. Populations that were on the fringe of the information revolution ten or fifteen years ago now find themselves in the middle of it.

For example, surveys say that most cellphone owners do not use most of the features on their phone, if they are even aware of what they do.[3] That is not important. What *is* important is that hardly anyone in America had a cellphone in 1987, whereas twenty years later just about everyone did. Similarly, most people do not consider themselves "Net savvy," but everyone uses automated teller machines (ATMs), which are found at nearly every street corner, kiosk, and convenience store. An ATM is a computer connected to the Internet.

It is this filtering-down effect that makes it possible for the organization One Laptop per Child to offer minimalist computers to kids in developing countries for less than $200 apiece—and for competing corporations like Intel and Microsoft to offer their own version, making the technology even more widely available.[4] Further down the technological ladder, wind-up shortwave radios connect the most remote villages in Chad with the outside world. The Internet continues to spread worldwide, node by node, via satellite and fiber, and sooner or later—more likely sooner—everyone will have easy access to information and the ability to use it. Even simple technology can have enormous impact. Those wind-up radios can educate hundreds of thousands of people about simple measures that can reduce malaria, HIV/AIDS, and other diseases—in the process raising countries to new levels of health and prosperity, and transforming demographic trends.

People began to notice how the new technology was changing global politics in the late 1990s when Jody Williams organized a shoestring network that ultimately succeeded in getting the Ottawa Treaty adopted to ban land mines. What was less noticed was how this technology not only pushed power to smaller groups; often the technology could fundamentally alter events even without anyone intending to do so—as the images of abused prisoners at Abu Ghraib prison demonstrated. As Secretary of Defense Donald Rumsfeld told members of the Senate Armed Services Committee with exasperation, "People are running around with digital cameras and taking these unbelievable photographs and passing them off, against the law, to the media, to our surprise, when they had not even arrived in the Pentagon."[5] In other words, you cannot contain, control, or escape from the technology.

The Abu Ghraib photos changed the entire momentum of the war in Iraq. Public support for the war plummeted among America and its allies. Reactions in the Muslim world were even worse. The effects linger still.[6] And it was all the result of a camera that one can buy at a drugstore or a military post exchange, consisting of just a cheap charged-coupled device and image processor, combined with flash memory and an Internet connection.

True, images have always shaped public support for wars and, thus, the ability of nations to conduct them. The difference today is the ubiquitous ability to capture such images, the speed of delivering them, and the means for distributing them. Recall, for example, the iconic image Eddie Adams captured in 1968 when Saigon police chief Nguyen Ngoc Loan executed a Viet Cong operative, Nguyen Van Lam. The police chief put a single shot through the side of the captive's head. Adams captured the picture by chance.

Later that day, Adams required twenty minutes to transmit a single "radiophoto" via telephone to New York. The Associated Press and United Press shared the same link and had to take turns using it.[7] Also, in 1968 the only way most people would see the picture was in a newspaper or magazine. This was before videocassette recorders or TiVo, so even if it had been shown on television, it would have been gone in an instant. Even photocopying machines were not yet common. For that matter, whether the image arrived on your doorstep or at the newsstand depended on the decisions of editors—at the time, almost all white, middle-aged Christian males. For the picture to run, one of them had to believe the pictures were newsworthy and suitable for a "family periodical."

Compare that situation to the Abu Ghraib images. Investigators found out later that the infamous images were actually just a few pictures on a compact disk containing probably hundreds of shots. Some reservists from a military police company based in western Maryland snapped the pictures to keep as mementos of their time in Iraq. However the images came to be taken, their digital nature made them easy to reproduce — so easy, in fact, that unlike a photo forty years ago that had to get through several hoops to be published, once they were taken it was almost *inevitable* that the photos from Abu Ghraib would eventually make their way into mass circulation.[8] The digital nature of the photos also ensures that they will exist forever on the Web, instantly available, poisoning the reputation of the United States.

Military Trends

The first military trend to keep in mind is that IT has gone to war. The effects of information technology on military operations are enormous, but they are not what are usually portrayed on the media. The revolution in military affairs is not just about big, sophisticated sensors and precision-guided munitions (although they are a major part of it). The September 11 terrorist attacks and the insurgency in Iraq show how *every* kind of military organization — regular armies, insurgents, terrorists — is finding the technology and tactics that offer it an advantage, and this is changing the nature of the threats we face. The most important developments are:

- *Networked warfare.* New communications technology makes it easier to exchange data between any two points. The result is that an organizational hierarchy is less important for effective command and control. All military organizations are organizing smaller, more agile units that rely on stealth and operating as flexible networks, all of which are adopting similar modes of operation.[9]
- *Precision weapons.* Again, everyone gets to choose their own technology, depending on their needs. Satellite-guided "smart bombs" and improvised explosive devices (IEDs) may appear completely different, but many of their essential features are remarkably similar. Both use disposable electronics to detonate a high-energy explosive at a precise time and location to destroy a target. The main difference is that a smart bomb is delivered to its target but an IED waits

for a target to come to it. Either way, electronics provide a higher probability of destroying a target, and potentially from a distance with stealth. These features have made the past twenty years of warfare fundamentally different from the preceding four thousand years—for everyone.

- *Commercial counterparts.* One reason why U.S. forces have no monopoly on the new way of war is because so much of the necessary technology can be bought over the counter and off the shelf. U.S. forces have global communication systems like MILSTAR; al-Qaeda gets by with commercial satellite telephones and one-time e-mail addresses using the Internet.[10] U.S. military planners locate targets and plan operations with imagery from the National Reconnaissance Office; our opponents have Google Earth. Everyone has encryption.

The second main military trend is developments in weapons of mass destruction (WMD). Nevil Shute warned about the dangers of cheap, widely available nuclear weapons a half century ago in his doomsday novel *On the Beach*: "The trouble is the damn things got too cheap. The original uranium bomb cost only about fifty thousand quid towards the end. Every little pipsqueak country like Albania could have a stockpile of them, and every little country that had that, thought it could defeat the major countries in a surprise attack. That was the real trouble."[11] Experts have been making similar predictions about chemical and biological weapons.[12]

The dangers are real but more complex than commonly portrayed. Nuclear weapons are not so cheap that "every little pipsqueak nation" can build or buy one. Today the bigger problem is that even a single weapon in certain hands can lead to tremendous risks and ripple effects, and it is becoming very hard to prevent a nation from developing a nuclear weapon if it is truly determined to do so. The bar is now so low that even developing nations with just a medium-sized industrial and technological base can build a nuclear weapon indigenously if they are truly determined—witness South Africa and Pakistan. Even a nation whose economy is otherwise in shambles, like North Korea, can build a nuclear weapon if it devotes itself fully to the task.

When countries such as these build nuclear weapons, the main danger is not the potential for hundreds of nuclear weapons spreading throughout the world and for *On the Beach*–style global annihilation. The danger is that even a single bomb being developed in a critical region—or even the plausible development of such a weapon—can radically transform the situation. It was the threat of Iraq having just one nuclear weapon that drew the United States into war in 2003, for example, and the test of a nuclear weapon by North Korea that polarized other nations in the region into taking action—including China, which had been reluctant up to that point.

So now the proliferation problem is low-level or covert proliferation—a threat that is harder to eliminate. Moreover, the appearance of new nuclear weapons technology—in particular, gas centrifuge enrichment—ensures that the problem will get only worse. Older uranium enrichment methods required enormous investments in diffusion plants or electromagnetic calutrons, and the only alternative for making fissile material, reprocessing plutonium, required a working (and readily observable) nuclear reactor. Today, centrifuges, in contrast, are easier to develop and harder to detect.

The technology for enrichment centrifuges dates back to the 1940s, when the Soviets seized German factories and scientists so they could develop new, advanced weapons. One of the scientists, Gernot Zippe, had heard of concepts originally proposed by Jesse Beams, a University of Virginia scientist, for separating fissile uranium. The process required combining uranium ore with fluorine, spinning the resulting gas at supersonic speeds, and then siphoning off the lighter molecules containing fissile uranium as they settled out. A working enrichment plant requires several thousand centrifuges linked together into a cascade so that each feeds into another, increasing the concentration of fissile isotopes in each step.

Zippe chose to work on centrifuges because he thought his Soviet captors would be more likely to allow him to return home than if he worked on more applied, sensitive technologies, like nuclear warhead designs or missiles. His instinct proved correct; the Soviets released him in 1956. From 1958 to 1960 Zippe worked with Beams in the United States to improve centrifuge technology. Eventually the West German government supported his research. A few years later the Germans contributed the technology to Urenco, a consortium to produce fissile uranium for commercial reactors that the Germans formed with Britain and the Netherlands.

The practice in such European consortiums is to parcel out contracts among countries, usually in proportion to their contributions (Airbus and the European Space Agency use the same approach today). So soon centrifuge blueprints were circulating among the three nations, each of which had its family of subcontractors. A. Q. Khan, a Pakistani working for one of the Dutch subcontractors, was able to get a set, and he smuggled it out of the country. The technology has since become available widely, at least to those, like Khan, who have an interest in obtaining it.[13]

The problem centrifuge enrichment presents is that, while industrial sized, they are still easier to conceal than older enrichment methods like gaseous diffusion or a production reactor that would produce fissile plutonium. Also, centrifuges use parts that are not that hard for a nation to obtain—mainly specialized bearings and carbon fiber or aluminum for the body of the centrifuge (recall the infamous aluminum tubes thought to be proof of an Iraqi nuclear weapons program in 2003; the tubes turned out to be intended for missile bodies).[14] Possibly most important, however, is the fact that centrifuges can be developed incrementally. This puts them within the reach of an inexperienced design team. One can first fabricate a single prototype centrifuge, spin it up, run it until it fails, and then fix the problem until one develops a successful working model. Then one can duplicate this design and build the cascade. In other words, centrifuges lend themselves to trial-and-error engineering, which is how Pakistan, Iraq, Iran, Libya, and North Korea have attacked the problem.[15]

Yet, as technology develops, we may even need to redefine what we mean by "weapons of mass destruction." Since World War II, "WMD" has meant "NBC"—nuclear, chemical, and biological weapons. Experts have been warning about threats from biological and chemical weapons for decades, and it is always possible that someone will make the technology breakthrough needed to make them into the kinds of weapons so many people fear. Recall that in 2002 it was Iraq's suspected chemical and biological weapons, not its nuclear program, that were the greatest concern of experts like the former UN inspector Richard Butler.[16]

For now, though, the more pressing problem is simply that all "energetic materials" have become more common in modern society and are so ingrained in the commercial economy that it is hard to control them. When combined with information technology, they are at least as lethal as chemical and biological agents, more readily available than nuclear weapons, and generally effective.

Countries began synthesizing explosives as soon as industrial-scale chemistry began; the chemistry for explosives and fertilizers is hard to keep separate, and the linkage between the two goes back to the late 1800s, when German chemists began to synthesize both. Agriculture could hardly manage today without ammonium nitrate, and that is what Timothy McVeigh used in the bomb that destroyed the Alfred P. Murrah Federal Building in the 1995 Oklahoma City bombing, killing 168 people. Other terrorists have used similar devices around the world.

It is the availability of energetic materials—potent explosives that can deliver enormous destruction for their size and weight—that presents the most immediate threat of mass casualties because the engineering thresholds are so low, especially when combined with the cheap information technology that makes it possible to detonate a bomb at a specific place and time for maximum effect. Currently this threat is most apparent in truck bombs and IEDs, but look for it to become an even greater problem when adversaries begin to use robots operating in the air, in the sea, and on the ground. A sophisticated unmanned aerial vehicle that can stay aloft for an hour or so and then land (or crash) within a few feet of its target sells today for as little as $35,000.[17]

The third military trend is new doctrine, strategy, and tactics. Technology aside, the range of military options that are available, accepted, and employed is changing and expanding. All military organizations are focusing more on how to use asymmetrical tactics—that is, they are developing forms of attack that specifically focus on where the target is weakest and draw on the advantages of the attacker.

The 1991 Gulf War was a great lesson in asymmetric warfare. Whenever a rout of major proportions occurs, military planners around the world take notice. Operation Desert Storm demonstrated that an industrial age army relying on prepared defenses would lose to an information age army that uses mobility and has better awareness of the battle space. Yet September 11 and the insurgency in Iraq will be at least as significant as Desert Storm as a demonstration of asymmetric warfare—in this case, against the United States. The intifada launched by the Palestinians against Israel and the mass missile attacks against Israel by Hezbollah, using mobile launchers shuttled between concealed sites in Lebanon, will also serve as lessons.

One especially significant asymmetric tactic has been the recent use of suicide bombers. Though Japan used kamikazes during World War II, and Soviet pilots occasionally resorted to *taran*—ramming—these were unusual acts of desperation or determination (or, as in the Charge of the Light Brigade, the result of blunder). Today suicide bombers are often an integral part of the doctrine, strategy, and tactics of several potential U.S. adversaries. They fit the classic definition of an asymmetric tactic. They are designed to strike where the target has the greatest difficulty of defending, and they are intended to break the underlying morale of an opponent while strengthening one's own support.

Robert Pape, a political scientist, has catalogued and studied hundreds of suicide attacks. (The fact that he has such a large sample reflects how significant the problem has become for military planners.) Although suicide bombers are probably most closely identified with Islamic terrorists today, it is interesting to note that the Tamil Tigers use the tactic even more than Hamas, Hezbollah, or al-Qaeda.[18] But whatever the motivation, the calculus of defense and deterrence changes when a would-be attacker does not plan to survive, and this changes the problem of planning and operations at every level. U.S. diplomatic facilities were redesigned to emphasize security after the 1983 suicide bombings of the embassy in Beirut and the 1998 bombings of the U.S. embassies in Kenya and Tanzania. Concrete walls, guard stations, and detailed inspection of incoming vehicles made the Americans safer, but it also made it much harder for them to reach out to local populations.

Suicide bombings have also affected how U.S. forces in Iraq and Afghanistan operate. The threat of suicide bombing has forced soldiers to wear cumbersome body armor and helmets, and discouraged them from interacting with the locals (U.S. convoys in Iraq often carry signs and use loudspeakers broadcasting in Arabic warning other motorists not to approach the vehicles). These precautions have created a social barrier at exactly the time the Americans are trying to win over the Iraqis. In effect, suicide bombing has been a countermove to our counterinsurgency doctrine. And suicide bombing has been effective. A high proportion of U.S. casualties in Iraq have been the result of suicide bombings. And, obviously, the September 11 terrorist attacks were suicide attacks.

Most troubling, however, are the implications of suicide bombings for U.S. assumptions about deterrence. During the Cold War, experts often debated about whether it was possible for a nuclear power to "extend deterrence" like an umbrella to protect an ally that lacked nuclear weapons of its own. Some experts also wondered whether Soviet or Chinese leaders even viewed deterrence the same way American leaders did. These debates were abstract and quickly devolved into vague assertions about foreign cultures and military doctrine.

Today's suicide bombings present hard evidence that at least some individuals in some cultures will act according to a different set of assumptions about values, morality, and, probably, their ultimate fate. Surveys say that public acceptance of suicide attacks dropped in Muslim countries during the first five years following September 11, but there are still pockets of strong support (70 percent of Muslims polled in the Palestinian territories in 2007 believed suicide bombings were justifiable). When such attacks are accepted among broad swaths of a population, one has to wonder what that means for traditional notions about deterrence, and especially about deterring the use of weapons of mass destruction.[19]

The net effect of all these developments is that many states and organizations can develop military forces that are very effective, especially for specific situations, such as making it costly for the United States to use its own forces in a particular region, to secure a particular area, or to deter an adversary under particular circumstances. Moreover, states and organizations can develop these capabilities quickly—as the insurgency in Iraq demonstrated. As a result, U.S. military capability, though uniquely powerful, can often be outflanked at the operational, tactical, and strategic levels.

Economic Trends

The big news for economic trends is that, though some may argue whether they like the effects of free market capitalism, hardly anyone argues that the alternatives are more efficient. Today, countries embrace capitalism, compromise with capitalism, or reject capitalism and get left behind.

This acceptance of capitalism is not the same as globalization (the greater interconnectivity of markets, information, ideas, and culture) or free trade (the lowering of tariff and regulatory barriers, increasing competition across national boundaries). It is a change in how people *think*, and about how they assume the world works. The acceptance of free market economics is like the general acceptance of the laws of physics and chemistry, or of the idea that the Earth revolves around the Sun and not vice versa. As more people adopt the assumptions of free market economics, it changes both their behavior and how we should expect them to behave.

Indeed, this change in most peoples' belief systems has led to the steady, worldwide trend toward deregulation, privatization, and removing barriers to international trade. Barriers to travel are also disappearing as countries extend common political and legal jurisdictions, like the European Union, or trade zones, like that established under the North American Free Trade Agreement. There have been some setbacks, such as tighter screening of visa applications and increased security measures by the United States and other countries since September 11. But the overall trend is clear, and this—again, often in combination with modern information systems—has created a truly global market with fewer constraints and much more competition.

In this kind of market, capital quickly moves to wherever it gets the best return. Indeed, the rapid movement of capital is probably more important than the ability of countries to outsource or import, because it can happen much faster. When capital moves at the speed of light, even a company that dominates the world market in its sector can be fatally undone in a matter of days if investors question its profitability or the security of their investments. Witness the collapse of Bear Stearns in March 2008.

Today companies can, without too much difficulty, locate their operations wherever offers them the best mix of talent, cost savings, and security. This means that national governments must compete for both capital and human talent. In effect, the general acceptance of market economics has created a new dimension in geopolitical competition, namely, the competition for talent that supports growth and, from that, power and influence.

In this competition, the measure of success changes from dominating and conquering your adversary to winning by identifying the market sector in which your country can best compete, and then offering the best package of opportunities, profits, and other benefits that attracts talent and promotes growth. As we will see, "talent" is not simply people with money and education. Rather, it is a subtle combination of attitude toward taking risks and an understanding of how to participate in a market.

Yet an even more important—though often overlooked—effect of the general acceptance of free market economics is that all leaders know, at least in principle, how to organize their economies in a way that sustains national power. This was not always so. During much of the twentieth century, the arguments over market efficiency and ideological correctness got blurred. Economists like John Maynard Keynes and John Kenneth Galbraith made a convincing case that markets were not only unfair but also wasteful because there was no one at the controls.[20] At the time, the evidence seemed to support them. Many planned economies were developing as fast or faster than their free market counterparts. It took a decade or two for the impact of the misdirected investment and perverse incentives that central planning usually causes to appear.

We have seen pragmatic behavior by leaders who really did not believe in capitalism before. But when Vladimir Lenin temporarily abandoned socialism in 1921 and adopted his New Economic Policy to get farmers back to work and avert famine, it was a grudging accommodation to reality. The Russian Civil War was at full tilt, and the New Economic Policy allowed farmers to sell crops for a profit. (Later Joseph Stalin decided that famine was not such a bad idea and resumed collectivizing the farms.)

What is going on today is more calculated. Where Lenin and his contemporaries saw these concessions as just a temporary measure for special conditions ("two steps forward, one step back"), leaders now understand the rules of the marketplace and carefully balance market efficiency with whatever other interests they are trying to achieve, like political control and personal enrichment. They also understand that they have to strike this balance continually, not as a one-time measure.

Some rulers, like Kim Jong Il in North Korea, may totally control their national economy, but they still accept the rules of supply and demand when it comes to selling drugs and weapons. In effect, they are institutionalizing a black market or underground economy, which is a time-honored procedure to evade the inefficiencies of market controls (even when they are your own). Other regimes, like China, take the opposite approach, adopting a market economy and clamping down on those transactions that might encroach into the political world (e.g., free markets do not apply in China when it comes to journalism or the Internet). Nations like Russia and, more recently, Venezuela, have taken a middle path, systematically taking control of key industries (in particular, oil and broadcasting) while leaving most of the rest of the national economy free.

The point is, today rulers are making these decisions more knowledgeably. They are drawing on two hundred years of experience that has demonstrated the general efficiency of free markets and the folly of interfering with them too much. So they have a better sense of where and when they can restrict markets for the sake of political control without incurring too great a cost.

The result is that modern dictators are less likely to drive their countries off an economic cliff in the name of a misbegotten ideology. Instead, they will willingly adapt and compromise—for as long as necessary, or even indefinitely. This changes the nature of the threats we face by making them more resilient, and thus requiring us to prepare to deal with them for the indefinite future.

Political Trends

Political trends are also shaping threats and challengers. But where technology development seems to be on a steady path toward greater capability and availability, and economics seems on a steady path toward capitalism, political trends and the underlying social attitudes that shape them are not as clear. Three pairs of conflicting trends have emerged.

The first pair is traditionalism versus modernism. Political scientists had written about the collision between traditional cultures and modernization for many years. The difference is that, where fifty years ago anthropologists, sociologists, and political scientists generally assumed that there is a natural tendency for societies to evolve from earlier forms of organization to more modern ones, today they are not so sure.

Samuel Huntington was one of the first to make this argument. He pointed out that historians up to then had usually talked about the development of political institutions when, in fact, the real question was not how long it would take governments to organize than how quickly they were apt to decay.[21] More recently, David Ronfeldt has argued that history is essentially agnostic when it comes to the form of social organization that emerges in a society, because it all depends on the local conditions. What is more, says Ronfeldt, one could even argue that some of the so-called primitive forms of organization are actually quite efficient and resilient. He is especially taken with tribes.[22]

To appreciate his argument, it helps to put oneself in the position of a tribe member and compare what the tribe offers to alternatives. Tribes come with predefined identity (you are born into a tribe), which creates ready-made trust relationships. Alternatives—like markets, democracies, and fluid networks—offer opportunity but also present risk. So tribes have an initial leg up on that half of the population that is neutral or averse to risk, and, whatever its constraints, many find tribe membership a valuable card to keep in a back pocket in case more modern forms of organization fail.

We have been seeing just how robust tribes are as an organizational form during the past two decades. No matter how hard Josip Broz Tito and Saddam Hussein tried, tribal identity was lurking just beneath the surface. Moreover, there were always those who had a vested interest in keeping the tribe going, even as the country appeared to modernize. So the tribes were readily available to fill the breech when the Yugoslav and Iraqi governments broke down. Indeed, many members of society always believed they were better off under tribal rule, so tribes were ready to compete for the allegiance of the people.

The kicker in this calculation today is that tribal organizations can use both modern technology and modern political techniques to compete with the parties or government authorities that might have thought they were the inevitable next step in social evolution. In Britain, the Scottish Nationalists have the same technology and know-how as the Labour Party. In a democracy, the political process does not care if you are a secular modernizer or a sectarian traditionalist—if you can be politic and bargain effectively, you can win an election, make yourself a critical member of a parliamentary coalition, or join an emergent political machine.

Turkey and Algeria are both examples in which religious movements, once submerged, reasserted themselves largely by competing in electoral politics more effectively than their opponents. Religious parties in Israel (like the Moral Majority and its descendents in the United States) have learned how to position themselves so as to be pivotal in many elections.

Hamas gained followers among Arabs in Gaza by offering benefits and patronage with an effectiveness that a Chicago politician would envy.

Indeed, thanks to technology and techniques that allow tribes to organize themselves effectively without actually controlling territory or government, in several countries these traditional cultures are giving so-called modern secular political systems a run for their money in winning the allegiance of peoples. Look at Western European countries like France, Germany, and the Netherlands, where Muslim subcultures have staked out such a high degree of autonomy that political authorities have grown concerned.

The Muslims in these countries present little threat to the legal government in the traditional sense of fomenting revolution. But they constitute a perceived threat in that they are able to enforce their laws and customs within their own societies. The threat is that they are not simply competing for control of the national regime. Rather, they offer a complete alternative system that could displace the government as the effective authority.

The second pair of conflicting trends is unification versus fragmentation. For most of the eighteenth, nineteenth, and early twentieth centuries, the clear tendency was for smaller states to unite and form larger states. It continued through the great age of colonial empires and mercantilism. The high-water mark may have been 1945, when the French and British empires were still intact and the Soviet Union had just extended its control over the Eastern European satellite states.

The rationale was that bigger states had the advantages of economies of scale—large populations, bigger tax bases, the ability to buy in bulk, the power to organize en masse. Even after the age of conquest had passed, early proponents of a voluntary European state like Jean Monnet argued that size was efficient and that as people lived under one economic union, eventually the hard edges of national differences would be worn away like rocks being smoothed in a stream, and eventually political union would be irresistible.

Yet the trend since World War II has not been for small states to form larger ones but for big states to come apart. After the breakup of the

European colonial empires and the Soviet bloc, even the states that resulted often split along ethnic lines. Local communities went their own way, or tried to. This was a result of four developments mentioned above: advances in information technology, the persistence of culture, the adoption of free market economics and free trade, and the declining importance of big, conventional armies.

Today, smaller political units are more viable. Before, they would have failed economically or have easily been crushed and absorbed by their neighbors. Now they can both sustain and defend themselves. So smaller groups of people bound by a traditional common culture who prefer to live under that creed now find there are fewer reasons not to do so. As self-rule on a smaller scale has become more feasible, many ethnic groups have chosen it. In many cases the result has been bitter civil war (e.g., Nigeria), sectarian violence (e.g., Sri Lanka and Iraq), or fragmentation (Pakistan and Yugoslavia). Even the Czechs and the Slovaks, with more than sixty years of peaceful union, could not hold together; once Soviet domination disappeared, they decided to go their own ways and have hardly regretted the decision. Québécoises seem to test the waters for independence from Canada every decade or so.

At the same time technology is making it more plausible to organize a viable nation on a smaller scale, free markets and free trade make national boundaries less relevant to securing a market, organizing production, or excluding competitors. Countries and even local governments can establish trading zones when it is efficient and can outsource or move operations offshore as needed.

So today the trend is for all kinds of international organizations to tailor their memberships and functions to optimize costs and benefits in the pursuit of specific goals. This is, in effect, the pragmatic, ad hoc alternative to the rigidly defined nation-state—and the mid-twentieth-century notion of the United Nations as a precursor to world government. All governments are tending to give up authority for efficiency and effectiveness, but just enough and no more.

The breakup of the colonial empires and the Soviet bloc demonstrated how hard it is to hold together very big political units. Meanwhile, the rejection by French voters of the European Union's proposed constitution in May 2005 demonstrated how hard it is today to merge smaller units together. Monnet's theory was proven wrong. Citizens of sovereign states did not taste unification and ask for more. Rather, having exploited most of the potential benefits—a common currency, the elimination of customs borders, free immigration—they decided they had what they needed and saw no reason to incur the costs of going further.

The third pair of conflicting trends is democracy versus authoritarianism. Official U.S. policy supports expanding democracy, and political scientists often argue that democracy reduces the probability of interstate war. Yet, though the idea of democracy gets more support than ever, the reality is that the spread of democratic government has almost ground to a halt.

Freedom House, a nonpartisan think tank in New York City, has conducted a survey of freedom in the world since 1973. A panel of experts rates each country for political freedom and civil liberties according to objective criteria. Its definition of "political freedom" is approximately synonymous with democracy. A country scores high if it holds elections, has universal suffrage, and so on. (The panel also evaluates countries for "civil liberties" based on whether it protects freedom of expression, organization, and assembly; whether its legal system is fair; and whether the police protect all residents against violence.)[23] Figure 1.2 tracks the progress of political freedom (i.e., democracy) from 1973 to today. The upper line shows the total number of sovereign states in the world. The lower line shows the number of nations Freedom House rated politically "free"—that is, scoring a "1" or "2" on its criteria, and which could thus be considered democratic.

Notice that, in Figure 1.2, the single event that has had the greatest effect in spreading democratic rule during the past thirty-five years was the breakup of the Soviet Union. States that had been part of the USSR, like Estonia, Latvia, and Lithuania, simultaneously became independent and democratic. States like Poland, Czechoslovakia, Hungary, Romania, and Bulgaria, which had Soviet-dominated communist regimes, adopted democracy when the Warsaw Pact came apart.

FIGURE 1.2
Trends in Political Freedom, 1973–2006

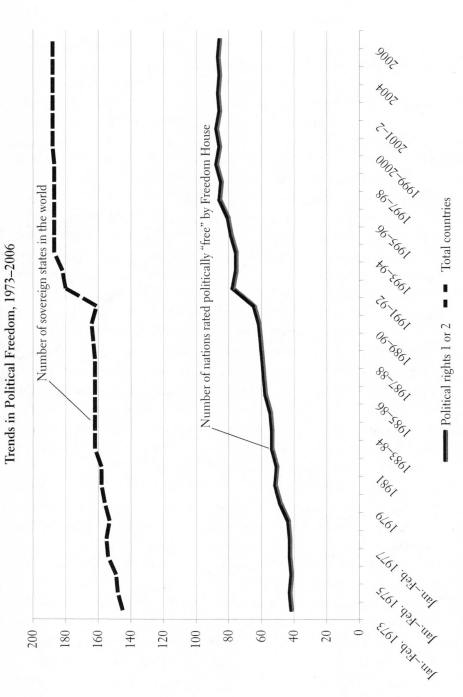

Number of sovereign states in the world

Number of nations rated politically "free" by Freedom House

Jan.–Feb. 1973 · Jan.–Feb. 1975 · Jan.–Feb. 1977 · 1979 · 1981 · 1983–84 · 1985–86 · 1987–88 · 1989–90 · 1991–92 · 1993–94 · 1995–96 · 1997–98 · 1999–2000 · 2001–2 · 2004 · 2006

0 · 20 · 40 · 60 · 80 · 100 · 120 · 140 · 160 · 180 · 200

—— Political rights 1 or 2   ■ ■ ■ Total countries

Source: Freedom House data.

This reflects a historic truth: There are exceptions like the military regimes in Asia and Latin America that allowed civilian democratic rule (e.g., the Philippines, South Korea, Brazil, Argentina), and some single-party states that allowed competition (e.g., Taiwan, Nicaragua). But, for the most part, not many regimes have transformed and adopted democracy. Democracy has been more likely to emerge from the fragments of nondemocratic nations. One can see this by tracing the two lines in Figure 1.2; they converge somewhat during the 1980s, reflecting a few existing states that moved from "not free" or "partly free" to "free." But for most of the period from 1973 to today, the lines mainly run parallel to each other, as the number of democratic states rises in tandem with the overall number of states. (Although it is not shown on the chart, the other step-changes in the trend toward democracy came with the dissolution of the European colonial empires, occurring in spurts from the end of World War II to the early 1960s. Many, though by no means all, of the states created by these breakups were democratic.)

Now notice another trend Figure 1.2 shows: Progress in expanding democracy during the past decade has been almost nonexistent. This is ironic, considering that this is when promoting democracy has been the explicit goal of U.S. policy. Both the total number of countries and the percentage of countries Freedom House has rated "free" with respect to political rights have been flat since around 1996. True, the number of "partly free" countries has grown, reflecting the fact that some of the least-free nations have allowed their citizens some rights. But, as a whole, the world lately seems stuck at a level at which about half of all the sovereign states have democratic government. One reason is that authoritarian regimes have become more adept at maintaining ultimate control, while allowing some rights in well-defined areas. This explains, for example, China, and Russia.

Another reason is that the countries that transformed into democracies in the 1980s or were liberated by the collapse of the Soviet bloc in the early 1990s had homogenous populations and could support a stable democracy. The countries that later had an opportunity to try democracy—most of the Balkan states, Lebanon, Iraq, and some former Soviet

republics—had segmented societies with cohesive, organized subpopula-
tions. So rather than practice democracy, they practiced sectarian war. As
hard as it is to get populations in a segmented society to live peacefully
together, it can be even harder to get them to do so under a democratic
government. Democracy puts in play control over schools, language, and
religion—all the things that define a culture. In segmented societies,
groups feel so strongly about these issues that they will not risk losing an
election.

Unfortunately, a willingness to lose elections is one of the things that
defines political groups in a stable democracy. Groups must prefer losing
and competing in the next election to taking to the streets or seceding.
Paradoxically, democracy works best when everyone cares more about
the opportunity to compete than about whatever is at stake.

If you are intent on holding a country together where groups are
unwilling to lose, then your only option is to change their calculus. You
have two levers: You can take the divisive issues out of the democratic
arena and let each group decide it for itself; or you can reduce the prospects for each group making a go of it alone. This is the challenge of
creating a federal government. It is, of course, also the essence of the
political problem that confronted the United States in Iraq once it
removed Saddam. Alas, brokering a federal agreement is one of the most
difficult diplomatic tasks. Anyone wanting a settlement had to undertake
several initiatives simultaneously, and often these initiatives were at odds
with each other. For example, the United States might arm and train
Sunnis in Anbar to fight al-Qaeda more effectively, but this would also
make them better able to resist Shi'ite pressure to join the central government. Or the United States might threaten to remove our troops in order
to pressure the Shi'ite-dominated central government to reverse its de-
Ba'athification program, a necessary condition for many Sunnis to join a
central government. But if U.S. forces did withdraw, we would be less
able to hunt down al-Qaeda terrorists.

The inherent complexity of this kind of situation helps explain why
diplomatic efforts to keep segmented societies together under peaceful,
democratic rule have such a poor record of success. In the 1970s some

political scientists believed they had figured out the formula for such "consociational democracy," and there were some examples of success—mainly in rich states with a tradition of democracy, where there was a lot to lose.[24] But, overall, the record has been poor. For every state like Belgium and Switzerland that was successful, one can show three or four where diplomacy, negotiation, and mediation failed: Nigeria, Sri Lanka, Lebanon, Cyprus, Rwanda, and so on, resulting in the breakup of the state, a long and inconclusive civil war, or domination of one group by another, possibly with mass killings or oppression.[25]

There is nothing in principle that would preclude a repeat of the 1980s, when several authoritarian counties transitioned peacefully and quickly into democracy. But the more likely scenario is that the rate of democratization will slow. There is no single empire like the Soviet bloc that could break apart today and produce a large number of new democratic states. Authoritarian leaders are determined to hold onto power and seem to be more adept at control and at separating the economic freedoms needed for efficiency from the political reforms that would undermine their rule. And many of the remaining nondemocratic states are culturally segmented; democracy can result from fragmentation or successful succession, but not likely otherwise.

So the optimistic analyst would say that democracy will proceed steadily, and inexorably, but slowly. The pessimist would say the progress of democracy will be irregular, with occasional wins but a lot of time in between. The net result will be a world that is generally more capitalistic, and with many democratic countries, but with many persistently nondemocratic countries, too. That is the world we will face; the issue, then, is: Will America have common cause with the democracies, or will the hard realities of international politics require it to align with authoritarian states? Much depends, oddly enough, not on ideology or high principle but on something more basic: demographics.[26]

Development and Demographic Trends

Scratch the surface of many issues, and you will find that where a country stands on them is driven, as much as or more than anything else, by its demographics. It is one of the most important factors shaping national security issues, but also one of the most overlooked—and hardest to do anything about. Take the issue of climate change. It turns out that the single best predictor of where a country stands on global warming is not science or high principle but demographics. Demographics also defines how the climate change issue will most likely play out.

First, some background. Most (but not quite all) climate scientists agree that average global temperatures are rising because greenhouse gases (GHGs) have been accumulating in the atmosphere. These GHGs include carbon dioxide, hydrocarbons, water vapor, and synthetic compounds like fluorocarbons. Once in the atmosphere, GHGs gradually warm the Earth by trapping solar energy that would otherwise be reflected back into space. The current consensus (again, with a few dissenters) also is that humans are responsible for the recent buildup of these gases. The National Oceanic and Atmospheric Administration has measured carbon dioxide in the atmosphere since 1959; atmospheric concentrations have tracked steadily upward for almost fifty years. They are now 20 percent higher than when the administration first started keeping records.[27]

The largest source of human-produced GHGs is the burning of fossil fuels—mainly coal, oil, and natural gas. These fuels produce carbon dioxide as a combustion by-product. Industry also releases GHGs, like solvents that evaporate during manufacturing processes. So does agriculture, mainly in the form of methane from fertilizers, plowed fields, and, yes, animal flatulence. Agriculture also reduces the tree cover, which would otherwise absorb GHGs.

Though most climate scientists are coming to agree that global warming is real, there is a lot of disagreement among political officials and government about how to deal with it. And that is where development and demography enter the picture. For instance, most European leaders support reducing the GHG emissions that each EU member country produces. Global warming is a huge issue throughout the European Union, and the EU was the strongest proponent of the 1997 Kyoto Protocol to the United Nations Framework Convention on Climate Change, which would require industrial states to reduce GHG emissions, in aggregate, 5 percent below 1990 levels. German chancellor Angela Merkel proposed at the 2007 Group of Eight economic summit that all countries agree to reduce their GHG emissions by 50 percent from the 1990 levels by 2050.[28]

To understand how governments have responded, it helps to keep some basic trends and facts in mind. As Figure 1.3 illustrates, global temperatures have been generally rising, and they generally follow growth in energy consumption (which, historically, has consisted almost entirely of fossil fuels).[29] But because they do not track perfectly, it is also clear that there are other factors at work. One can see a general correlation between historical energy consumption levels and warming, but there is a lot of unexplained variance and it is hard to quantify a precise

FIGURE 1.3
Energy Consumption and Global Temperatures, 1851–1995

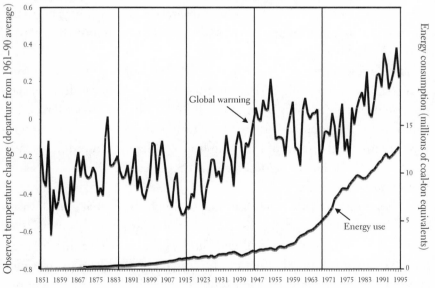

Sources: For temperature change, the data are from the Hadley Centre at Britain's Met Office. For energy consumption, the data are from the Correlates of War Project, a social science database originally developed by J. David Singer and Melvin Small and currently based at the University of Illinois.

relationship. For example, from about 1935 to 1965, energy consumption doubled but global temperatures remained essentially flat. From 1850 to 1880, energy consumption increased little but temperatures increased significantly. And between 1880 and 1910, energy use doubled but temperatures actually declined. Scientists would argue that thirty years is a very short span for climate change, and they are correct—but it is a very long time in politics and economics.

Most people probably do not realize that estimates of GHG production are not based on actual emissions but are extrapolated from fuel consumption and energy production, with adjustments for the kind of fuel being burned and the efficiency of the plant in question. Similarly, restrictions on GHG emissions would actually take the form of regulations on the various forms of fuel consumption, with some allowance for mitigation measures, like planting trees or technologies for capturing carbon.

Because proposals to control GHGs are really proposals for regulating fuel consumption, the lack of a tight correlation between actual historical fossil fuel use and observed changes in global temperatures is problematic, to say the least. Officials will find themselves unable to answer basic questions from their constituents, such as how much cost they must bear to achieve a specific reduction in global warming.

Another insight one gets by comparing the two trend lines in Figure 1.3 is a sense of the scale of the regulatory measures that are potentially involved. It is ironic that many of the political officials who are most concerned about climate change seem to be the most sanguine about the difficulty of solving the problem. In fact, if one is serious about cutting fossil fuel consumption to reduce GHG emissions, there is nothing in the data that would suggest the task is anything but hard. Figure 1.3 suggests that, if we wanted to return to the environment of, say, the 1960s, one would need about a 50 percent reduction in fossil fuel consumption—a *very* significant reduction, no matter how it is handled. And that does not even consider how to accommodate the countries that have yet to industrialize.

There is no simple way to finesse this collision between demographics and thermodynamics. The Kyoto Protocol and most current proposals to limit GHGs include trading systems that allow industries to "buy" rights to emit, or would impose a carbon tax. These do not solve the core problem. Trading schemes and taxes may produce an *efficient* allocation of regulation costs, but they do not answer the question of what the overall emission levels should be or whether we can sustain development without significant warming. Some officials and writers argue that a carbon tax or a trading system will provide incentives that will lead to new technologies that produce fewer GHGs. This is a misunderstanding of both economics and technology.

Incentives may be a necessary condition for innovation, but they do not guarantee that such technologies will be found. At least two other outcomes are possible. One is that the economy might simply decline as productive activities are regulated and made unprofitable, and no technology is discovered to fill the gap (as happened when stringent environmental restrictions resulted in a shortage of oil refineries). Or industry might adapt in unexpected ways that accommodate the tax or regulation but do not reduce GHGs (as happened when U.S. automobile manufacturers started building more large trucks and sport utility vehicles that people bought for personal transportation—circumventing fuel mileage standards that applied only to cars and light trucks).

So the issue of how to allocate the costs of controlling climate change might seem challenging, but it is really the easier part. The more difficult question is the total cost the world is willing to accept—or, to put it another way, how much economic development the world as a whole is willing to forgo for the sake of maintaining the current environment or returning to the environment than existed before the Industrial Revolution. This is where demographic factors enter the picture and underpin the positions countries take.

To see this, observe Figure 1.4, which depicts shares of GHGs produced since 1980. The figure shows that the United States generates more GHGs than any other country. But it also illustrates a fact that gets much less publicity: The amount of GHGs America produces has

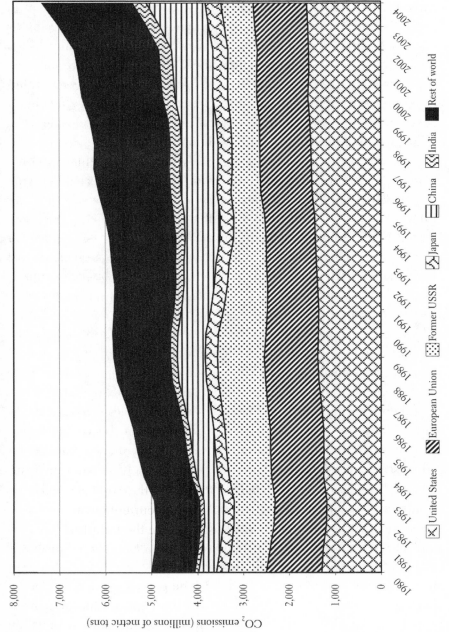

National Share of Carbon Dioxide Gas Emissions, 1980–2004

Source: U.S. Department of Energy data.

increased little for the past quarter century. Almost all the recent growth in GHG emissions during the past decade has been from developing countries—in particular, China. This is because, historically, when nations have begun to industrialize, the GHGs they produce on a per capita base increase quickly. As they mature, per capita energy consumption, and thus GHG emissions, reaches a plateau. Energy efficiency slowly improves as a country industrializes. Also, dirty industries, like manufacturing, move to countries with lower labor costs.

This pattern has been true for virtually all industrializing countries, beginning with Britain in the early 1800s. This fact is reflected in Figure 1.5, which tracks the per capita emissions of carbon dioxide, a major GHG. Though the United States is often criticized for being ever more profligate, in reality, the quantity of carbon dioxide that we produce per capita has not changed significantly since 1980. The small increase that the nation as a whole emits (about 1 percent per year) has been entirely from our growing population. Per capita emissions by European countries have changed little, too—despite Kyoto.[30]

Meanwhile, the decline in GHGs from the former USSR reflects the collapse and extensive deindustrialization of the old Soviet economy. It also suggests something about what it would take to reduce GHGs 30 to 40 percent over the course of a decade. It is not a pretty picture.

One interesting feature of Figure 1.5 is how Canada's per capita carbon dioxide emission levels closely follow those of the United States. This is to be expected because, however much it may trouble our famously independent neighbor to the north, the United States and Canada are geographic and demographic twins, and per capita fuel consumption has historically been driven by geography and level of economic development.

The United States and Canada have similar population densities—about 3 persons per square kilometer for Canada, about 30 persons per square kilometer for the United States. The population densities of the United States and Canada are even closer if one adjusts for the sparsely populated Canadian north; about 90 percent of all Canadians live within 100 miles of the U.S./Canadian border. By comparison, the population

FIGURE 1.5

World Emissions of Carbon Dioxide per Capita, 1980–2004

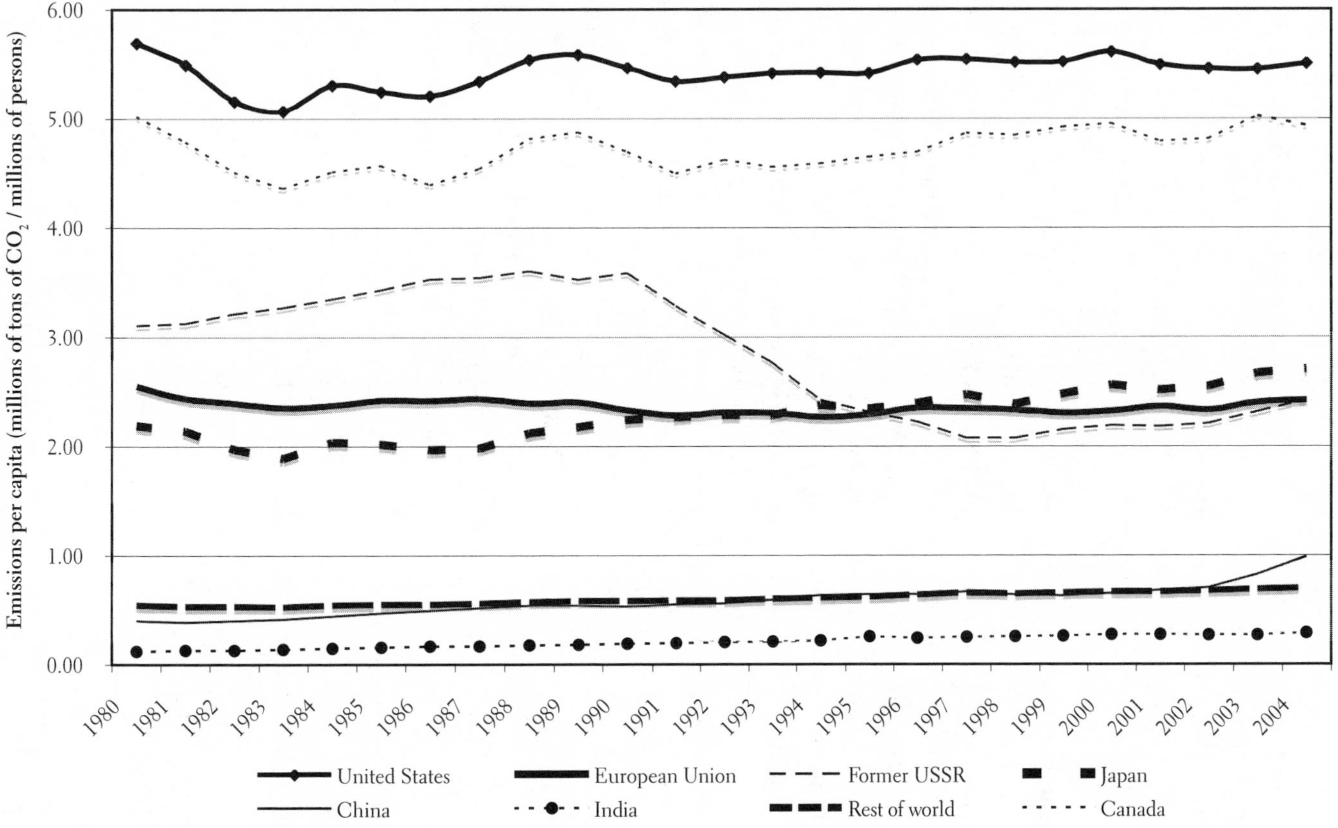

Emissions per capita (millions of tons of CO_2 / millions of persons)

United States · China · European Union · India · Former USSR · Rest of world · Japan · Canada

1980 1981 1982 1983 1984 1985 1986 1987 1988 1989 1990 1991 1992 1993 1994 1995 1996 1997 1998 1999 2000 2001 2002 2003 2004

0.00 1.00 2.00 3.00 4.00 5.00 6.00

Source: U.S. Department of Energy data.

density of France is about four times that of the United States (about 100 persons per square kilometer), while Germany and Britain have populations that are *eight times* denser than that of the United States (about 230 persons per square kilometer). Europeans have shorter commutes and do not have to expend as much energy getting stuff to each other.[31]

Therefore, it is little wonder that Canada's per capita energy consumption has tracked U.S. levels since the mid–twentieth century, when Canadian standards of living and per capita gross domestic product approached that of the United States. Figure 1.5 also shows how China's per capita carbon dioxide emissions have just begun to take off and India is still in the early stages of industrialization. Notice also that per capita carbon dioxide emissions in the EU, despite its adoption of the Kyoto Protocol, have also remained flat. Total fuel use patterns are hard to change without major economic disruptions.

To see the final piece of the picture of how demographics shapes the positions countries take on climate change, look at Table 1.1, which shows the populations and population growth rates of ten representative

TABLE 1.1
**Selected Populations and Population Growth Rates of
Ten Representative Countries**

Country	Population (millions)	Annual Growth Rate (percent)
China	1,311	.61
India	1,122	1.61
United States	301	.89
Pakistan	166	1.83
Nigeria	135	2.38
Russia	142	−.48
Japan	128	−.09
Brazil	187	1.00
Germany	82	−.03
Ethiopia	76	2.27

Source: U.S. Census Bureau International Database.

countries. The important thing to notice here is the differences in growth rates among countries. What is going on in negotiation rooms has a lot to do with what is—or is not—going on in bedrooms.

Current projections say that the population of Germany will be about 15 percent smaller by 2050.[32] Thus, it was easy for Germany to adopt the Kyoto limits or Merkel's proposed ceilings; demographic trends alone would get Germany much of the way to the targets, and incremental technologies would do the rest.[33] One can also now understand why Russia also signed onto Kyoto. It not only has a shrinking population but also has a smaller, less industrial economy compared with 1990.

The crunch only occurs if a country is industrializing, has a growing population, or both. This is why China (which did not object to Kyoto because, as a developing country, it was not covered) resisted Merkel's proposal even more vociferously than the United States. Mai Kai, the minister of China's State Development and Reform Commission, put it concisely: "The consequences of restricting the development of developing nations will be much more serious than the consequences of global warming."[34] China must create 25 million new jobs each year just to keep up with an expanding workforce and to accommodate workers laid off by the restructuring of old state-owned enterprises.[35]

Similarly, Indian leaders said they would go along with a global warming treaty if it recognizes that a country is a low polluter on a per capita basis (Merkel's proposal required cuts from a country's current base, regardless of size). After a country modernizes, its national energy consumption is driven mainly by population trends. It is not by chance that the three developed countries that have resisted the Kyoto Protocol—the United States, Canada, and Australia—happen to be the ones with growing populations. In all three cases, this growth is mainly because they admit significant numbers of immigrants—a policy that also distinguishes them from EU members, which mainly allow either guest workers or immigration only within the EU. (Canada signed the Kyoto Protocol but withdrew in April 2006 after the election of Stephen Harper and the Conservative Party, so it never actually had to meet its targets; Australia ratified the protocol in December 2007 after the election of

Kevin Rudd and the Labor Party but has not explained how it will comply.)

In short, the positions that countries have taken on global warming, almost without exception, are largely defined by their state of development and their demographics. Everyone understands the climate change problem, but no one will adopt measures that hurt their own economic future. This is just one example of how basic demographics will shape the positions governments take on big geopolitical issues. It could upset traditional alignments, like the partnership between the United States and Western Europe, and create new ones, like the mutual interest in accommodating economic and population growth that China, India, and the United States now share.

From the perspective of U.S. national security, it is as important—perhaps even more important—to anticipate how events are likely to play out as how America might like them to play out. Countries like China and India are unlikely to forgo development. The risks are simply too great. The pressures to sustain economic development are enormous.

For example, some experts warn that global warming will cause millions of people to lose their homes and be forced to move as the result of flooding as ocean levels rise. Other potential consequences from climate change could include the spread of disease as tropical regions expand, and the extinction of entire species from the loss of habitat. Yet those are *exactly* the types of harm that China is accepting as a result of the Three Gorges Dam, which it built across the Yangtze River and will bring into operation in 2009. The dam will inundate 2 cities and 1,351 villages and displace 1.1 million people. Environmentalists and other opponents had no effect on the Chinese government's decision to proceed. Chinese officials said the dam was critical for economic development. One can expect that the Chinese government will have similar views of climate change.

Indeed, when Merkel presented her plan at the Group of Eight meeting, China offered its own proposal (the first Chinese policy to address climate change), which would commit it to improve its energy efficiency by 20 percent in 2010 from 2005 levels and increase forest coverage by

1.8 percent. The Chinese government also said that China would increase its cooperation with other developing countries "within the framework of South–South cooperation." It committed "to do what we can to help African countries and small island developing states build capacity to tackle climate change." In effect, it told the West to butt out, and, with enough boats, everybody is going to make it.[36]

The positions all governments take on controlling GHGs inevitably reflect their parochial interests and, in reality, it is hard to say that one plan is objectively better than another. Any system of controls contains arbitrary decisions about such factors as the base year from which controls will be measured, how emissions will be measured, the rate at which reductions in emissions will be required, and so on.

For example, the United States could argue that, instead of reducing national GHG emission levels, as Merkel proposed, the world should adopt per capita reductions from current levels. This would have aligned America with China's and India's positions. And, in fact, one could reduce total GHGs just as effectively that way.

Indeed, even though U.S. per capita emissions have been flat for the past quarter century, the U.S. gross domestic product has grown about three times faster than its national GHG emissions—which would seem to be the very definition of sustainable growth. One could also argue that measuring GHGs country by country is unfair and ineffective because, as noted above, dirty industries move to countries with lower labor costs—even as developed countries reap many of the benefits. Germany may show a reduction in its GHG emissions when Volkswagen builds fewer Jettas in Wolfsburg and more in Puebla or Chengdu, and the decision improves Volkswagen's bottom line, but the net benefit to the world's climate is nil.

Similarly, defining a ceiling on a per capita basis rather than a national basis is no more arbitrary than, say, choosing to cut GHGs from 1990 levels rather than from 1995 levels. Russia has no problem with the former but many problems with the latter, because it would force it to make reductions from a lower base. By the same token, France agreed to the EU proposal only when it was given credit for its nuclear plants. France generates 80 percent of its electricity from nuclear power, which does not emit GHGs. But France built most of these plants in the 1980s, so it has already used up that option, which is one of the few proven ways to reduce GHG emissions on an industrial scale and an option other EU members plan to employ in the near future.

China and India have officially acknowledged the potential costs of climate change, but agreement on these facts is not the issue. They simply have other priorities, and they are unlikely to sacrifice growth to control climate change. The hard, cold fact of global warming is that China, India, and the rest of the developing world cannot reach Western standards of living without producing significant warming. Therefore, the most likely outcome is that global temperatures will rise.

Conflict on climate change is just one example of how global demographics will shape U.S. national security concerns. There are others. For example, in most countries that are on course to have large populations, 50 percent or more of the people are under the age of thirty. Historically, countries with many young people tend to have "interesting" times—big political, economic, and social shifts, for good or bad. The result can be rapid economic expansion and innovation, or it can be revolution or chaos. There is a lot of human energy about to be released, and it will undoubtedly shape events. And one must wonder how changing demographics will affect the United States. What does it say for a country if domestic politics is dominated by issues like paying for pensions and Social Security rather than creating jobs and building schools?

Technology, economics, politics, and demographics are the tidal trends that will determine the main contours of national security. They are hard to change because they are not fully under the control of any authority, and such changes usually outstrip the lifetime of any official. The challenge is to navigate these trends. How well a country succeeds goes a long way toward deciding whether it remains predominant, which is the question we turn to next.

CHAPTER TWO

Power

IN THE SIMPLEST TERMS, here is the long-term problem the United States faces in keeping its current position of predominance: By almost any measure you choose, it is currently the most powerful country in the world. This predominance is because of its size (third largest in population, or fourth if the European Union is considered a country), combined with its advanced level of economic and technological development. But when countries like China, India, and other developing nations with larger populations and comparable territory modernize, they will be growing from a bigger base. That will give them greater "upside," which is another way of saying that, when they reach their full potential, they could be more powerful and influential than the United States.

Currently Americans generate, on average, about $44,000 in goods and services annually. Chinese generate about $7,700. Indians generate about $3,800. The difference is due to modernization—better technology, better infrastructure, and more intellectual property. In short, person for person, Americans produce more because they have modernized more—for now.

As China, India, and other countries modernize, their people will also become more productive. At current rates, Chinese per capita gross domestic product (GDP) will be about 40 percent of U.S. per capita GDP by 2060; India's will be about 20 percent.[1] Modernization and economic development are generally good things. Wealth is not necessarily a zero-sum proposition. But, from a geopolitical perspective, modernization will give China more power. With a projected Chinese population of 1.4 billion in 2060, and a projected U.S. population of just under 400 million, even this lower level of productivity would still mean that the Chinese economy would be larger than America's.

A wealthier China could obviously spend more money on military forces. But a nation's productive capacity—that is, its economy—is usually more important today in that it defines a nation's broader influence—in politics, trade, and culture. In addition, smaller nations present their own challenges. Their economies may not match that of the United States in sheer size, but as they modernize, they will also find niches in which to compete and may challenge America in specific geographic areas and economic sectors and on certain strategic issues.

To understand all this and the issues it presents, let us first look at the concept of power itself. Power, how we think about it, and ideas about predominance and the rise and fall of nations are all closely linked.

A Brief History of Measuring National Power

National power is all about influence and the ability to shape events. It inevitably raises the issues of who has more, who has less, and in what direction these relationships are moving. So it should not be surprising that ideas about national power evolved directly from efforts to measure it. Estimating national power has always been about counting heads and counting wealth, and governments have been doing *that* for more than four thousand years. One reason, and usually the main reason, was to collect taxes.

Indeed, most of the written records we have for ancient civilizations deal with one of two subjects: religion and gods, or taxes and revenues.

Wall paintings in Egyptian tombs built around 2500 BC depict armies in battle, workers building monuments, farmers cultivating fields and— inevitably—Egyptian subjects paying taxes to the pharaoh, with rows of scribes recording the annual audit.[2] Egyptians were taxed a flat 20 percent of their crop. So in the process of the audit, the scribes also generated statistics on the size of the Egyptian economy. Written records and taxes were two sides of the same coin (so to speak).

The other reason countries began to collect statistics was to determine how many men were available for the army. Cuneiform records say that was why Babylonia conducted one of the earliest censuses, also around 2500 BC. The Old Testament also recounts how, as the Israelites wandered in the desert around 1400 BC, the Lord ordered Moses to count, tribe by tribe, all the men over the age of twenty who could serve in the army. The Levites got an exemption as guardians of the Tabernacle, and the remaining population totaled 603,550 men, or just under the number of soldiers currently on active duty in the U.S. Army.[3]

The Romans combined both these forms of records—tax data and census data—to implement a head tax. As the Nativity story says, "A decree went out from Caesar Augustus, that a census be taken of all the inhabited earth." Everyone had to "register for the census, each to his own city." Joseph, a descendent of David, was obliged to travel to Bethlehem with his pregnant wife Mary to be counted, and so that was where Jesus was born.[4] Were it not for taxes, we would presumably be singing, "Oh, Little Town of Nazareth" each Christmas. But the Romans did have reasonably accurate measures of how much money the government had, how many people it ruled, and, thus, a good sense of their power.

Record keeping, along with the ability to measure national power, disappeared in Western Europe with the Dark Ages, with just a few exceptions. One was the *Domesday Book*, again demonstrating the close relationship between taxes, record keeping, and measures of power.

The *Domesday Book* traces its origin to Robert, duke of Normandy, who fathered an illegitimate son, William, sometime around 1028 (as noted, record keeping was less than rigorous in the Dark Ages). Referred to as "William the Bastard," the son was an ambitious man, and so, after vanquishing all his rivals in Normandy, he crossed the English Channel to challenge the throne of England. Defeating the Saxons in 1066 at the Battle of Hastings, he thus became, of course, William the Conqueror.

To control the countryside, William granted estates to the noblemen who supported him. They, in turn, built castles to defend their estates. This system of about 180 estates provided an army of up to 5,000 knights. All of them had to be fed and supported, as did their horses (a knight typically required six), plus their entourage of squires, pages, common foot soldiers, and so on.

By 1085 the costs of maintaining this army were mounting, and William had no systematic process for raising taxes or, for that matter, even knowing how much he was owed. So he ordered the first British national tax assessment, to be based on the amount of land each nobleman owned. The king ordered his nobles to report their holdings, and he then sent tax commissioners to each estate to verify the owner and the property. As one subject recalled: "He sent his men all over England in every shire and had them find out how many hundred hides there were in all the shire, or what land and cattle the king himself had in the country, or what dues he ought to have in twelve months from each shire. . . . So very narrowly did he have it investigated, that there was no single hide nor a yard of land nor indeed. . . . One ox nor one cow nor one pig that was left out, and not put down in his record; and all these records were brought to him afterward."[5]

The "hide" that the author was referring to was the amount of land (between 40 and 120 acres) that was sufficient for a family to live on and cultivate with a plow. The *Domesday Book* also illustrated the linkage between national power and record keeping. A country's arable land, mills, and plows determined how many knights a king could support and, thus, its military power.

The results were compiled into a single, all-encompassing, authoritative ledger that came to be called the *Domesday Book* because it was the kind of eternal record akin to what one might encounter upon arriving at the Pearly Gates. William died before the survey was published, but the *Domesday Book*—now residing in the office of the British Records

Department in Kew—was remarkably complete. About 95 percent of all the 13,418 locations cited in the 888 parchment leaves of the two volumes can be found today. It was to be the last record of its kind taken for seven hundred years, and there was nothing like it anywhere else in Europe.[6] Then progress on statistics stopped until the seventeenth century, when William Petty got to work on the problem.

Petty was the son of a tailor who journeyed to the Continent in 1643 at the age of twenty. Britain was in the midst of its civil war, and it was a good time for Petty to get out of Dodge, so he traveled around in Utrecht, Leyden, and Amsterdam for three years, studying and making money as a trader, before finally landing in Paris. There he met Thomas Hobbes, the philosopher, who was working in France as a tutor. Hobbes hired Petty as his assistant. Returning to England three years later and £10 richer than when he had left, the tall and strikingly good-looking Petty married well, mixed in the right circles, and, already successful at business, sealed his fortune with lands confiscated from Irish Catholics.[7]

Petty's early wealth gave him time to study science and philosophy— and write. One of his first opportunities came from Edward Chamberlayne, the author of *Present State of England,* a popular handbook on English politics. Chamberlayne knew Petty as an Ireland expert, and he asked the young man for help for the next edition. Petty thought it was such a good idea that he decided to write his own pamphlet, *Political Arithmetick.* Petty had a novel idea for political analysis: objectivity and quantification. "The Method I take to do this,' he wrote "is not yet very usual; for instead of using only comparative and superlative Words, and intellectual Arguments, I have taken the course (as a Specimen of the Political Arithmetick I have long aimed at) to express my self in Terms of Number, Weight, or Measure."[8]

Until then, authors wrote about politics poetically and described nations using adjectives. Chamberlayne, for example, described England as "blessed with a very fertile wholesome Soyle, watered abundantly with Springs and Streams, and in divers parts with great Navigable Rivers; few barren Mountains or craggy Rocks, but generally gentle pleasant Hills, and fruitful Valleys, apt for Grain, Grass, or Wood."[9]

Chamberlayne can be forgiven for his lack of precision. He was writing in an era with few maps and no idea of how geology worked, and when Galileo still was still trying to convince people that the Earth revolved around the Sun. Even so, Petty wanted to quantify. The challenge was that, though Petty was determined to express himself in "Numbers, Weights, and Measures," all three were hard to come by. To be sure, local authorities and parishes recorded events, like "Timothy was christened on the Second of July the Year of Our Lord, 1601." They also recorded deaths, in the form of a Bill of Mortality, which would list the numbers of people who died in a village or London neighborhood during a given month. But no one was keeping systematic records.[10]

So Petty, working with his friend John Graunt, estimated and surmised. (Graunt, who compiled Bills of Mortality into tables, is now considered one of the principal founders of demography.) Deaths eventually equal births, so one gives a rough estimate of the other, and, over a span of time, one can estimate total population. This all might seem crude today, but at the time so little data were being collected that the mayor of London had only an approximate idea of how many people lived in the city he was supposed to govern. Petty's estimates, rough as they were, represented a major breakthrough in assessing a country—and measuring national power.

For example, one of the pressing issues of the time was whether France could threaten Britain. This hinged largely on the question of sea control, so Petty looked at whether France might possibly match Britain's navy. Petty focused on the underlying economic and demographic factors, and concluded it was unlikely. He presented the issue thus:

> Some will say that other Nations cannot build so good Ships as the English; I do indeed hope they cannot; but because it seems too possible, that they may sooner or later, by Practice and Experience; I shall not make use of that Argument, having bound my self to shew, that the impediments of France, (as to this purpose) are natural, and perpetual. Ships, and Guns do not fight of themselves, but Men who act and manage them; wherefore it is more material to shew; That the King of

France, neither hath, nor can have Men sufficient, to Man a Fleet, of equal strength to that of the King of England.[11]

In other words, Petty believed he had identified a key variable that determined overall power—in this case, skilled manpower—that he would measure. Today we would call this a "critical parameter" or "the long pole in the tent." (Manpower, and in particular, reducing its cost, remains a huge issue for the U.S. Navy even today, which is why it has tried so hard to reduce crew size via automation.) But to continue: Petty considered the time required to train various classes of seamen, and he then made some rough calculations:

> The King of Englands Navy, consists of about seventy thousand Tuns of Shipping, which requires thirty six thousand Men to Man it; these Men being supposed to be divided into eight parts, I conceive that one eighth part, must be persons of great Experience, and Reputation, in Sea Service: another eighth part must be such as have used the Sea seven years and upwards; half of them, or parts more, must be such as have used the Sea above a twelvemonth, viz., two, three, four, five, or six years, allowing but one quarter of the whole Complements, to be such as never were at Sea at all, or at most but one Voyage, or upon one Expedition; so that at a medium I reckon, that the whole Fleet must be Men of three or four years growth, one with another.[12]

Petty then referred to an outside authoritative, impartial source for additional information to complete the analysis:

> Fournier, a late judicious Writer, makeing it his business to persuade the World, how considerable the King of France was, or might be at Sea, in the ninety second and ninety third pages of his Hydrography, saith, That there was one place in Britany, which had furnished the King with one thousand four hundred Seamen, and that perhaps the whole Sea-Coast of France, might have furnished him with fifteen times as many: Now supposing his whole Allegation were true, yet the said number amounts but to twenty one thousand; all which, if the whole Trade of Shipping in France were quite and clean abandoned,

would not by above a third, Man out a Fleet equivalent, to that of the King of England: And if the Trade were but barely kept alive, there would not be one third part Men enough, to Man the said Fleet.[13]

In all, it was a sophisticated inferential assessment not too different from what a Beltway Bandit might sell to the Defense Department today. A king could use it to estimate his power and make plans accordingly.

Information gradually became easier to come by over the next two hundred years. Some of the reasons were traditional—collecting taxes and preparing for war—but soon there was a new factor. When Britain began to settle North America, it authorized its colonies to establish legislatures. The legislators had to apportion seats. The result was the rebirth of the census. Indeed, the first regularly scheduled modern national census resulted from the compromise between big states and small states at the Philadelphia Continental Convention.

Having agreed to peg taxes and representation to a state's free population and three-fifths of its slaves, the delegates realized they needed a head count, with a regular update. This is why the U.S. Constitution requires a census every ten years. The Founders were familiar with the census process in several colonies, and so they simply adapted it to the national level.[14] U.S. marshals, the only federal representatives who existed throughout the states at the time, conducted the first national census in 1790. The marshals and their assistants rode on horseback from house to house and farm to farm, and simply asked who lived there, how many were free, and how many were slaves. The enumeration took a year and a half. A standard printed form did not come along until 1830.[15]

As governments began to gather these kinds of data, some officials realized the information might be useful for something more than just measuring revenues and counting voters. John Sinclair, a wealthy Scottish politician in the late 1700s, was one. In the process of demonstrating this, he adopted the word to describe them that we use today: "Political arithmetick" became *statistics*.[16]

Sinclair was known in Parliament as an expert in finance, economics, and, especially, farming. This eventually earned him the nickname

"Agricultural Sir John." He had both an insatiable appetite for information and the means to chase after it. Taking time off from Parliament
during the last half of 1786, he set off on a tour of Europe, aiming to see
twelve cities in seven and half months, averaging more than thirty miles
a day. (For the time, this was an extraordinary effort.) Armed with a
hundred letters of introduction that he had gathered—the eighteenth-
century version of social networking—he set off for the Continent.

Sinclair took notes constantly. He recorded with concern that the
French seemed to be everywhere, spreading their influence by recruiting
foreign officials and secretly buying access into the media (at the time,
broadsheets). He discovered that Russia was adopting British naval technology and that Prussia had a new system of military drill. He also noted
that German governments had adopted a new practice of collecting
detailed information about their national economy and population. They
called the process *statistik*, or "information for the state," using a term
coined sometime around 1749 by Gottfried Achenwald, a scholar of politics from Leipzig.

Other Continental governments were also compiling statistics for
planning purposes. Sweden had even begun taking a national census as
early as 1749, and Spain had conducted one in 1787.[17] All this gave
Sinclair the idea to compile a collection of data for his own country,
Scotland. Aside from the fact that he could afford to pay a staff, he had a
special privilege that made the project feasible: as a member of Parliament, was allowed to frank. In 1790 virtually all long-distance communications still depended on the mail, and it was very different from the
postal service of today. The post office at the time was usually a local inn
designated as a "letter receiving house," where an innkeeper accepted
letters for delivery and turned over letters when an addressee came to
call. It was not until the 1800s that such postmen would have their servants deliver a letter for a fee of 1 to 2 pence (about $1 in today's
currency).

Just as important, Sinclair was on good terms with the clergy. At the
time, local churches were usually the only reliable source of information
about a community. Sinclair prepared a letter with a list of 166 questions

about births, deaths, weddings, harvests, trade, and commerce—that is, a survey—to each of the 938 parishes in Scotland.

This survey, moving at the speed of mail and parish clerks, took months to complete and even longer to compile and disseminate. Sinclair called the resulting product *The Statistical Accounts of Scotland*, which was printed in twenty-one volumes over an eight-year period beginning in 1791. But unlike Achenwald's *statistik* and the Swedish and Spanish censuses, the *Statistical Accounts* was designed from the start for public release. "Real statesmen, and true patriots, no longer satisfied with partial and defective views of the situation of a country," Sinclair wrote, "are now anxious to ascertain the real state of its agriculture, its manufactures, and its commerce."[18]

As data began to trickle in, the very first compilations of national statistics across countries began to appear. The earliest book of its kind in the English language seems to be William Playfair's *Statistical Breviary*, published in 1801, and adapted from a compilation of tables collected by Jacob Boetticher of Königsberg.[19]

The *Statistical Breviary* is sort of an early-nineteenth-century equivalent of the *World Factbook*, which the Central Intelligence Agency publishes today. There is a section for each nation in Europe (in 1801, there were only fifteen), plus Hindustan—present-day India and Pakistan. For each nation, Playfair provided a short commentary on political conditions. He also included a table indicating the nation's area, population, revenues, debt, size of army, size of navy, and balance of trade—just as the *Factbook* does today.

The most remarkable thing about the *Statistical Breviary* is that Playfair, using Boetticher's data with some corrections, was able to do this *before* most national governments began compiling official statistics on a regular basis. Comparing estimates of geographic area with what is known today, one finds that the data in the *Statistical Breviary* were remarkably close to the true figures. Extrapolating backward from the early 1800s, when actual census data were collected, one finds that Playfair's estimates of the population of continental nations were just 10 to 20 percent under the true population, and were 20 percent high for

Britain. At the time, no one was really sure whether France was more populous than Britain or vice versa, which was one reason why power was such a contentious issue and why it was of great concern.

Britain carried out its first systematic census in 1801; that, and the American census taken after the Continental Convention, marked the true beginning of national statistics collected on a regular basis. The idea had been kicking around in Britain for at least fifty years but could never get through Parliament. Some members were afraid a census would expose Britain's weaknesses to its enemies. Others thought it was a back-door means to a military draft. Yet others warned that its results would be used to raise taxes. Even then, learned people knew something of the history of statistics, and why authorities collected them. A census taker coming to your door was apt to be the equivalent of the taxman, or even the Angel of Death.

Then, in 1796, John Rickman, a twenty-five-year-old clerk in West-minster, drafted a paper proposing a census, this time using an economic crisis and its military implications as the rationale supporting a head-count, rather than the argument for avoiding one. As noted, Britain was straining to keep up with France, and a disastrous harvest in 1800 had caused a major economic crisis. Rickman believed that getting a handle on these problems required some kind of ground truth, beginning with knowing how many people actually lived in Britain. He gave his paper to George Rose, his representative in the House of Commons. Parliament passed the Census Act on December 31, 1800, and the census—under Rickman's supervision—was taken on March 10, 1801.

Rickman later also supervised the censuses of 1821 and 1831. He died in 1840, but by then the process had become routine, and the British government had put more rigor into the count. Civil registration—the regular recording of births, deaths, and marriages—began in England in1837, and the 1841 census was linked to these databases. The entire staff of the General Register Office was five men.[20]

Once countries started taking reliable measurements, it was inevitable that someone would want to compare one country with another—basically, reinventing Playfair's *Statistical Breviary* with official data. Sure enough, sometime in the mid-1800s the British Prime Minister, Robert Peel, asked the publisher Alexander Macmillan whether it might be possible to compile a "handbook" of the world, and the first edition of *The Statesman's Yearbook* was published in 1864, followed by *The World Almanac* and its British counterpart, *Whitaker's Almanac*, both first published in 1868.

The final dimension of national power to be measured was, paradoxically, military capability—even though much of the rationale behind the development of modern statistics was to prepare armies and navies. The problem here was that, like just about everyone else, armies and navies took a more casual approach to record keeping than today. Playfair estimated in his *Statistical Breviary* how many warships each country had, but that was a one-off book, not a periodical. With industrialization, navies could change significantly year to year. An enterprising young Briton was the first to spot a market opportunity.

Fred T. Jane, the son of a clergyman, was born in 1865 in Richmond, Surrey. Like many boys, he liked to draw pictures of ships. Jane was creative and curious, and a classic Victorian eccentric. As a student, he had a penchant for brewing explosives in chemistry class, and, when he grew older, he earned a reputation as a daredevil driver and instigator of prank kidnappings of waiters, friends, Labour members of Parliament, and a younger Winston Churchill.[21]

Not unexpectedly, Jane struggled to find a profession, and at the age of twenty he left home to become a hack writer and illustrator of science fiction and imaginary war stories. As it happened, the Royal Navy was trying to boost its public image at the time and was offering cruises to reporters willing to write about the fleet.

It was just the kind of opportunity and adventure Jane wanted. So in 1895 he found himself attached to the Royal Navy during mobilization exercises on the *HMS Northampton*, a third-rate battleship. That was where he found both his niche and his method. Jane compiled data on the characteristics of warships simply by looking around. He took careful notes, and—a daring leap in class-conscious Britain—talked to the crew and engineers who actually made the ship run.

Many writers had already published books about navies and warships. W.F. Mitchell had published *Ships of the Royal Navy 1872–1880*, and Lord Thomas Brassey, the son of a railroad magnate, had published the *Naval Annual* in 1882. The Royal Navy itself published the annual *Navy List* of officers and ships, but it was simply that—a list. It did not describe the features of the ships, said nothing about foreign navies, and did not have pictures.

Jane had a new idea: a comprehensive listing of every fighting ship in the world, organized by nation and ship type—one ship, one picture, one description, each in a single entry. A reader could easily thumb to, say, "Spain," and see a short entry describing the size, armament, and capabilities of every ship in the Spanish navy, from the largest battleship to the smallest tender, along with the technical features of each. In other words, Jane created the first modern naval database.

It is hard to appreciate today what a breakthrough this was. At the time the public had few reliable data for measuring military capabilities across nations. For that matter, even the professionals were not in great shape. Royal Navy culture had always regarded officers who spent any time handling paper and pens as "theoretical"—a kiss of death for promotion. The British Naval Intelligence Department had only been around since 1887 (five years after its American counterpart), and its sources of information were spotty at best. Even if you could see a foreign warship (and this was not always easy), portable cameras were still rare. So the only way to record the information was with paper and pen, usually while peering through a telescope or binoculars.

The first edition of *Jane's Fighting Ships* appeared in 1898, coinciding with the previous year's Diamond Jubilee Review at Spithead, when more than two hundred warships from Great Britain and several invited navies sailed in a procession for the queen. The book was an immediate hit. For the first time, a captain could match a silhouette of a warship on the horizon with an entry that gave its speed, size, and armament, and the navy to which it belonged. Similarly, a landlubber could get a thumbnail sketch of the entire navy of a foreign country in just a few pages and mentally tabulate its total power.

Jane may have been a bit of a flake, but he knew how to make money. Two years after publishing the first edition of *Fighting Ships*, he released the Jane Naval Wargame. The Wargame (which, in fact, Jane had thought of before his book) came in a box with tokens that could represent the ships of various navies; each had a table of capabilities assigned to it from the information in the book. Players could simulate "maneuvers" and do battle against an opponent. The book and the game were integrated, and although the Admiralty never endorsed it, it was popular with naval officers and armchair strategists alike.

Jane sold a quarter of his publishing interests to Sampson Low & Company in 1908, and so the business survived his death in 1916. Today Jane's Information Group is a subsidiary of IHS, Incorporated, which bought it in 2007 for $183 million. Jane's has annual sales of $58 million and about 260 employees, and it is considered one of the leading providers of "open source intelligence." It is a safe wager to say that every significant military organization uses its products in one form or another.

So, in sum, by 1900 it was possible to "weigh" with reasonable accuracy the total economic and demographic capacity of each major nation in the world. Most European governments had statistics offices by the time World War I began. When the League of Nations was established, it convened a commission in 1920 to organize a system of global statistics, which was gradually designed through the 1930s. Alas, the League's Committee of Statistical Experts was as weak and lackadaisical as the League itself, so not much came of this effort. When the United Nations was set up, however, one of its first undertakings was to organize a Statistical Commission, which met at the UN's temporary headquarters on Long Island in May 1946. It adopted the terms of reference for a new UN Statistics Division, which published its first directory of international statistics in 1951.

Throughout the twentieth century more and more governments compiled a wider variety of statistics. The reason was almost always something other than power politics, but at every step it became more possible to describe the characteristics—that is, the power—of nations, groups, and other players on the world scene. And that is how the modern language of national power came to be.

Growth, Decline, and Hierarchy

It was not long after measures of national power were available that people began thinking systematically about what caused nations to rise and decline, both in an absolute sense and relative to others. Writers had been chronicling the fall of empires since ancient times, but these were usually in the form of an epic or a myth. The first account that a modern historian would recognize as serious research (i.e., an objective narrative based on original documentary sources) was probably Edward Gibbon's *The Decline and Fall of the Roman Empire.*

Though Gibbon focused on a story about a single state, he believed his tale illustrated some general principles about why nations fail, which, in the case of Rome, he thought were self-apparent:

> "The rise of a city which swelled into an empire may deserve, as a singular prodigy, the reflection of a philosophic mind. But the decline of Rome was the natural and inevitable effect of immoderate greatness. Prosperity ripened the principle of decay; the causes of destruction multiplied with the extent of conquest; and as soon as time or accident had removed the artificial supports, the stupendous fabric yielded to the pressure of its own weight. The story of its ruin is simple and obvious; and instead of inquiring *why* the Roman empire was destroyed, we should rather be surprised that it had subsisted so long."[22]

Gibbon's theme—the ascent and descent of a nation—is a recurring one in history, economics, and political science. The explanations generally fit a pattern: Some factor—technology, geography, natural resources, political reforms, or something else—causes a country to grow stronger in wealth, power, and influence. Over time, however, this growth factor is offset by some debilitating factor that causes collapse. Often the debilitating factor is one that unavoidably accompanies the growth factor, so the decline or collapse of the state is really just a question of when one outpaces the other.

For example, wealth might lead to corporations that seek monopolies, which ultimately act as a drag on competition and economic productivity. Or a favorable geographic location might put a nation at the hub of trade routes, bringing prosperity—and foreign disease. Or political reforms might lead to broader participation, offer the energy of nationalism and public support—and, eventually, political factions, lobbies, and interest groups that make it impossible to get anything done.

It is the template for a Greek tragedy, and, indeed, ancient Greece follows that storyline: Democracy leads to an enlightened state whose culture and trade produce prosperity—and softness and sloth, allowing less refined neighbors to topple it. Gibbon's tale of Rome offers a similar story arc: Superior organization and culture enables Rome to conquer the known world, but eventually also causes it to overextend itself. The riches of conquest in time undermine the society.

This basic plot line endures today and, as one might expect, because it deals with winning and losing and how to achieve one and avoid the other, the topic quickly gets intensely political. Books that focus on the downside of the cycle usually get published as criticisms of current policies or as explanations of when things seem to be getting tough for the United States.

For example, just over two hundred years after Gibbon, another historian, Paul Kennedy, took his basic idea—empire overreach—and retooled it as an implicit warning for the United States in *The Rise and Fall of the Great Powers*.[23] Kennedy's book resonated in the late 1980s with critics of the Reagan administration's defense buildup and budget deficits—though his predictions proved completely off the mark. The boom economy of the 1990s created unprecedented wealth, and the United States dominated the world like no power since, well, the Roman Empire.

Jared Diamond, a geographer, presented a new variation of this storyline in *Collapse*, looking at a half dozen primitive societies that initially flourished because of their proximity to natural resources but that later failed because their success drove them to overfarm, overforest, overfish, or otherwise exceed the capacity of the land.[24] This struck a chord at a time when the public was increasingly concerned about the environment. More recently, as more Americans worried about their place in the world following the September 11 terrorist attacks and the start of the Iraq war, a spate of books appeared predicting the decline of the United States. The titles describe their authors' views: Chalmers Johnson published *Nemesis: The Last Days of the American Empire*; Charles Kupchan published *The End of the American Era*; and, lest anyone miss the point, Cullen Murphy published *Are We Rome?*[25]

William Playfair and the Elements of National Growth and Decline

Credit for the first attempt at a general theory of the rise and fall of nations seems to belong, however, to William Playfair, whom we have already met as the author of the first comprehensive catalogue of the capabilities of nations—the *Statistical Breviary*. The two achievements are related.

Playfair is almost forgotten today, which is ironic, because the average person probably uses his ideas more than those of any other political economist who ever lived. That is because Playfair invented statistical graphics—that is, the visual presentation of data. All the pie charts, bar graphs, and time series diagrams we use today—including those in this book—trace their origin to Playfair, the first to use such illustrations. Indeed, when Playfair is remembered at all today, it is almost always because of his inventing statistical graphics.

Yet that was not Playfair's only contribution or even his most important. He was enormously proud of his graphics and promoted them throughout his life, but he considered himself mainly a writer and analyst of politics and economics. In that sense, his slipping through the cracks of history is doubly unfortunate, because his most important works deal with precisely the challenges facing the United States today. He was a pioneer, identifying the basic principles underlying the disciplines of strategic studies and international political economy, the two fields of study most relevant to understanding these challenges.

In the late 1700s and early 1800s Great Britain was still recovering from a long, controversial war (shades of Iraq). Britain remained the most powerful country in almost every respect, just as the United States is now. Even so, Britons worried about the future—again, just as Americans do today. No two eras are perfectly parallel, but their underlying problems—in particular, maintaining stability in a world gone topsy-turvy, and promoting growth to retain predominance—echo each other. As it turns out, many of Playfair's observations about the rise and decline of nations are also relevant today.[26]

One reason Playfair does not get the credit he deserves is probably because he did not have a scholar's pedigree. He never went to high school, let alone college. But that may have been just as well, because he would have been a hopeless fit in any academic institution. He was a swashbuckler, a wheeler-dealer, an unabashed patriot, a bit of a rogue, and radically creative.

Playfair was born in 1759 in Dundee, Scotland, and his father died when he was just thirteen. His older brother John took charge of the family and tutored him. (John later himself became a famous mathematician, played a leading role in developing modern geology theory, and was a protégé of Adam Smith.) At the time the countryside around Dundee was the epicenter of the Scottish Enlightenment. Edinburgh and Glasgow were home to a remarkable number of smart, ambitious thinkers—Adam Smith, David Hume, James Hutton, and the first generation of industrialists, like James Watt. Playfair knew many of these great men through his brother.[27]

Alas, in this crowd, Playfair was not just second-string; he could hardly make the bench. He was supposed to become a tradesman. Soon after his father died, he was apprenticed to Andrew Meikle, an Edinburgh engineer later famous for inventing the first practical threshing machine. Having learned the basics of drafting, in 1777 he moved on to Birmingham to become an assistant to Watt, who at the time was developing the first practical steam engine. From Birmingham, Playfair left for London in 1781 with William Wilson, a partner he met during his employment with Watt, to set up a silversmith company. He filed several patents for metalworking techniques, but these never paid off. It was at about this time that Playfair first tried to earn a living as an author.

Playfair published his first known book (actually, more of a monograph, at 122 pages), *The Increase of Manufactures, Commerce and Finance, with the Extension of Civil Liberty, Proposed in Regulations for the Interest of Money* in 1785. He was just twenty-six. This book was an analysis of British economic and monetary policy, focusing on interest rates and taxation.[28]

A born writer, Playfair was incredibly prolific, publishing more than one hundred-fifty books, pamphlets, and monographs in a career extending over thirty-six years. This was a remarkable accomplishment, given the time and effort required to produce any kind of publication. Remember, at the time every published work began as handwritten script. Even getting paper could present a challenge, and for their first drafts writers like Playfair often used the backs of old broadsheets, leftover ledgers, or whatever scraps came to hand.[29]

The following year, Playfair published *The Commercial and Political Atlas*.[30] It was here that he introduced statistical graphics. He used time series charts to depict the balance of trade between Britain and other nations. (Then, as now, trade deficits were a frequent worry among political officials and scholars alike.) At the time, it was a challenge to produce any kind of picture or diagram for a book. Each figure required an etching or engraving that could be inserted into a printing press. Because he had trained to be a draftsman, he was familiar with the process and was comfortable with drawings in general. His contemporaries, who worked solely with the written word, were not.

Looking for new opportunities, Playfair moved to France in 1787. An acquaintance gave a copy of *The Commercial and Political Atlas* to a French diplomat who, in turn, presented it to King Louis XVI. The king liked the charts because they made statistics easy to understand. Playfair was given liberty of the court, and he become acquainted with French high society and the American expatriate community, including Thomas Jefferson, who was the U.S. ambassador at the time. He also met Joel Barlow, who was something of a celebrity in the United States for his epic poem *The Columbiad*, and later became famous as the first American diplomat to die in the line of duty.[31] Playfair and Barlow became the talk of Parisian society when they collaborated on an ill-conceived scheme to sell land in the Ohio territories. This resulted in the first great scandal of American politics, known as the Scioto Affair, after the river along which the land was located. When several hundred French settlers became marooned in southeastern Ohio, bailing out the settlers became an urgent matter for the new American Congress when it convened in Philadelphia for its first session.[32]

King Louis's patronage notwithstanding, Playfair sympathized with the Republicans and, depending on whose account you believe, he either witnessed or took part in the storming of the Bastille in 1789.[33] However, Playfair soon soured on the French Revolution, as it took a hard radical turn. French "Jacobinism" had roughly the same standing that Islamic fundamentalism does today (they did not call it the Reign of Terror for nothing), and British leaders feared that radicalism might cross the Channel.

So Playfair assumed yet another career: covert operator. William Windham, the British War Secretary, secretly put Playfair on His Majesty's payroll, and Playfair began publishing counterrevolutionary pamphlets.[34] This inevitably got him in trouble with the authorities, and he fled France, returning to Britain via Germany and Holland. En route he encountered an émigré in Frankfurt who, in conversation, described the French semaphore telegraph, an early communication system that could transmit a short message across France in about thirty minutes and was critical to its defense. Playfair made a model of this device and sent it to the Duke of York, at the time the Commander in Chief of the British Army.

Returning to England in 1793, Playfair led an economic warfare operation against France aimed at flooding the French economy with counterfeit currency. He had first proposed the idea a few years earlier and later wrote that, if only officials had "taken his advice in the year 1791 in making war upon the credit of France instead of combating her troops, . . . we would not had now to arm in England, so many men would not have bled in the field." Playfair even estimated the rate at which the French currency would fall in value as it grew in quantity.[35] The bogus money was printed on paper manufactured at mills scattered across the English countryside. The Duke of York carried the counterfeit notes with him to the Continent when British forces deployed to Flanders, and he distributed the notes by using them to pay his troops. The British also gave the notes to the foreign armies that it was funding.[36]

With this background in international finance and foreign intrigue, Playfair eventually turned his attention back to political economy, publishing *The Statistical Breviary* in 1801. Then, Adam Smith's publisher asked Playfair to edit a new edition of *Wealth of Nations*, which he published in 1805, adding a commentary and update. (Smith had died fifteen years before; Playfair knew Smith through his brother, John.)[37]

Playfair next took the issue Smith raised—why countries prosper—and asked the logical follow-on: What causes them to decline? The result was *An Inquiry into the Permanent Causes of the Decline and Fall of Powerful and Wealthy Nations, Designed to Shew How the Prosperity of the British Empire May Be Prolonged*, also published in 1805.[38] The book begins with one of Playfair's engravings (Figure 2.1), portraying the rise and decline of empires from 1500 BC to AD 1805. Playfair described it thus:

> It is constructed to give a distinct view of the migrations of commerce and of wealth in general. For a very accurate view, there are no materials in existence; neither would it lead to any very different conclusion, if the proportional values were ascertained with the greatest accuracy.
>
> I first drew the Chart in order to clear up my own ideas on the subject, finding it very troublesome to retain a distinct notion of the changes that had taken place. I found it answer [sic] the purpose beyond my expectation, by bringing into one view the result of details that are dispersed over a very wide and intricate field of universal history; facts sometimes connected with each other, sometimes not, and always requiring reflection each time they were referred to. I found the first rough draft give me [sic] a better comprehension of the subject,

FIGURE 2.1

Playfair's Depiction of Wealth Migration and the Rise and Decline of Empires

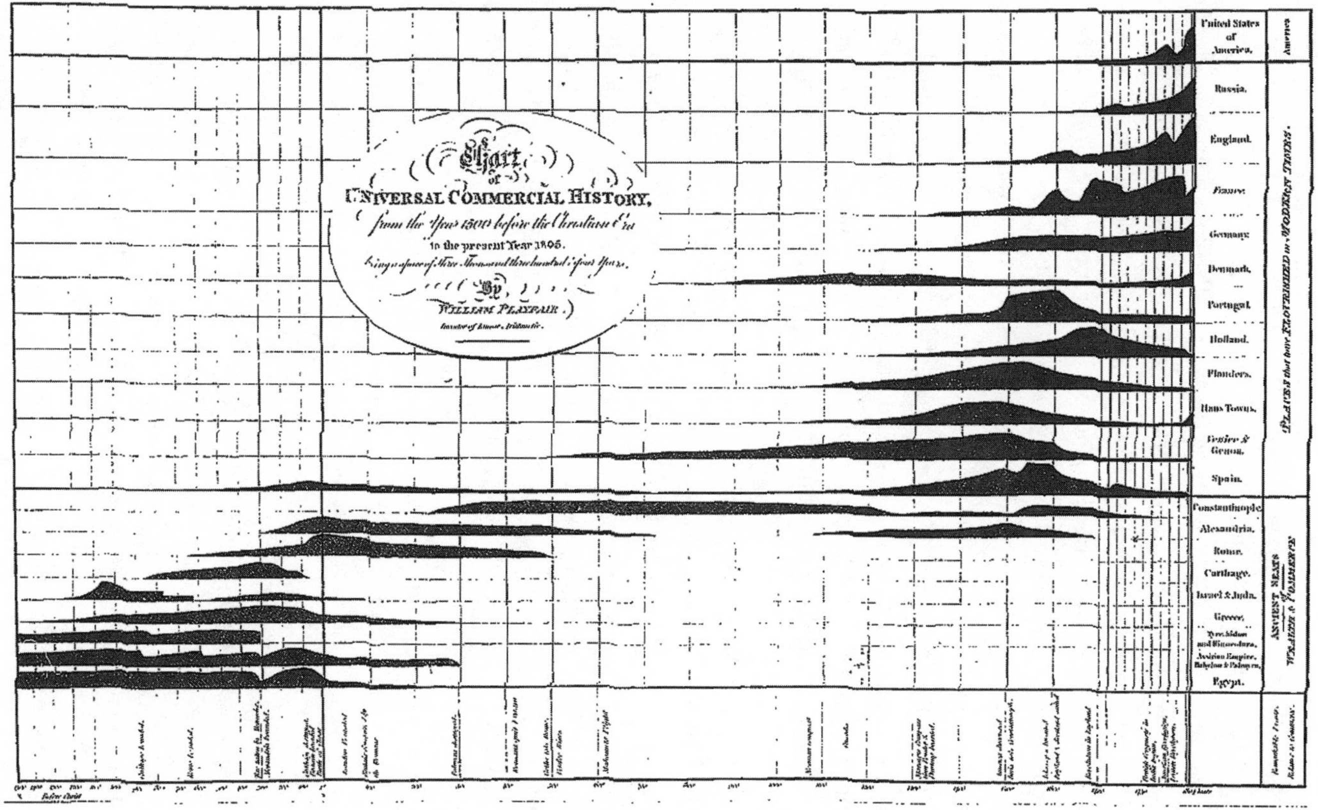

In this "Chart of Universal Commercial History" Playfair attempted to illustrate the transition of power and influence over the course of three millennia. The vertical axis on the right lists ancient empires like Egypt, Greece, and Rome, and modern nations like Spain, Portugal, France, England, and, at the top, the United States. The width of the band is Playfair's estimate of each nation's wealth at a given point in time, and, thus, its rise and decline.

than all that I had learnt from occasional reading, for half of my life-time; and, on the supposition that what was of so much use to me, might be of some to others, I have given it with a tolerable degree of accuracy.[39]

Playfair conceded that the chart was not based on hard, specific documentation and lacked precise quantification, but that is why the *Inquiry* and the *Statistical Breviary* should be read as a pair. One provides the theory; the other provides the data. Together, they represent the state of the art of political economy in the early 1800s.

Playfair made several specific contributions that are important to how we think about the rise and decline of nations. He rarely gets credit for these ideas. Nevertheless, they are largely his own, and, in some cases, one can even document a path through which they influenced other, better-known scholars. These ideas include:

- statistical databases to describe national capabilities;
- the idea that one could, in fact, develop a general theory explaining the rise and decline of nations;
- the concept of comparative advantage;
- the concept of entrepreneurship based on individuals maximizing expected value under conditions of uncertainty, and the linkages between this risk-taking activity, economic growth, and national power;
- the adverse, cumulative effects of special interests as societies mature; and
- the concept that a geopolitical balance of power, combined with free trade, will reduce conflict and produce prosperity.

Let us consider each of these ideas in turn.

Statistical Databases to Describe National Capabilities

To the degree that people know of Playfair at all today, it is almost always in connection with his inventing the graphic presentation of data, as in the *Statistical Breviary*. It is easy to miss an equally important invention simply because it is so obvious: In addition to its graphs, the *Statistical Breviary* provides a country-by-country summary of the capability of every country in the world. It presents estimates for population, land area, revenues, size of army and navy, and so on. It predates *The Statesman's Yearbook, Whittaker's Almanac,* and *The World Almanac* by sixty years, and it can be considered the distant ancestor of databases now used in strategic studies and international political economy.[40]

The main omission in the *Statistical Breviary* is that it did not include the United States, but Playfair corrected this four years later by publishing the *Statistical Account of the United States of America,* a translation of materials collected by the French writer D. F. Donnant (Donnant himself had translated the *Statistical Breviary* into French, which Playfair, as we have seen, had based on translations of tables originally compiled by Boetticher). In effect, this was a predecessor of the present-day *U.S. Statistical Abstract.*[41]

The Possibility of a General Theory Explaining the Rise and Decline of Nations

The possibility of a general theory explaining the rise and decline of nations, of course, was the objective of *Inquiry in the Permanent Causes of the Decline and Fall of Powerful and Wealthy Nations,* which continued the commentary that Playfair had provided in the edition of *Wealth of Nations* he had edited. He explained that he wrote *Inquiry* partly as a response to Edmund Burke, who did not think such a general theory was feasible. Burke believed one could describe the life arc of individual humans, but he thought that nations were too complex. Playfair said that such a theory was indeed possible because the details of day-to-day events washed out when one took in the big picture.

No one seems to have tried to present such a theory before. Gibbon had looked at a single country in *Decline and Fall of the Roman Empire.* Others had looked at the conditions necessary for prosperity, like Smith in *Wealth of Nations,* but he did not connect it to a nation's power and predominance. One can assume that Playfair was trying to echo these books with his own title, combining the question posed by Gibbon ("What caused national collapse?") with the issue posed by Smith ("What causes nations to grow wealthy?). In *Inquiry*, Playfair catalogued what he believed was a systematic list of the reasons for the growth and decline of national power. Eventually the field of political economy focused on this problem and took a similar approach, but that was not until much later. For example, John Stuart Mill founded the Political Economy Club, which included David Ricardo, Thomas Malthus, and other early practitioners, in 1821.

The Concept of Comparative Advantage

Ricardo is generally credited with introducing the idea of "comparative advantage." This is a central concept of economics that underlies arguments for free trade. The concept refers to the edge that one country has in a specified activity and is noteworthy because it leads to the conclusion that the world as a whole benefits most when each nation concentrates on making the things it makes best, or at least those things that it makes "least bad." As Ricardo wrote in his 1817 book *On the Principles of Political Economy and Taxation,*

> Under a system of perfectly free commerce, each country naturally devotes its capital and labour to such employments as are most beneficial to each. This pursuit of individual advantage is admirably connected with the universal good of the whole. By stimulating industry, by regarding ingenuity, and by using most efficaciously the peculiar powers bestowed by nature, it distributes labour most effectively and most economically: while, by increasing the general mass of productions, it diffuses general benefit, and binds together by one common tie of interest and intercourse, the universal society of nations throughout the civilized world. *It is this principle which determines that wine shall be made in France and Portugal, that corn shall be grown in America and Poland, and that hardware and other goods shall be manufactured in England.*[42] (emphasis added)

Yet Playfair wrote this analysis ten years earlier in *Inquiry*; notice the similarity between the two passages, even down to the examples that each author uses:

> Variety of soil and climate, difference of taste, of manners, and an infinity of other causes, have rendered commerce necessary. . . . *Some nations are situated by nature so as to be commercial, just as others are to raise grapes and fine fruits; therefore, though one nation has more than what appears to be an equal share of commerce, it ought not to be a reason for envy, much less for enmity.* . . . *Some nations also find it their interest to attend chiefly to agriculture, others may find it necessary to attend more to manufactures; but that ought to be no cause of enmity or rivalship.* . . . Britain, the wealthiest of nations, at this time, sells little of the produce of her soil, and a great deal of the produce of her industry; but she purchases a great deal of the produce of the soil of other countries, though not much of their industry: in this there is great mutual conveniency and no rivalship. . . . *If France would cultivate her soil with the same care that we attend to manufactures, (at the same time manufacturing for herself as much as she did before the revolution,) she would be a much richer country than England, without having a single manufacture for exportation. Her wines, brandies, fruits, &c. &c. would procure her amply whatever she might want from other nations. Let France make good laws to favour industry; and, above all, render property secure, and she will have no occasion to envy England.* (emphasis added)[43]

Playfair's statistics on land area and population made clear that Britain could not compete with France in agriculture, which was larger and more fertile. This was even truer of Russia. If Britain had any hope of maintaining its power and influence, Playfair concluded, it had to find those activities in which it could excel and concentrate on them—in other words, its comparative advantage. Trying to match France or Russia across the board would ultimately fail.

Ricardo is generally credited with introducing the idea of comparative advantage, but he seems to have been influenced by Playfair, even borrowing some of the language the earlier writer had employed. Playfair also anticipated the potential benefits that resulted from a global economy based on each nation focusing its efforts in that activity in which it enjoyed a comparative advantage. International trade at the time was based on mercantilism, in which European nations established monopolies based on national control of land. Each nation regulated all the trade with its colonies. Free trade, based on comparative advantage, would organize markets on competition and economic activity rather than geography and control.

Playfair believed that if every country were encouraged to find something it could do well, there would be less pressure to protect the exclusive trading rights that go with having colonies. Mercantile competition had been a source of conflict between countries, and especially between Britain and France, triggering the Seven Years' War (also known as the first true world war), the American Revolution, the French Revolution, and, ultimately, the Napoleonic wars. Where Ricardo stressed that free trade would be efficient trade, Playfair stressed that free trade would promote peace—and allow Britain to remain predominant.

The Concept of Risk Taking and Expected Value in Investment, the Adverse Effects of Usury Laws, and the Linkage of Risk Taking to Growth

Adam Smith argued that free markets and free trade would create more wealth for a nation as a whole. However, Smith also believed that, for the good of society and for moral reasons, authorities should limit interest rates. In other words, Smith, the father of capitalism, believed in anti-usury laws.

Jeremy Bentham usually gets credit for making the argument against interest rate ceilings in his essay A *Defense of Usury*. But Playfair was first, and his argument was much more sophisticated and is much more relevant today.

Bentham had read Playfair's work. In a letter Bentham wrote in May 1787 to George Wilson, a barrister and friend, he told Wilson that he was working on *Defense of Usury* and that one of the few works he had

seen on the subject was one by Playfair. This seems to have been Playfair's 1785 monograph *The Increase of Manufactures, Commerce and
Finance.*[44]

Bentham did not think much of it. He suggested that it was just a
polemic, whereas he was writing a more thoughtful, philosophic piece.
In his letter to Wilson, Bentham wrote dismissively, "Nine-tenths of it is
bad writation about the origin of society, and so forth: the other tenth is
a perfectly vague and shapeless proposal for relaxing the rigour of the
anti-usurious laws in favour of projectors; yet without any argument in it,
or any other idea, but that vague one thrown out in almost as general
and vague a way as I have stated it. I understand it has been well enough
spoken of by several people."

In reality, Playfair was much more profound than Bentham believed,
and his argument has proved more enduring than Bentham's. One has
to parse the language some to appreciate the points Bentham and Playfair
were each making.

Bentham's argument for lifting usury limits was philosophical. Usury,
he said, might appear unseemly, but it provided the greatest good for the
greatest number of people. That, indeed, was the essence of Bentham's
concept of utilitarianism.

Playfair was making an entirely different argument. In 1785 the "projectors" Bentham referred to were investors who worked on projects—
that is, venture capitalists. The "bad writation" that Bentham referred to
was Playfair's historical analysis of the evolution of investment practices,
which was essential to an argument for an economic policy. Playfair was
arguing that a government cannot limit the upside return of investments
if it expects investors to raise capital for risky ventures. This, of course, is
now the conventional wisdom, and, notwithstanding the importance of
utilitarian philosophy, it is a much more significant argument today.

Moreover, Playfair, unlike Bentham, had a modern understanding of
how investors make decisions. Playfair used the concepts of probability,
expected value, and calculations under conditions of uncertainty in making his argument. Again, some parsing—and background—are necessary.

The concept of probability is about 350 years old. Gambling, of course, is as old as antiquity (recall the Roman soldiers casting lots for the clothing of Jesus when He was crucified), and national lotteries date back to the 1500s (France appears to have been first, although the city-state of Venice seems to have run one earlier).[45] But just because someone played a game of chance does not mean that they knew what they were doing. Girolamo Cardano, a scholar of Milan and a compulsive gambler, wrote about odds in games of chance in the 1500s, but his manuscripts were not published until a century after his death. So probability theory dates only to 1654, when Blaise Pascal and Pierre de Fermat developed the basic ideas.

Pascal also introduced the idea of expected value—that is, the net value, or utility, calculated when multiple outcomes are possible for an event. Pascal used the idea as a part of his well-known argument for believing in God. As Pascal put it, when you consider the rewards of Heaven and the discomfitures of Hell, the probabilities of each, and the cost of living a virtuous life, it makes sense to believe in a deity. Christiaan Huygens adopted the idea and applied it to gambling when in 1657 he published what appears to be the first book on expected returns under conditions of uncertainty, *Calculating in Games of Chance*.[46] The formal definition of an expected value is

$$E(U) = p_1(x_1) + p_2(x_2) + \ldots p_n(x_n)$$

where N is the total range of possible outcomes, x is the cost or benefit of each outcome, and p is the probability of each.

Even so, the financial world was slow to adopt the concept of a probabilistic return on investment. In Britain, for example, the price of an annuity was not linked to the age of its buyer (and, thus, the likelihood of death) until 1789, and insurance was considered vaguely immoral because it seemed one was betting on the likelihood of personal disaster. Nevertheless, Playfair used an expected utility equation (described in words, rather than symbols) to explain the calculation projectors (i.e., venture capitalists) make when considering an investment. His point was that the government must ensure that there is an environment where such a calculation yields a positive value—that is, a profit. Playfair wrote in *The Increase of Manufactures, Commerce and Finance*:

> ALL projecting partakes of the nature of gaming, in a very considerable degree; the risque incurred is of the same nature, and the effect produced on the mind of those concerned is often the same. The circumstances under which, as well as the extent to which it may be prudent to adventure, may be reduced, in some measure, to calculation also. When projecting is compared to gaming, we must allude to that deep species of play which raises to the summit of fortune, or involves in misery and ruin; for such is the case with projecting in general.
>
> IT is only, however, in some things, that projecting and gaming resemble each other; for gaming is useless labour, at all events; projects are only so when they fail; when they answer, they are the most advantageous sort of productive labour.
>
> PREVIOUS to engaging in any new thing, it is customary to reckon the advantage that will arise from success even among the most sanguine, and to consider what may be the expence of a trial. The more prudent consider the chances. It is not, however, the nature of men, to allow their minds to dwell on the unfavourable parts so long, nor so accurately, as they do on the pleasing and agreeable. The comparison is therefore very seldom made fairly. This is the cause of many failures.
>
> THERE are, besides the circumstances that are usually considered, numbers of others equally necessary to be acquainted with, previous to the undertaking of any new thing.
>
> THE ability of the projector to give a fair trial, and, after it is proved to be a good thing, his further ability to prosecute it.
>
> THE consequences that a FAILURE OF SUCCESS will have upon his circumstances.
>
> THE consequences that SUCCESS will have upon his circumstances.
>
> THESE, then, in addition to the four other great and important considerations; the chance of gain; the risque of loss; the probable amount of gain; and the probable extent of loss, make the chief previous considerations.
>
> AS these do partly depend on the nature of the project, and partly on the circumstances of the projector, they become pretty intricate; and

the more so as each of these things involves in itself a considerable degree of uncertainty.[47]

Linking entrepreneurship to expected value was essential to Playfair's thesis. He believed growth was essential for Great Britain to remain predominant, and that entrepreneurship was essential for growth. He argued that, if the "consequences of success" were limited, projectors would calculate that the expected value of their investment might not be worth taking the risk. When he wrote, the idea of expected value was only a hundred years old, was still controversial, and was not widely applied to public finance. He understood, however, that when governments limited the potential returns of "projects" or taxed too heavily, the most productive members of society seek a more favorable venue. That is, he anticipated tax flight.

The concept of expected value was further developed in the twentieth century and became an integral part of economics in the form of game theory. The calculation Playfair presented in words is now often referred to as a "von Neumann–Morgenstern equation," after John von Neumann and Oskar Morgenstern, who used it as a method to calculate a cardinal measure of utility in their treatise *The Theory of Games and Economic Behavior*. Bruce Bueno de Mesquita and others later adopted the idea to explain a very different kind of "project" central to international relations theory—namely, the calculation one nation's leadership makes when considering whether to attack another.[48]

The Concept That Nations Become Less Productive as Their Economies Mature Because of an Accumulation of Laws and Regulation, and Because of an Aversion to Risk

The concept that nations become less productive as their economies mature because of an accumulation of laws and regulation, and because of an aversion to risk, is important because Playfair's goal was to identify the factors that stopped growth and led to decline. Playfair listed what he called "internal" and "external" causes of decline. Internal causes included all "which arise from the possession of wealth and power, operating on the habits, manners, and minds of the inhabitants; as also on the political arrangements, laws, government, and institutions." External causes resulted from the "envy of other nations; their advancement in the same arts to which the nations that are rich owe their wealth, or their excelling them in other arts, by which that can be rivalled [sic], reduced or subdued."

Almost two centuries later, Mancur Olson proposed a theory in *The Logic of Collective Action* explaining how factions in society inevitably mobilize to get laws and regulations adopted that to benefit themselves — that is, special interest groups. These groups benefit their own members but reduce the efficiency of the economy as a whole. Olson later used his idea to propose a model of why nations decline, in a 1982 book titled, aptly enough, *The Rise and Decline of Nations*.[49] Playfair's analysis of the internal causes of decline anticipated Olson's arguments. In explaining in *Inquiry* how democracies stagnate, Playfair observed how special interests and their advocates — trial lawyers — accrete as a nation matures:

> This is, perhaps, one of the greatest and most crying evils in the land, and calls out the most loudly for redress, as the effects are very universal. In a commercial country, so many interests clash, and there are such a variety of circumstances, that the vast swarms of attorneys, who crowd the kingdom, find no difficulty in misleading one of the parties, and that is the cause of most law-suits.
>
> As commercial wealth increases the evil augments, not in simple proportion, but in a far more rapid progression; first, in proportion to the wealth and gain to be obtained, and, secondly, according to the opportunities which augment with the business done.
>
> In addition to the real dead expense, the loss of time, the attention, and the misfortune and misery occasioned by the law, are terrible evils; and, if ever the moment comes, that a general dissatisfaction prevails, it will be the law that will precipitate the evil.[50]

Playfair said that anyone worried about the decline of their nation's power should watch for warning signs — specifically, the multiplication

of special interest groups, which freeze wealth; the accumulation of regulations and laws that impede entrepreneurs; and taxes that cause the
most productive citizens to leave. In other words, he not only anticipated
today's concept of tax flight but also understood how a nation can offer
a package of benefits to would-be entrepreneurs to compete for their
allegiance. We will return to this idea of a "national brand" in Chapter
3.

The Idea That the Proper Geopolitical Configuration of Power, Combined with Free Trade, Will Reduce Conflict and Produce Prosperity

In *An Inquiry into the Permanent Causes of the Decline and Fall of Powerful and Wealthy Nations*, Playfair considered a world organization to
preserve peace—in effect, anticipating the United Nations. But he
believed it was impractical at the time:

> There appears to be only one real cause for war, so far as it is occa-
> sioned by a wish to obtain wealth; and that arises from possessions in
> the East and West Indies, and in America. If there were no such posses-
> sions, or if they were more equally divided, there would be very little
> cause for war amongst nations.
>
>   It may, very possibly, at some distant time, be an object for a general
> congress of nations, to settle this point; so that it shall be no longer an
> object of jealousy. This can be done only by abandoning entirely, or
> dividing more equally; but, at present, the animosity and enmity occa-
> sioned is considerable, though not well founded.[51]

As an alternative, he proposed a strategic coalition to contain France.
In *Outline of a Plan for a New and Solid Balance of Power in Europe*, a
monograph he published in 1813, he used the measures of national
power he presented in *Statistical Breviary* to show how an alliance led
by Britain and Russia would benefit both and stabilize Europe. Britain
would provide the military force in the coalition; Russia would provide
the people and geographic depth. This kind of quantitative analysis of

international relations did not become common in political science until the 1960s.[52]

Playfair's study, which apparently is unknown to most scholars in international studies today, may have been the first time anyone had tried to analyze grand strategy with measures of national capabilities. He presented a "Statistical Table" listing the fifteen major nations of Europe and their power as measured by fourteen variables: area, population, revenues, military personnel, and so on. He then showed how an alliance between Britain and Russia would offset the power of France. The other states would remain in play but would affect the balance only marginally. This paper was a remarkable piece of analysis for its time, and it would stand up well even today. A professor teaching an upper-division class in international relations would likely give it a grade of B+ or better if he or she were unaware of its true origin.

No significant idea or school of thought develops in total isolation, of course, and Playfair's contributions must be seen as one step in our modern understanding of world politics. However, William Playfair was the first writer to describe international relations in a manner that one would find familiar today. His use of statistics, theory, and history, combined with how he analyzed events in his own time, makes him the first modern practitioner of strategic studies and international political economy.

Demography and Power

As far as we can tell, A. F. K. Organski never heard of William Playfair, but the two men probably would have hit it off. Both were wanderers, looking for opportunity. Both had a taste for the art of the deal. From a theoretical standpoint, both understood that, though national security specialists tend to focus on relations among nations, it is usually what is going on inside that is most important.

Kenneth Organski was a Jewish refugee who migrated from Italy to America shortly before World War II. He went on to serve in the U.S. Navy during the war. One day, when his ship was anchored somewhere in the Pacific, he looked around at all the warships and aircraft assembled in one place and was struck by the sheer military power around him. He could not believe that any nation could ever be more powerful through mere policy.

The only things that could upset this balance, Organski believed, were the tidal forces of modernization and demographic change. He took cues from the evolving field of demography, which had taken off dramatically in the late 1800s as more governments started taking censuses and maintaining systems of national accounts. The new data provided more and better material for developing and testing theories, and led to ideas like the "demographic transition model."

According to this model, countries go through four stages in modernizing. Before modernization, populations have high birthrates, but also high death rates, so they have small, stable populations and short life expectancies. Modernization brings better nutrition, sanitation, and medical care, and life expectancies grow. Because birthrates remain high, however, total population also grows. It is only in the later stages of modernization, as more people move to cities and take manufacturing or service jobs, that birthrates fall. Then population stabilizes at a higher level, with longer life expectancies. In the last stage of this model, population levels may even decline if birthrates are too low. These societies shrink and, on average, grow older.

Although the data eventually showed that relationships between modernization and population growth were more complex than originally thought, the demographic transition model became widely accepted. National leaders implicitly referred to it during the late 1800s and into the early 1900s, when population size was a major concern in Europe. Ironically, considering the worries European leaders have today, their concern was about having *too few* people, and whether they would have enough laborers for their farms, workers for their factories, and soldiers for their armies.

But scholars who studied international relations did not think much about the impact of demographics. To be sure, they acknowledged that some countries had more growth potential than others, but they mainly thought in terms of alliances and of the motivations of countries that created them. The chief difference of opinion among international relations scholars was over whether countries were motivated more by principle or by simply seeking power—the classic collision between idealists and realists.

The realists based their arguments on "the balance of power," the idea that nations tend to align themselves so that no one can dominate the others. It is hard to be sure, of course, but David Hume seems to have introduced the term into common usage in an essay in 1742, "On the Balance of Power." Hume himself did not claim to have invented the idea, noting that even the ancient Greeks were aware of the concept. He wrote of how "the Athenians (as well as many other republics) always threw themselves into the lighter scale, and endeavoured to preserve the balance."[53] Gradually the term began to morph, probably because the Enlightenment led to a better understanding of physics. Since the Athenians or the British always seemed to throw their capabilities to whichever side needed assistance to prevent another country from dominating, it was a short additional step of logic to assume that they would naturally always do so, much as two connected columns of water would balance out. Thus, the "balance of power" became not only a strategy (which was how Playfair used the term in his 1813 monograph) but also a theory about how the world worked and an explanation for events.

Hans Morgenthau popularized the idea during the mid–twentieth century, making "balance of power" synonymous with "realpolitik," or the amoral pursuit of national power. It was a counterpoint to Woodrow Wilson's argument that governments—especially that of the United States—should promote democracy to promote peace. Morgenthau believed the cynical competition of nations seeking their own interests was more likely to produce an equilibrium of power that would avert war.[54] The idea sort of resembled Adam Smith's "invisible hand," where the selfishness of individual buyers and sellers would produce the most efficient allocation of resources and the greatest levels of overall wealth.

Unfortunately, the balance-of-power argument begged a question: Why would one believe any country would act to restore a balance? It seemed much more logical that, if a country had the choice, it would be at least as likely to join the winners in a conflict and share in the gains as to take a chance with incipient losers. For that matter, why would *any* government join a coalition whose main purpose was not to win but to keep anyone from winning?[55]

This was where Organski proposed an alternative argument, drawing on concepts from demography. He observed that a country's *potential* power is roughly equal to its population and physical size (and, thus, natural resources), multiplied by its level of modernization. When a country modernized, he said, the multiplication effect of industrialization kicked in. If it were working from a large enough base, it could develop enough power to upset the existing alignment among nations. Countries faced with the rise of a new power had three options: They could try to deter it, they could try to crush it, or they could bargain with it and accommodate it peacefully. So, in Organski's interpretation, modern history is a series of phases in which one country after another modernizes and dominates, fails, or accommodates. World events were not defined by movement toward *balance* of power but by efforts to consolidate or seize the *preponderance* of power.[56]

This interpretation of history was actually much more consistent with what political scientists and economists were finding in other situations. In legislatures, for example, there is a tendency over time for members to form coalitions that are "efficient" or just big enough to win, so they are obliged to share the winnings with as few partners as possible.[57] Similarly, in Organski's view, the most powerful nation set the agenda for the world's culture, politics, and economics. Less powerful nations could either seek a place (of lesser standing) in the dominant nation's coalition or could try to overthrow it.

So Organski would interpret the period from the late 1700s to the late 1900s as a process wherein Britain was challenged first by France and later by Germany. Both failed to upset the hierarchy. Then the United States, building from a larger base, displaced Britain as it modernized and gained power. But because the American view of how the world should operate was not that much different from Britain's, the transition was peaceful. Later, in the twentieth century, Russia modernized and (in the guise of the Soviet Union) challenged the United States for predominance. Because its views of how the world should operate were very different from those of the United States, accommodation was impossible. But Russia failed in its challenge and collapsed in the process.

In effect, Organski was proposing a process similar to what William Playfair had described a century and a half earlier. Indeed, one can illustrate Organski's idea and show what a power transition looks like, and the results look a lot like what Playfair tried to illustrate with his copperplate etchings.

The Correlates of War Project, which we visited earlier in the book to look at patterns in world energy consumption, also provides a composite index of national power. Look at Figure 2.2, which shows how this index fluctuated for eight countries between 1816 and 2001. I have included three of the traditional European great powers, Britain, France, and Russia; the major emerging powers of Asia and Latin America, China, Japan, India, and Brazil; and the United States. The wider the band for a country in a given year, the higher it scored on the power index. The result is a chart that sort of resembles the one Playfair put at the beginning of *An Inquiry into the Permanent Causes of the Decline and Fall of Powerful and Wealthy Nations.*[58]

This resemblance is no coincidence, since Playfair and Organski were both trying to explain and illustrate the same phenomenon: power transitions. Some of the trends that appear in the current-era charts include the following:

- Britain grew less powerful relative to other states throughout the period. The United States grew more powerful. Over the 185 years depicted in Figure 2.2, that is the main event: a power transition from Britain to the United States as both countries modernized, and the United States' population and resources outstripped the British population.
- The same advantages and problems that applied to Britain also applied to France, but on a smaller scale.

- Russia cratered in 1990 with the breakup of the Soviet Union and the collapse of the Russian economy. Prior to that, it had been a significant power under both the tsars and the Soviets, thanks to its large population, large army, and respectable level of industrialization.
- China has always been a significant presence because of its size but only recently started to grow economically (the boom of the early parts of this century is not yet included in the Correlates of War data set, because the researchers require data for all countries to add a year to the series).
- Brazil and India are also just beginning to show growth in recent years.

One can imagine what Figure 2.2 might look like in 2015 or 2025. China will probably begin to approach or even surpass the United States in this index of power. Brazil and India may be near where China is presently. The European nations will continue to diminish. Organski anticipated these developments, and he was not too far off in predicting the time frames in which they would occur.[59]

From the perspective of power as it is traditionally defined and measured, one would have to bet on China and India gaining predominance, unless they do something precipitous that stalls their economic growth and limits their military power. And that, as we said at the beginning of the chapter, is the long-term challenge to the United States: How do we retain our place in the world in which the basic numbers run against us?

Avoiding the Power Transition: What Are the Options?

Playfair and Organski arrived at similar conclusions about how nations moved up and down the pecking order, but they disagreed on how the competition would play out and what a nation could do about it. Playfair believed that Britain, with the right strategy, could remain predominant. It would have to shed the deadweight of its colonies, support education

FIGURE 2.2

Playfair Revisited: Illustration of a Power Transition in the Nineteenth and Twentieth Centuries, Using an Index of National Power

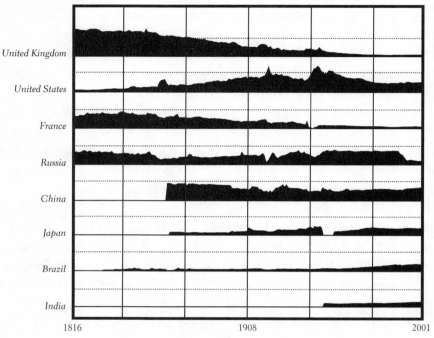

This chart shows the rise and decline of national power from 1816 to 2001 using the Correlates of War index of national capabilities. The index is based on each nation's share of the world's steel production and energy production; total population and urban population; and military personnel and defense expenditures. The wider the band for a country in a given year, the higher it scored on the power index.
Source: Correlates of War Project.

to create new industry, manage alliances to conserve power, and promote free trade so its industry could concentrate on those things it did best. Britain might not lead in every category of trade but, with the right incentives for entrepreneurs, it would maintain the wealth and prosperity to stay on top.

Organski was not so optimistic. He believed demographics could not be denied. Eventually—in the early twenty-first century, or perhaps two, three, or four decades later—China would modernize. Even if it achieved a fraction of the United States' progress, its huge population would make it predominant. "Athenians, Romans, Arabs, Turks, Zulus and Sioux, Spaniards and Swedes, and even Frenchmen and Englishmen have found it possible to continue living with their days of greatest power past," Organski mused. "Perhaps Americans will find it possible as well."[60]

Who is correct? Or do we have a choice in affecting the outcome? Generally, when two logical arguments reach different conclusions, it is because there is an unstated variable critical to the outcome. In this case, the critical variable is the nature of power. There are two central issues: Can the United States use its special strengths to develop critical forms of power that enable it to stay competitive with larger nations? And can it retain these special strengths even as other countries modernize?

In effect, for the United States—which currently is playing a losing hand in the traditional competition of demographics, modernization, and global hierarchy—there is one key question: Can America change the nature of the game? In the process, it may also have to change what it means to be a world power.

Whether and how the United States can do this is the question we turn to next. As we will see, America may now *seem* to have a losing hand, but it still holds cards—culture, political institutions, past investment—that other countries do not have or cannot play. These offer it countermoves. They do not guarantee success, but they can keep America in the game and provide the basis for a winning strategy.

CHAPTER THREE

The American Edge

IT IS EASY for Americans to get discouraged by the war in Iraq and all the other problems that seem to trouble us in the later years of the first decade of the third millennium. Yet, despite these problems, the United States still has more power—defined almost any way—than any other nation in the world today. Name any accepted measure of national power—military capabilities, economic clout, social influence—and America has a clear edge over every other nation. Indeed, we are so accustomed to this advantage that most Americans take it for granted and do not think about it. (The rest of the world is keenly aware of it.)

The question is, can we retain this advantage? The short answer is, "Yes, but." The United States has a shot at remaining predominant, but it will be a different kind of predominance. As we have seen, other countries are bound to develop economically and technologically. Several are working from a larger base, and it will be a more crowded field of competition in any case. So, in the future, the American edge—if we retain it—will depend on whether we are able to take advantage of three fields in which we enjoy special strengths relative to most other countries.

The first field in which we have a special strength is military capability. No other nation currently matches America's military capabilities, and our superiority rests on political, economic, and cultural factors that are hard for other countries to replicate. While support for defense spending in most other countries has virtually disappeared, Americans still support the funding a large standing military requires. The U.S. military also has a level of professional skill that most other countries lack and cannot easily match.

The second field in which we enjoy a special strength is economic. The U.S. economy is still the largest in the world, and we achieve our success largely because we offer a combination of opportunities, incentives, and protection under a reliable rule of law that are all deeply engrained in our culture, politics, and legal system. Other countries will inevitably modernize and grow—indeed, that is our hope—and as the world prospers, the United States will become a bigger fish but in an even bigger pond. Because they are starting from a larger population, countries like China and India will eventually overtake us in sheer size. The economic clout of the United States will depend on whether we can offer something other countries cannot by continuing to reinvent ourselves and by attracting people with ambition and talent.

Our third special strength is cultural. American culture continues to be the only true global culture. Indeed, the phenomenon that is called globalization is really, in many respects, the diffusion of American culture throughout the rest of the world. This spreads our values and perspectives, and that gives the United States influence. The issue here is that culture is hard to control and even harder to direct so as to influence events.

America's ability to remain predominant depends on whether it uses its special strengths and maintains its military, economic, and cultural capabilities, and whether it has the pacing and agility to sustain its capabilities effectively. But underlying all this is the question of *why* Americans want power, or even whether they should. So we first need to say a few words about that.

The Jacksonian Tradition

A few years ago, Walter Russell Mead wrote a perceptive essay in which he observed that, though foreign policy specialists tend to portray Americans as either isolationists or internationalists, experience says they are neither.[1] As a matter of principle, they do not want to shut out the world. But they do not want to get deeply involved in it, either. The average American, said Mead, is a "Jacksonian," a point of view defined by Andrew Jackson, the seventh President of the United States, who served from1829 to 1837.

Jackson was the first populist to occupy the White House. Previous Presidents had won office with the support of elites—northern traders or southern planters. Jackson won with a philosophy and platform aimed at "commoners"—small farmers, laborers, merchants, and frontiersmen. This philosophy, Mead claimed, reflected the no-nonsense mindset of the Scots-Irish immigrants of the late 1700s–early 1800s. Their values— self-reliance, respect for anyone who pulls his own weight, individualism, willingness to take risks, and courage—defined what most Americans admired, and, wrote Mead, continue to admire today.[2]

A Jacksonian is a pragmatist. Like his unruly Scots-Irish ancestors, he believes that the government should keep its nose out of everyone's business—unless there is a good reason to do otherwise, in which case it should act decisively, fix the problem, and then let people get on with their lives. A Jacksonian brings the same mindset to national security. He does not want to get involved with the rest of the world any more than is necessary, but when it is necessary, he wants the U.S. government to take charge and fix whatever is wrong on its terms and then move on. That is where national power enters the equation. Power gives a country the margin needed to stand aloof and the capability required to take charge.

Jacksonians opposed Alexander Hamilton's constituency, Yankee traders, who wanted greater engagement with the Old World, their biggest market. Hamilton said the principal purposes for the federal government included "the regulation of commerce with other nations and between the States; the superintendence of our intercourse, political and commercial, with foreign countries."[3] The key word was "superintendence," which means, "care, oversight, and direction" and has synonyms likes "guidance" and "control." The Hamiltonians favored building institutions for governance, both at home and abroad; they were the predecessors of today's "internationalists." The Jacksonians rejected that.

Yet, at the same time, the Jacksonians also rejected the political philosophy of the southern planters—Thomas Jefferson's constituency—who wanted as little of foreign affairs as possible. As Jefferson put it in his inaugural address in 1801, "Peace, commerce, and honest friendship with all nations—entangling alliances with none."[4] The Jeffersonians were the predecessors of today's "isolationists," believing that the United States, with its vast lands and resources, could mainly be self-sufficient or, at worst, could simply put its corn and tobacco on a ship, deliver it to a foreign buyer, and come home with the proceeds.

The Jacksonians came down in between these two extremes: Diplomacy and national defense were distractions but were a tolerable cost if they got rid of bigger distractions. As Jackson said in his own inaugural speech, "With foreign nations it will be my study to preserve peace and to cultivate friendship on fair and honorable terms, and in the adjustment of any differences that may exist or arise to exhibit the forbearance becoming a powerful nation."[5]

The Jacksonian formula was a strong navy, combined with fortifications and militia. The Jacksonians were willing to spend money on defense, but they were suspicious of large standing armies like those of European nations, and which might threaten the government and drain the economy. It was a national security policy that tried to keep the world at arm's length—not too close but not letting go completely, ready to deal with it when necessary, and forcefully if need be.

This is, admittedly, a simplistic sociological analysis, but it does seem that the Jacksonian ethos is an accurate description for what most Americans want out of international affairs even today—at least it is closer than the Jeffersonian or Hamiltonian alternatives. Americans are determined to keep the world at a distance, while not isolating ourselves from it completely. If we do need to take action abroad, we want to do it on our terms. But our main focus is at home, and while we are willing to pay attention to foreign developments, we do so selectively.

For example, Americans are, on average, much more insular than people from other wealthy, industrial countries. We travel abroad less, preferring instead to stay at home within the vast boundaries of the United States. Only about one in four Americans has a passport. Germans and Britons spend four times as much per capita on foreign travel as their American counterparts; French and Italians spend about twice as much.[6] As for knowledge of international politics—Americans, true to the Jacksonian tradition—will pay attention to issues we think are important, but only *when* they seem important, and no more. Yet this is not apathy. A closer look at real data suggests that something subtler is going on.

Several years ago, Michael X. Delli Carpini and Scott Keeter conducted a "survey of surveys," reviewing several of the major studies that measured the typical American's knowledge of political affairs.[7] As expected—Americans are famously ignorant of politics—there were huge gaps in the respondents' knowledge of how a bill becomes a law. They were often unable to name past Presidents, current legislators, and just about anyone who has served as chief justice of the Supreme Court. Generally, people who were affluent, educated, and engaged in work that got them involved with government scored better than those who did not.

But Delli Carpini and Keeter also found that an impressive number of Americans *do* know the important facts that define the essential principles of American democracy—the length of a President's term, the requirement for a warrant before police can conduct a search, guarantee of jury trial, and so on. Three-quarters of Americans know that the Constitution prohibits a religious test for office holders. A similar number can name at least one of their senators. That is, Americans understand the basic rules of the political game, whom to complain to when the government is not working—and whom to hold responsible. Similarly, on foreign affairs, almost all Americans surveyed know that the United

States is a member of the United Nations; half can name the Secretary of State, and between 25 and 50 percent can correctly associate a major foreign leader with the country he or she heads.

What emerges is a picture of a country whose practical people take a practical approach to knowledge about national security. Americans do not bother with the details most of the time because, for most Americans, the details do not matter most of the time. But we *do* know the outlines of the big picture and what we need to worry about, so we know when we need to pay greater attention and what is at stake. This is the kind of knowledge suited to a Jacksonian.

Americans do not mind being *engaged* with the rest of the world; it is just that we are reluctant to get deeply *involved* with it. For the sixty or so years that pollsters have surveyed Americans on national security issues, the results have reflected this dual mindset. For example, when polled, most Americans do not agree with the statement that the United States should be the "sole leader" in world affairs. Most support the idea of the United Nations, U.S. membership in the World Bank, the World Trade Organization, and the International Monetary Fund. Most Americans polled favor closer relations with Western Europe.[8]

Conversely, more than 80 percent of Americans surveyed would support unilateral air strikes or ground operations to attack terrorist bases. More than two-thirds favor the assassination of terrorist leaders. More than half believe the United States should be able to overthrow governments that support terrorism. And even though most support international organizations in principle, fewer than half of all Americans have a favorable impression of them.

In short, pollsters find a set of mixed results that reflect a thoroughly pragmatic approach, and national power makes it all possible. National power provides the margin needed to stand aloof, and the capability to take charge. This mindset both creates a well of support for maintaining national power and, as we shall see, sets hard limits on how these capabilities can be used. For now, let us consider the magnitude and essential features of American power.

American Power, Measure by Measure

A good way to appreciate the "American edge" is to look at the three dimensions mentioned above in which the United States currently stands out from other nations—military capability, economic heft, and cultural influence—and especially at the U.S. special strength in each.

The Military Dimension

Talk about American security, and you very quickly start talking about the U.S. military. To get an idea of the sheer size of the American military, let us start with people—specifically, the number of people we have in uniform compared with other countries.

The data in Figure 3.1 come from the International Institute for Strategic Studies (IISS), a London-based think tank that publishes *The Military Balance*, an annual summary of defense data for most countries. The IISS gets its information from a variety of official and unofficial sources, but most experts consider it mainly on the mark. The IISS says there are about 20 million active duty military personnel in the world today. About 1.4 million of them are in the U.S. armed forces. Our nearest competitors are China, with 2.3 million, and India, with 1.3 million. North Korea has 1.1 million people in uniform (5 percent of its total population!). Russia has just over a million.

Most of the countries that have big armies also have a draft. The chief exception is the United States, for a combination of reasons that are worth examining more closely. They explain both why our military forces are so capable and why we cannot expand them quickly or easily.

One often hears that the United States has an "all volunteer force." That is incorrect. That label makes it sound as though our military personnel are a bunch of dilettantes, which they most definitely are not, and that they are underpaid, which is also untrue. It is more accurate to say that the United States has an "all-*professional* force."

It is hard to get rich on a military salary, and there are easier and safer ways to make a living. But the U.S. armed services do pay market rates

FIGURE 3.1
Share of World Military Personnel

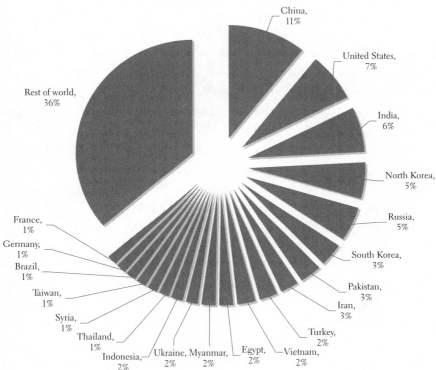

Source: International Institute for Strategic Studies data.

for talent, and, all things considered, a military career is not a bad deal at all. Starting pay for a private, seaman recruit, or airman basic straight out of high school is about $17,000 a year, plus health, housing, and education benefits. A twenty-five-year-old enlisted man or woman with five years in service would probably be a sergeant or petty officer and earn about $28,000 a year. A career enlisted man or woman can earn a top salary of around $60,000 after serving twenty-five years and would be eligible to retire at about two-thirds salary.

In other words, enlisted personnel earn a solid middle-class wage. They can work though their late forties, get an inflation-adjusted pension of $40,000 for life, and then go fishing, write poetry, or move on to a second career and a very substantial income. It is about the same as being a cop or a firefighter for a city, a state, or the federal government.[9]

Similarly, for college-educated officers: A thirty-five-year-old "O-4" (an Army, Air Force, or Marine Corps major, or a Navy or Coast Guard lieutenant commander) earns about $70,000 a year, plus health and housing benefits. An officer who decides to make a career in the military has about a one in four shot at making O-6 (an Army, Air Force, or Marine Corps colonel, or a Navy or Coast Guard captain) in his or her early to middle forties.[10] These O-6s earn about the same as a full professor, a senior engineer, or a corporate or government lawyer with comparable experience—around $120,000 to $135,000 a year. Promotion to flag rank (i.e., general or admiral) is more of a lottery and depends much on chance, organizational politics, and personal diplomacy. But that is true of the executive suite in most professions.

All these facts are reflected in the U.S. military workforce. Military personnel are broadly representative of American society. Even in the thick of the war in Iraq, when the Army was receiving unfavorable publicity for offering more waivers to recruits who did not meet its personnel standards, first-time enlistees in 2006 were still, on average, better educated than young Americans as a whole. More than 90 percent had high school diplomas (compared with 75 percent of their peers), and two-thirds scored in the fiftieth percentile or higher in math and verbal scores. Most came from middle-income families. The main difference between military recruits and the general population is that a disproportionate number of recruits come from the South (a trait they share with American Presidents). Approximately 41 percent of military personnel come from the South, compared with 36 percent of the eighteen- to twenty-four-year-old U.S. population as a whole.[11]

Although the war in Iraq has made it harder to meet recruitment targets—in particular, for the Army and Marine Corps—the bigger problem these days is not a lack of recruits but a shrinking pool of candidates who can meet entry standards. According to the Army's Center for Accessions Research, only 27 percent of young men and women between the ages of seventeen and twenty-four can meet Army entry standards. The remainder, to quote General William Wallace, commander of the Army's Training and Doctrine Command, "are morally, intellectually, or physically" ineligible. "It's the lowest it's been in more than ten years."[12]

That is a polite way of saying that most young Americans are too fat, too dumb, or temperamentally unsuited for military life. A remarkable number of young Americans cannot pass an Army physical, which says as much about the candidate pool as it does the standards. To get through basic training, a seventeen- to twenty-one-year-old man must do thirty-five pushups, forty-seven situps, and run two miles in under sixteen minutes and thirty-six seconds; for women, the requirements are thirteen pushups, thirty-one situps, and a twenty-three-minute, twelve-second two-mile run. After one enters the Army, the standards required to stay in are somewhat stiffer.

Take all this together, and you see that the U.S. military consists of professionals, not merely "volunteers." Everyone in uniform has signed on to make the military their career, at least for part of their lives or part time, and they must work to remain in the service. The salary is a fair wage, but as with most jobs, the money is usually not the main reason people choose a military career. Patriotism, a desire for opportunity, and a sense of adventure are factors, too. (Where else will someone actually pay you to jump out the back of an airplane from 1,000 feet?)

An all-professional force costs more and is harder to maintain, but professionals can do more. Yet America not only pays our people better than the adversaries they may have to face; we train and equip them better, too. You can get a sense of the difference when you calculate how much money the United States spends per person in uniform, which is another way of saying how much it invests in each soldier, sailor, airman, or Marine.

Figure 3.2 gives a breakdown of the world's estimated military expenditures in 2005, the most recent year for which data are generally available. As pundits often note, the United States spends as much on defense as the rest of the world combined — 46 percent, or about $520 billion in 2005. China is second (and rising at a rapid clip) at about 7 percent, or

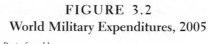

FIGURE 3.2
World Military Expenditures, 2005

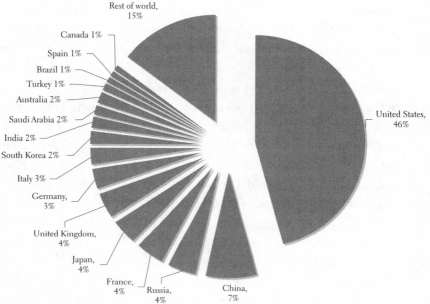

Source: U.S. Central Intelligence Agency, *World Factbook.*

about $80 billion. Russia is third, at about $50 billion (though still hard to measure because of state secrecy). Allies like France, Japan, Britain, Germany, and Italy spend between $25 and $45 billion annually. Then there are several countries that each account for 1 to 2 percent of military spending, or roughly $5 billion to $20 billion each.

Do the math, and you find that the United States spends about $365,000 for every person in uniform. Compare that to China, which spends about $36,000. Britain and Japan, which have professional armies like our own, spend about $180,000–$250,000 per person. In contrast, Russia—which still has a traditional conscript force—spends just $48,000 per person, and India just $14,000.

Granted, not every dollar spent yields a dollar's capability, and currency exchange rates and the cheaper labor costs some countries enjoy have to be considered. But even with these adjustments, America is still investing more than the competition. (To get the rough equivalent purchasing power of a U.S. salary in, say, China, divide by five; the $365,000 we spend becomes $73,000, meaning that we are still spending more than twice as much per soldier.)[13] And at some point, dollars do make a difference.

Compared with the adversaries the United States is likely to face, it spends five, ten, or even thirty times as much to pay, train, equip, and support every man and woman in the armed services. This investment we make in each person is also why a draft does not make sense for the United States. Conscription does not fit our "business model." We will look at this more closely in Chapter 4.

But as long as we are comparing military spending, notice some other facts. First, as mentioned, the United States spends about as much on defense as the rest of the world combined. That is a sign of will as well as of wealth—the Jacksonian mindset kicking in, and the determination to deal with the world on our terms. The size of the combined economies of the members of the European Union, for example, is roughly equal to ours. Yet, all together, the members of the EU spend only about a third of what we spend on defense. Our European friends—like most other countries—do not share our priorities.

The difference in priorities becomes clear as soon as you compare forces, and especially big-ticket items that require multi-billion-dollar investments over many years. Even when you consider the price advantages that countries like China and Russia enjoy, we still have a huge edge over our competitors in "force structure." To wit:

- Of the world's 36 aircraft carriers, 23 belong to the United States. Each is two to three times as large as its foreign counterparts.[14]
- There are approximately 220 operational long-range bombers in the world; 170 belong to the United States.[15]
- There are an estimated 13,000 operational nuclear weapons in the world; approximately 5,700 belong to the United States.[16]

- Of the world's 3,870 tons of nuclear explosive materials (plutonium and highly enriched uranium), the United States owns about 1,250 tons.[17]
- Of the approximately 150 nuclear submarines operating in the world, 69 are in the U.S. Navy.[18]

This gap becomes even more apparent when you shift focus from mere numbers and compare what the U.S. armed forces can actually *do*. For example, of all the countries in the world, the United States is really the only one that can support a military operation of any size far from home. No other nation except Britain and France has anything like this capability, and they are far behind.

How far? Recall how many troops Britain contributed in the initial invasion of Iraq—about 9,000 soldiers, compared with about 150,000 from the United States. Each sent about the same fraction of its standing army; there are about 137,000 soldiers in the British army, compared with the 1 million soldiers in the U.S. Army.

Or, to look at it another way, recall the earthquake that rocked northern Pakistan in December 2005. The temblor killed about 75,000 people and left about 2.5 million homeless. Much of the destruction occurred in remote mountain regions. Landslides or bridges that had collapsed usually blocked the few roads that reached the damaged areas. The only organization in the world that could assist Pakistan was the U.S. armed forces, which airlifted food and medical support into the region. Other countries sent money or rescue personnel, but it is fair to say that the U.S. Department of Defense was the backbone of the effort.

Just about every opinion survey says that Europeans are quite happy spending a larger share of their taxes on welfare, farm subsidies, and state-funded health care instead of their armies and navies. French taxes consume about half the total French gross domestic product (GDP), but the government spends only about one-twentieth of that on defense.[19] Nicholas Sarkozy won the French presidential elections in 2007 promising policies that most would consider right of center, but these did not include increasing the defense budget. To the contrary; Sarkozy promised to "maintain" (meaning, not to increase) defense spending at about 2 percent of GDP, and, indeed, he had opposed a larger defense budget when he was finance minister a few years before.[20]

Countries cannot expect to have military influence if they have not made a military investment. This is worth keeping in mind when the United Nations debates whether to authorize the use of military force. For most national governments, it is really an academic discussion. They have little force to use. Bangladesh and Nigeria, for example— traditionally, two of the largest contributors to UN peacekeeping missions—may send troops, but not for outright combat. They do not train for it, and they could not fight through any serious opposition. They could not even get to the scene without assistance, because they do not have the ships or aircraft. (The U.S. Air Force typically provides transportation.)

The same is true for Russia. The old Soviet army was designed for a 500-mile strike across Western Europe. The Soviets invested in bridging engineers, pipeline layers, and thousands of tanks, trucks, and armored personnel carriers. Today's Russian army, in contrast, can hardly operate much beyond the old Soviet borders. And the same is true for China. The People's Liberation Army Navy (yes, that is what it is called—or, for short, the PLAN) is modernizing, but for now it cannot operate more than a few hundred miles beyond its coast.[21]

In effect, since the Cold War, every nation other than the United States has been designing armies for local operations—to keep the neighbors out, keep order at home, and, every so often, grab territory just beyond the border. Indeed, most nations are spending less and less on combat forces each year, and the only military powers other than the United States, Britain, and France that have a significant capability to strike far from home are, oddly enough, international terrorist groups like al-Qaeda—as the 2001 terrortist attacks on the World Trade Center and the Pentagon demonstrated.

Because long-term investments are needed to develop the infrastructure, professionalism, and institutional knowledge required for an effective military force, the United States has a military edge that will take several years for anyone to overcome. Consider China's navy again, for example. Some analysts believe China intends to build aircraft carriers, partly to challenge the United States in the Western Pacific and partly to support a potential attack on Taiwan. And, sure enough, during the past few years, Chinese companies have bought some old, retired aircraft carriers—the *Melbourne* from Australia in 1985, and the *Minsk* and *Kiev* from Russia in 1995 and 1996. The PLAN itself bought the *Varyag* in 1998 from Ukraine. (Many Chinese companies have ownership and management ties to the Chinese military, so it is hard to say whether a purchase was for military or commercial reasons, and it may be a distinction without a difference in any case.) Even so, building the ship might be the *easiest* task; watch a carrier in operation, and you soon realize that the hard part is mastering the complexities of making all the bits and pieces work together in a sustained, effective fashion.

Tradition, culture, and institutional knowledge are hard to build. They require sustained investments. More important, they require a cadre of people who want, by inclination and upbringing, to devote a lifetime to develop the skills and dedication a modern professional military organization requires. The United States has this culture and tradition. Most other countries do not.

These barriers to entry limit the competition, and so the United States will have a unique military capability for the foreseeable future. This will give it a dimension of power that will make it distinct from all other countries for several decades. To be sure—and as we shall see—U.S. military power is far from unlimited, and our adversaries will concentrate their own efforts to take maximum advantage of our weaknesses. Even so, our past investment and distinctive culture favoring military service together carve out a special role for the United States that other nations cannot perform.

The Economic Dimension

Now let us look at our second dimension of national power: the economy. Figure 3.3 shows the world's total GDP, and how much of it each

FIGURE 3.3

Distribution of the World's Gross Domestic Product, 2005

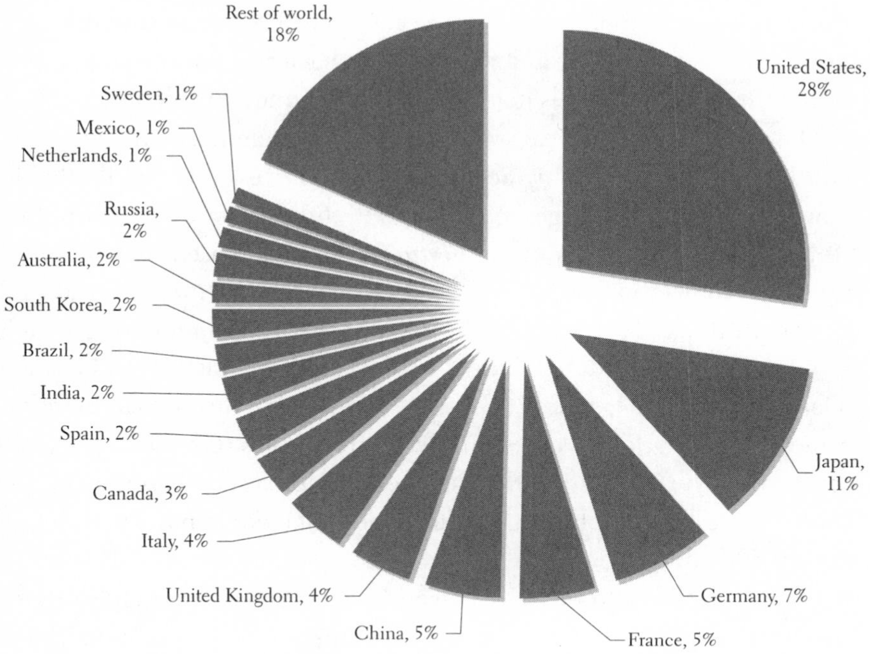

Rest of world, 18%

Sweden, 1%
Mexico, 1%
Netherlands, 1%
Russia, 2%
Australia, 2%
South Korea, 2%
Brazil, 2%
India, 2%
Spain, 2%
Canada, 3%
Italy, 4%
United Kingdom, 4%
China, 5%
France, 5%
Germany, 7%
Japan, 11%
United States, 28%

Source: United Nations Statistics Division.

country generates. GDP is simply a measure of how much stuff—goods and services—a country produces. In effect, it measures the size of a nation's economy.

So, according to the pie chart, the world currently produces about $65 trillion worth of stuff each year—cars, computers, crops, counseling, cosmetics, accounting services, advertising, aircraft, oil, NFL football, World Cup soccer, Hollywood movies, greeting cards, and illegal drugs (roughly $300 billion per year for that last item; for comparison, General Motors has annual revenues of about $200 billion).[22] You name it, and it is in there.[23]

Of this, we in the United States produce about 20 percent, or around $13 trillion worth. Or, again, to put it another way, about a fifth of the world's economy is the American economy. If California were a country, it would rank between Canada and Italy. All things being equal, countries with bigger economies can raise more taxes for their armed forces, public works, education, and so on. They have more money to invest, more to spend, and all this together gives them more influence.

The same pattern appears when one looks underneath the top line. The United States not only accounts for the largest share of the world economy; most of the largest companies in the world are American, too. Of the top 10 companies in the *Fortune* 500, 6 are based in the United States: ExxonMobil, Wal-Mart, General Motors, Chevron, Ford, and ConocoPhillips. Two are British (BP and Royal Dutch Shell, which could also be considered based in the Netherlands), 1 is German (Daimler), and 1 is Japanese (Toyota). About 100 of the 500 largest companies in the world are based in the United States. China now has 40 companies in the listing. No European country comes close to the United States, though the European Union as a whole has about 200 of the top 500 companies.[24]

Or to look at wealth in a very personal way: There are as many billionaires in the United States as in the next nine countries combined (432 vs. 304; Germany is second with 55). Two of the three richest people in the world are Americans: Bill Gates and Warren Buffet; Mexico's Carlos Slim has alternated with them in the top three slots.[25]

But to get a complete picture of nations' comparative power, we need to know more than just the size of a nation's GDP, where businesses base themselves, and who has wealth. What are the trends?

Figure 3.4 shows the average growth rate of a sample of countries during the past ten years and the past fifteen years. Five key observations make it easier to understand economic growth and its potential impact. First, mature, industrial countries have low growth rates. Economies take advantage of the "low-hanging fruit" when they first begin to develop. Cheap labor moves to the cities. Few safety or environmental regulations get in the way of business. Putting in basic infrastructure—roads, electrical power—yields big gains. Later on, interest groups mobilize—industry associations, unions, and consumers—and get subsidies, wage floors, and

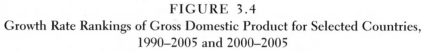

FIGURE 3.4

Growth Rate Rankings of Gross Domestic Product for Selected Countries, 1990–2005 and 2000–2005

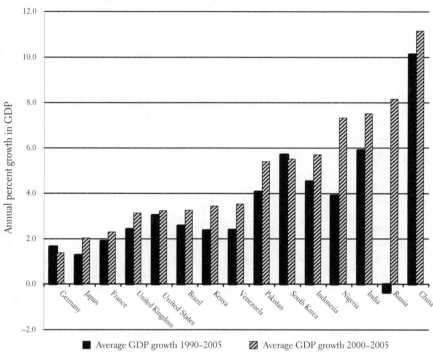

Source: United Nations Statistics Division.

regulations. Taxes go up. These special interests may provide important benefits to their constituents and even society, but they also weigh down the economy as a whole.

The second key observation is that the countries with the highest growth rates currently fit into two categories. Some are in the initial stages of industrialization—like South Korea, India, and China. They are getting the big gains that come from early investment, and they are not yet bogged down by special interests. Go to Beijing and look at the sky; most days you will not see it. It is worse than Manchester in the 1800s. In both cases, cheap coal, lax or nonexistent pollution controls, and a workforce that would rather work in sweatshops than subsistence farms equal double-digit growth rates.[26]

Third, the other fast-growing countries are oil exporters—Nigeria, Russia, Indonesia. Their growth is directly related to the rising cost of energy and that, despite the cost, the world is using more of it. (Gozprom, the Russian state-owned oil monopoly, accounts for about a quarter of the nation's entire GDP.) The big question for these countries is whether their growth is a temporary historical blip or something that fundamentally changes their economies and, thus, their standing in the world.

Fourth, notice that Russia's economy had "negative growth" in the early 1990s—it actually shrank as Russia disengaged from communism and made a painful transition to capitalism. Its growth during the past few years has more than made up for that. If you ever wondered why Vladimir Putin was popular despite his disdain for civil liberties, now you know. For better or worse, his success with the economy is one of the most important factors shaping Russian politics today.

And, fifth, of the mature, developed economies, the United States stands apart. For the past twenty years, it has outpaced Japan and Europe.

Now, look at Figure 3.5 to put all these factors together and get a sense of how the economic clout of different nations has been evolving. The rankings shift somewhat from year to year, but the overall pattern has persisted for almost two decades.

Everyone is growing, but the United States is growing a little faster than its industrial competitors. You can see how China and India have entered the scene, and you can see the downward dip the economy took (as a whole and Russia in particular) when the Cold War ended. The rapid growth in China, India, and other developing countries is the result of manufacturing jobs moving there. Millions of peasants are moving from rural areas to cities. This process is being accelerated as new manufacturing cities are being built in rural areas.

In effect, China can "offshore" its industry without going abroad. If the labor rates 500 kilometers from the coast are ten cents too high to make a business case for a new factory, a company can choose a site 200

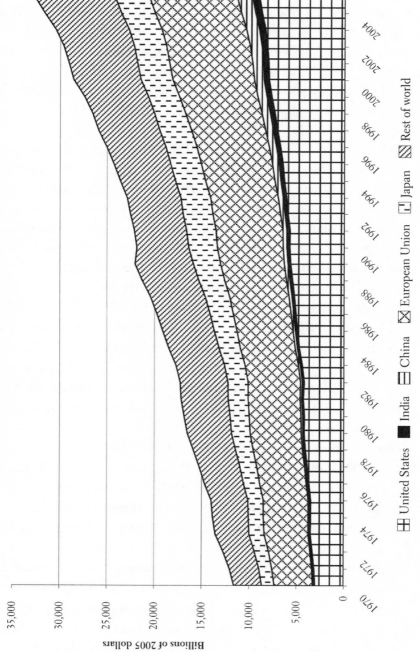

FIGURE 3.5

Distribution and Rates of World Economic Growth, 1980–2005

Billions of 2005 dollars

⊞ United States ■ India ⊞ China ⊠ European Union ⊡ Japan ▨ Rest of world

Source: United Nations data.

kilometers further inland where the labor rates are cheaper still. Moreover, these factories are mainly new and modern, designed to take advantage of cheap land and laid out for maximum efficiency. The work is
hard, but the pattern is the same we have seen since the beginning of
the Industrial Revolution. People would rather work long hours in a
sweatshop, live in company dormitories, and shop at a factory store than
try to eke out a living as a subsistence farmer.

This same process is being played out, if only on a slightly smaller
scale, in other countries. Forget Rio de Janeiro; the soul of Brazil today
is São Paulo—the fourth-largest city in the world. Coming over the
mountains and first seeing it, it is impossible for one to take it all in. The
houses, factories, and office buildings stretch from one horizon to the
other. As in the case of Shanghai (and Mumbai and Jakarta), it is impossible to stop millions of people from seeking a better way of life for themselves and their families, and so they move to the city.

Immigration has also been critical to U.S. economic growth, and it is
one of the chief reasons our growth outpaces that of other developed
economies. Without immigrants, the United States would begin to look
more like Western Europe, growing older, smaller—and less productive.
Immigrants are more likely to start new businesses, ranging from Rupert
Murdock's latest megaventure to the local cleaning service or construction contractor. Immigrants also account for a disproportionate share of
American inventions, as measured by patent filings.[27]

Requests from American high-technology firms for more H-1B visas
(the temporary permits that allow workers with specialized skills to
remain in the United States) reflect a major trend: the rapid growth of
"skilled human capital" outside the United States. Fifty years ago, about
half of all research and development was conducted in America. Today
three-fourths of all of the world's research and development is conducted
overseas—40 percent in Asia alone. On a per capita basis, the United
States currently scores well in measures of human capital—only Japan,
Sweden, and Finland have more scientists and engineers—although we
are turning them out at a lower rate than many of our competitors.[28]

But the larger issue is about absolute numbers, and whether we want the center of gravity of the world's science, medicine, research, invention, and engineering to move overseas. This is another example of development and demographics shaping national security issues and presenting choices. Skilled human capital outside the United States will continue to grow. To respond, we can admit foreign workers as guests, in which case they will have little incentive to assimilate and switch their allegiance to the United States. We can create more immigration slots and encourage them to become Americans. Or we can watch more and more of the world's know-how move overseas. (As it is, about 1 million would-be applicants compete for about 100,000 H-1B visas).[29]

As everyone knows, however, immigration policy has become incredibly controversial in the United States. On the one hand, immigration is a fundamental part of America. At some level, all Americans can trace their ancestry to someone who took a risk to leave their home and find greater opportunity somewhere else. On the other hand, intense pluralities oppose immigration in varying degrees and for different reasons: homeland security, economic interests, or ethnocentrism.

Yet, in fact, immigration has been controversial literally from the beginning of U.S. history. The earliest English settlers objected to the poorer Scots-Irish immigrants who arrived after them. (Immigration was an important part of the Scots-Irish culture; before homesteading in America, Scottish lowlanders had immigrated to Ulster for the same reason: land and opportunity.) The issue reemerged in the 1840s when the "Know Nothings" and their successors opposed Irish Catholic immigrants and then reappeared in response to each successive wave of foreign arrivals—Germans, Chinese, Jews, Italians, Eastern Europeans, South Asians, and, most recently, Hispanics. Pat Buchanan used the issue to rally supporters in his presidential campaigns in 1992 and 1996, Pete Wilson used it to win the California gubernatorial election in 1994, and, more recently, Lou Dobbs used it to revive his career as a television personality.

American attitudes toward immigrants are complex. Polls show that Americans generally have favorable attitudes toward Asians and Hispanics (who today constitute the majority of immigrants). Americans tend to overestimate how many immigrants—both legal and illegal—are in the country. Perhaps not surprisingly, unfavorable views of immigrants are more likely in places where immigrants are most visible; about twice as many respondents in Phoenix say immigration is a "very big" community problem as in Chicago, Raleigh-Durham, or Washington.[30]

The evidence for the common complaints about immigrants—that they take jobs from citizens, impose burdens on public services, contribute to crime, and refuse to assimilate—is at best ambiguous and often wrong. For example, though both legal and illegal immigration have increased rapidly since the mid-1990s, unemployment has hovered at about 5 percent, which most economists believe is the rate that occurs when the workforce is effectively fully employed and workers are simply moving between jobs. So it is hard to argue that immigrants take jobs from native-born Americans.[31]

Most studies indicate that immigrants commit crime at about the same rate, or less, than the rest of the population,[32] and that Hispanics are assimilating at about the same rate as previous generations of immigrants; 23 percent of first-generation Hispanic immigrants speak English well, and this share rises to 88 percent for the second generation and 94 percent for the third generation. About half of all foreign-born Hispanics speak only Spanish at home, while 90 percent of their children speak English at home.[33]

In other words, Hispanics are assimilating at about the same rate as previous immigrants. The main difference is that their presence in American society is greater than the presence immigrants had forty or fifty years ago because there were then greater restrictions on immigration. Their presence, as a percentage of the American population, is about the same as that of immigrants in the late 1800s and early 1900s, and so perhaps it is not surprising that xenophobia is running at about the same rate.

However, from the perspective of maintaining a strategic advantage for the United States in global politics, the immigration controversy itself poses a significant threat for U.S. national security. Resistance to immigration undermines America's ability to compete for the world's ambitious, motivated, and talented people—which would be ironic, because assimilation of foreigners to take advantage of their talents was a key component of the Scots-Irish culture on which the Jacksonian philosophy of foreign affairs is based.

The Scots-Irish were assimilators. James Webb (D-VA), the Marine-turned-novelist and current U.S. senator, writes in his history of the Scots-Irish that "the Scots-Irish, like other cultures, have always had their group prejudices as well as their fiercely held internal codes." But, he goes on to say, "On the whole they are an embracive people who have tended to focus more on shared concepts such as family loyalty and personal honor than on simple ethnic similarities."[34] Mead described the process this way:

> Most progressive, right thinking intellectuals in mid-century America believed that the future of American populism lay in a social democratic movement based on urban immigrants. Social activists like Woody Guthrie and Pete Seeger consciously sought to use cultural forms like folk songs to ease the transition from the old individualistic folk world to the collective new one that they believed was the wave of the future. . . . What came next surprised almost everyone. . . . In what is still a largely unheralded triumph of the melting pot, Northern immigrants gradually assimilated the values of Jacksonian individualism. Each generation of new Americans was less "social" and more individualistic than the preceding one. . . . Outwardly, most immigrant groups completed an apparent assimilation to American material culture within a couple of generations of their arrival. A second type of assimilation—an inward assimilation to and adaptation of the core cultural and psychological structure of the native population—took longer, but as third-, fourth- and fifth-generation immigrant families were exposed to the economic and social realities of American life, they were increasingly "Americanized" on the inside as well as without.[35]

In short, the United States does not have an immigration problem so much as it has a border security problem and an assimilation challenge. The solution is to separate and fix the true security concerns, like preventing unauthorized border crossings; create incentives for assimilation, like learning English and American culture; and then deal with the rest of the immigration issue as a strategic issue, in which the United States must cast as wide a net as possible for talent and anyone with a proclivity to take risks for the promise of reward.

The Cultural Dimension

Joseph Nye coined the term "soft power" in his 1990 book *Bound to Lead*.[36] Nye, a Harvard professor who has occasionally served in government, contrasted soft power with traditional forms of "hard power," like military force or economic clout. According to Nye, soft power is the ability of one nation to shape the behavior of others because they wanted "to follow it, admiring its values, emulating its example, aspiring to its level of prosperity and openness."[37] Nye believed soft power would play a larger role in world affairs with the end of the Soviet-U.S. confrontation. But the idea of influence—the ability of a nation to inspire, cajole, or shame people in another nation to take action—dates back at least two thousand years.

For example, sometime around AD 80 the Greek historian Plutarch wrote about how Cimon, a general and politician in ancient Athens, habitually used neighboring Sparta (also known as Lacedaimon) as a role model. According to Plutarch, Cimon was "a favorer of the Lacedaemonians even from his youth." He even named one of his sons Lacedaemonius, and he had a penchant for ending arguments in the assembly by simply asserting, "This is not the Spartan way."[38] He was implying that the Athenians ought to adopt the methods, values, and judgment of the Spartans because it would make Athens stronger. That is soft power.[39]

Soft power has gotten a lot of attention lately, partly because, at least by some measures, the United States seems to be faring so poorly in using or developing it. One widely cited poll, the Pew Global Attitudes Project, reported that the United States is "broadly disliked in most countries surveyed."[40] Andrew Kohut, who directed the survey, and his coauthor Bruce Stokes summarized their results concisely in the title of a book:

America Against the World: How We Are Different and Why We Are Disliked.[41] Surveys such as these report that in Muslim countries like Turkey and Pakistan—U.S. allies—only 23 percent of the public had a favorable view of the United States. Even in Lebanon, where the United States was critical to the success of the Cedar Revolution in 2005, support ran at only 42 percent. Other surveys have produced similar results.

What surveys taken abroad say about the United States may be disconcerting, but a different picture emerges if you measure actual behavior. When people vote with their wallets or vote with their feet, the United States comes off better. For example, statistics on foreign direct investment consistently put the United States in the top ranks of places where investors put their money (e.g., in 2006 the United States was second, behind Great Britain).

One reason is that the United States offers a combination of opportunity and security. The Heritage Foundation and the *Wall Street Journal* publish an annual Index of Economic Freedom, similar in concept to the Freedom House survey, except that, instead of using criteria that define democratic government, economic freedom experts grade according to criteria that define a nation's business environment: tax rates, inflation, corruption, amount of regulation, fairness of the legal system, and so on. Other organizations, like the Fraser Institute, publish similar indexes.[42]

The United States always ranks near the top in these studies (4th in the 2006 Index of Economic Freedom, behind Hong Kong, Singapore, and Australia). China is ranked 119th, just ahead of Russia, but generally investment rates are correlated with high scores of economic freedom. Investors flock to Russia and China because the potential return on investment is so attractive, despite the risk and hassle. Basket case economies, as expected, rank lowest in economic freedom; North Korea ranked last, at 157th. Cuba (156th), Libya (155th), Zimbabwe (154th), and Burma (153rd) fill out the bottom rungs; none are known as capital magnets.

Similarly, surveys may say the United States is unpopular, but by almost any measure it is the most popular place in the world when people look for a new home, a place to study, or a base for doing business.

Tourism to the United States from abroad dipped about 15 percent after the September 11 terrorist attacks, thanks largely to restrictions that make traveling to America a hassle. But, in general, the United States still attracts talent and commerce.

Some background on this point about the global market for talent and ambition is useful. Migration patterns are changing. In the nineteenth and twentieth centuries, nine-tenths of all migrants were making a once-in-a-lifetime decisions to leave poorer "countries of origin" to resettle in a few "countries of destination" like the United States, Canada, and Australia. Today migration is constant and networked. People are shopping for opportunity. Cheap airfares make it easier to move, and telephone calling cards and Internet cafes make moving less traumatic. The result is that about 200 million people today live in a land other than the one of their birth. If this nation of migrants were itself a country, it would be the seventh largest, ahead of Brazil and just behind Indonesia. Migration is, in effect, a huge economic sector in the global economy, like manufacturing, services, or energy. For many developing countries the remittances that migrant workers send home to their families members represent 10 to 20 percent of their total GDP.

In this market for talent and ambition, no one attracts workers like the United States. One in five of all migrants in the world comes to the United States (about 1 to 1.2 million a year legally; about 400,000 to 800,000 illegally). Just over one of every ten Americans, or 38.4 million, is foreign born. But there is competition. Germany attracts slightly more migrants on a per capita basis. Russia, perhaps surprisingly, comes in second in overall number of migrants; its booming economy attracts workers in Europe seeking opportunity the same way the United States does in the Western Hemisphere and the Pacific.[43]

Similarly, when people choose a place to study abroad, the most frequent choice by far is the United States. No one attracts as many foreign students. In 2006, 564,766 non-U.S. students were enrolled in American colleges and universities. (This was a rise back to pre–September 11 levels after a dip of a few years.) By comparison, the next five top-ranking destinations are the United Kingdom (about 340,000 foreign students), Germany (246,000), France (238,000), China (141,000), and Japan (118,000). The largest number of students visiting the United States, incidentally, comes from India (13.5 percent), China (11.1 percent), South Korea 10.4 percent, and Japan (6.9 percent)—another example of how the United States is shifting many of its traditional ties from Europe to Asia.[44]

If you probe a little deeper, you get an even better appreciation for why so many people want to come to the United States, and why the United States is so successful in competing for the world's talent. The Council on Competitiveness, a nonpartisan research organization that promotes economic growth, rates countries on an index of "business friendliness." It measures variables like the number of steps required for incorporating, the cost of setting up a company, and so on. The easiest place in the world for a person to go into business is Denmark, where the cost of starting a company is close to zero. New Zealand and Ireland come next; both have seen a lot of small business growth. The United States is fourth, where starting a new business costs an average of 0.7 percent of a person's income and requires five days. (By comparison, in Germany, setting up a business costs about 5 percent of per capita income and requires twenty-four days; in Japan it is 7.5 percent of income and twenty-three days.)[45]

Similarly, once an immigrant arrives in the United States, his or her chances of moving up are good. Despite frequent assertions about growing inequality and income stagnation, statistics say that the "American dream" of rising from rags to riches still comes true. Using a sample of almost 100,000 tax returns filed from 1996 to 2005, the Treasury Department found that Americans in the lowest income rungs (e.g., day laborers, store clerks, janitors, and laundry workers) have the highest income growth rates—90.5 percent over the ten years, compared with an average of 24.2 percent for all groups. In other words, the U.S. economy offers mobility, which translates into opportunity—all features essential for a nation to compete for the world's talent.[46]

So why does the United States do so poorly on the Pew surveys and similar polls? One reason is that they are really measuring whether foreigners *like* the United States or U.S. policies, and that also has to be put in context.

Recall Cimon. The Athenians may have admired Sparta, but the two states were in fact bitter rivals. And there was nothing soft about the Spartans; they were apt to hurl a newborn infant off a cliff if the city elders thought the kid was not up to snuff and might weaken the state as an adult. In other words, soft power is often not nearly as warm and cuddly as the term would imply. Having influence is not the same as being liked or being approved of. Influence is simply being able to shape the behavior of individuals, organizations, and governments with a message and, over time, with a reputation—that is to say, a *brand*.

Power and Brands

In today's world, if you want power, and especially soft power, you need a brand. Brands attract the people, capital, and other resources that generate power. On the cultural front, brands are both the means to make a culture more effective and a measure of how effective your cultural power happens to be.

Consider recent global affairs, and you can see the power of brands. In the summer of 2002 Abu Musab al-Zarqawi was just a middle-ranking figure in the world of Islamic militants. "Zarqawi" was a nom de guerre—that is, a personal brand. The Jordanian had been born Ahmad Fadhil Nazzal al-Khalayleh thirty-six years earlier, and he took a pseudonym from his hometown of Zarqa. The accepted story is that Zarqawi was a street tough who found religion while serving time in prison in Jordan during the 1980s. Once released, he traveled to Afghanistan for the tail end of the war against the Soviets. He did another stint in jail in Jordan during the mid-1990s, this time for plotting against the government. Freed in 1999, he fled first to Pakistan and then back to Afghanistan, where he set up a camp for Jordanian militants. Like other terrorists, he competed for recognition and followers.

After September 11, Zarqawi reportedly took refuge in Iraq, heading the Jamaat al-Tawhid wa'l-Jihad, or the Unity and Jihad Group. When Colin Powell addressed the UN Security Council in February 2003, he cited Zarqawi's presence in Iraq as evidence that Saddam Hussein gave refuge to terrorists. Unfortunately, in the process Powell unknowingly enhanced the terrorist's stature. Before the UN session, Jamaat al-Tawhid wa'l-Jihad had been just one of several jihadist groups in the region. With Powell's imprimatur, Zarqawi became a recognized, validated threat to the United States—and his group became the one to join as the insurgency heated up.

Zarqawi's "brand strategy" was to portray himself as the most ruthless insurgent of all. He was one of the first to capture and behead Western hostages, and he put videos of the murders on the Internet. The execution of Nick Berg, a young American businessman, in May 2004 was the tipping point. After it appeared on the Web, word seeped out that the hooded murderer was none other than Zarqawi himself, and he became the most recognized and feared leader of the insurgency.

Even so, Zarqawi was a Sunni—a minority in Iraq, and a foreigner, to boot. So he needed a way to expand his base. This is where his interests converged with those of al-Qaeda.

Zarqawi presented both a problem and an opportunity to al-Qaeda. After the U.S. campaign in Afghanistan in late 2001, Osama bin Laden and other al-Qaeda members took refuge in the tribal lands straddling the Afghan/Pakistani border. As they laid low, thousands of miles from the action, Zarqawi was becoming a rock star among the Sunni extremists, doing battle against both the American "Crusaders" and the Shi'ite apostates in Iraq. Al-Qaeda was in danger of becoming passé, and its solution was, in effect, to "franchise" the brand. Sometime in late 2004, Zarqawi swore allegiance to bin Laden and renamed his organization Tan'im Qa'idah il-Jihad fi Bilad ir-Rafidayn, or al-Qaeda in the Land of the Two Rivers—or, as it became known in the West, al-Qaeda in Iraq.

This was a win–win. Al-Qaeda got an army in the middle of a war and could take credit for whatever mayhem it achieved, enhancing its reputation and attracting more recruits worldwide. Zarqawi got an affiliation with an organization that let him go global, and bin Laden's endorsement gave him a leg up on his local competition. In fact, few if any of Zarqawi's terrorists went to al-Qaeda's "home office" for training. Few if any physical assets were exchanged. The deal was all about the brand.

American forces killed Zarqawi in an air strike in June 2006, but al-Qaeda in Iraq continued. Meanwhile, rival groups fought to establish their own brands by highlighting the faults of al-Qaeda in Iraq and touting their own merits. Groups developed their own styles and identities in Internet videos. Some even have logos. For its part, al-Qaeda acquired additional affiliates as other terrorists in the Middle East and North Africa swore allegiance to bin Laden.[47]

Al-Qaeda, in other words, developed a strong brand. It is instantly recognizable and, like many brands, tells a story through its very name ("al-Qaeda" means "The Base," harkening back to the resistance against the Soviets in Afghanistan, when bin Laden set up a support network for mujahideen). The brand provides the organization tangible benefits. It focuses attention on its activities; whenever terrorists strike, one of the first questions reporters ask is, "Was it al-Qaeda?"

This brand also provides context for what might otherwise seem like a random string of incidents. The media links al-Qaeda's attacks to the organization's program and objectives, even if they are carried out independently by the "franchisees." And the brand attracts and funnels recruits, so it sustains the organization. In short, it does just about all the things an effective brand should. If we do not understand al-Qaeda as a brand, we will not be able to defeat it.

The modern phenomenon of brands and branding began to emerge in the mid-1800s with the arrival of large-scale production, mass marketing, and national distribution channels. By the late 1800s, companies like Heinz and the National Biscuit Company introduced products that they hoped would become familiar to consumers across the nation.[48] Some products, like the Gillette safety razor and Kodak camera, also required a customer to invest time to learn how to use them. This created a sort of personal, continuing relationship between an individual and the corporation through the brand.

Ironically, however, the idea of brand management as we know it today—and consider it a component of soft power—was the brainchild of Neil McElroy, a man who eventually held the one job that epitomizes hard power—Secretary of Defense.[49] McElroy was born in 1904 and grew up in the Cincinnati suburbs. His parents, both teachers, sent him to Harvard, where he majored in economics. Returning to Cincinnati, he went to work at Procter & Gamble (P&G, as it is universally known) in the mailroom. P&G was a Cincinnati mainstay—thanks to pigs. Up until 1865 or so, more hogs arrived for slaughter at the Cincinnati stockyards than anywhere in the world. Hogs give you pork, pork gives you carcasses, carcasses give you renderings—and renderings are the stuff candles and soap are made from. Cincinnati lost its lead in meatpacking to Chicago, but not before two brothers-in-law, William Procter (candles) and James Gamble (soap), set up their company.

P&G grew like gangbusters during the Civil War selling to the Union Army. It continued to expand after the war, gradually becoming known as one of the best-run companies in the world. It earned its reputation by succeeding in a tough business. Selling soap is tough because, left to itself, soap is, well, soap. It is hard for one bar to be better than another. The advantage goes to whoever can create a reason for a customer to reach for their soap instead of the competition, and to do so time after time. In other words, the winner will likely be whoever has the best brand.

All brands consist of two parts: reality and image. And this is precisely how P&G succeeded. It understood how to combine *real product features* with a *well-crafted message* ("Ivory: The Soap That Floats").

Working his way up from the mailroom, McElroy become something of a wunderkind in business and marketing. One of his insights was that products needed an identity. Soap had to get clothes clean, of course, but it also had to capture how buyers saw themselves and—how they *wanted* to see themselves: rich (Tide), frugal (Duz), glamorous (Ivory

Snow), exotic (Camay), cutting-edge (Oxydol), and so on. McElroy collected his thoughts in a three-page memo in 1931that established the basic concepts of brand management. Even today companies use his principles about how to define a brand, manage it, and position it in the market. By 1948 McElroy was president of P&G. He was just forty-four.[50]

In 1957 Dwight Eisenhower asked McElroy to serve as his Secretary of Defense. Eisenhower, the former supreme U.S. military commander during World War II, had all the military expertise any administration needed. He wanted a business executive who could manage the enormous day-to-day operations of the Defense Department. McElroy served through 1959, when he returned to Cincinnati and P&G, where he became chairman of the board.

Brand management is so important today that some consulting firms have even developed methods for estimating the market value of a brand. This is important for a company both to manage its brand and to set a value for the intangible assets of a company if someone wants to buy it. Interbrand Corporation, for example, reports that the most valuable brand in the world is Coca-Cola, with an estimated worth of at least $67 billion, followed by Microsoft ($59.9 billion), IBM ($53.4 billion), and General Electric ($47.0 billion).[51]

Simon Anholt, a British writer and consultant, has tried to apply this idea to international politics. He estimates the value of nations as brands the same way P&G might measure how consumers feel about Tide. His Nation Brands Index takes surveys and calculates a composite score based on how respondents size up a country along six dimensions: quality of exports, quality of governance, attractiveness for investment, attractiveness as an immigration destination, desirability to tourists, and whether its people and culture have favorable images. In his recent surveys, Sweden was the top-ranked nation brand.[52]

These kinds of indexes, of course, encounter the same problems that affect the Pew Global Attitudes project and other surveys that try to measure public opinion. Surveys of attitudes are often poor predictors of actual behavior. Recall the Edsel and New Coke. In both cases, companies designed products tailored to survey results, and customers fled in droves.

Also, these surveys are based on samples designed to represent the entire population of a nation, whereas in many cases a national brand only needs to cater to a *segment* of the population—potential immigrants, entrepreneurs, or investors, for example. Foreign public opinion of U.S. policies may become more important now that more countries have democratic government, but opinions of the United States will still be just one of many issues that get batted around in the politics of a foreign nation, and it is hard to count on how it will really affect the nation's politics and policies. (A case in point: Polls consistently say that only about a third of the French people have a favorable view of U.S. foreign policy, and few French politicians are as supportive of the United States as Nicolas Sarkozy, yet he still won the 2007 election. French democracy is as complex as our own.)

Besides, a brand does not always have to be likable to be effective; the issue is whether and how a brand influences its targeted audience. No one really *liked* Ty Cobb, Dave Schultz, the old Oakland Raiders, or Allen Iverson, but they all have had strong brands. They attracted fans who liked a rough game, and their reputations were good for a point or two whenever they played anyone with a rational concern for their well-being. Dale Earnhardt (brand: "The Intimidator") became one of the most successful stock car racers in history precisely because he was *not* nice and made it clear that he did not care. Sometimes, alas, the United States may not want a positive brand—something to be supported, favored, or emulated. Rather, it may need to sell itself as a force to be joined, acceded to, complied with, or simply steered clear of. Indeed, the most important decision in creating a brand is to choose what the brand should do. It must achieve its desired effect, and it must be something that the brand holders themselves can live with.

In any case, the United States has distinct advantages in conveying a brand because American culture has greater presence and penetration than any other. It attracts more people who (wittingly or not) operate within its terms of reference and language, and they (wittingly or not) add to the influence of American culture and the impact of the American brand. Consider the news and entertainment industry, for instance. It is much more fragmented today, thanks to technology, globalization, and deregulation. Even so, more people are employed in news broadcasting and publishing in companies based in New York than anywhere else. The same is true of entertainment; India makes more movies than the United States (almost a thousand each year), but Hollywood is still the top maker of, let us say, "exportable films."

People from around the world wanting to work in news and entertainment come to the United States for opportunity. When they do, to one degree or another, they get assimilated or at least speak from a largely American context, if only because everyone has to deal with at least some part of the existing industry during contract negotiations, hiring, production, distribution, and so on. Moreover, once an industry takes root, it develops a self-sustaining critical mass of social networks and technical know-how that create a culture. There are so many advantages to being close to this critical mass that, even if someone starts their career elsewhere and is successful, it is hard to avoid dealing with the existing culture dominating a field, and even being drawn into it.

Recall, for example, Jeff Douglas, the Nova Scotia–born actor who played "Joe" in the "I Am Canadian" Molson beer commercials. This ad campaign created a wave of patriotic fervor across Canada. Websites sprung up responding to the ad in which Canadians poured out their feelings about their nation. It was a spontaneous mass social phenomenon. Yet, soon after his striking success, Douglas moved to the United States—in the footsteps of Peter Jennings, Arthur Kent, Jim Carrey, Lorne Greene, Lorne Michaels, Alanis Morisette, William Shatner, Avril Lavigne, and many others seeking a larger market, greater exposure, and a shorter commute to the studio and their agent's office. Even the hockey player Wayne Gretsky—perhaps the greatest Canadian ever to play the Canadian national sport—finished his career in New York.

The same is true of other industries that have an extended cultural impact. The centers of the world's software industry are Northern California and Washington State, so the manner in which people interact with their computers is defined by people who program in an American context. Similarly, though more manufacturing is moving overseas, the "look and feel" of most products still have an American accent; half the top design schools in the world are in the United States—like the Art Center College of Design in Pasadena, the University of Cincinnati, and Pratt Institute in Brooklyn. This is almost ten times as many as any other country. China is second, making inroads with four of its nearly four hundred design schools ranked in the top sixty, followed by Italy and the Netherlands.[53] Students of design come to the United States to learn how to make things look, and they either find jobs here or take this intangible piece of cultural influence back home.

Or consider language. English is the world's language for science, popular culture, and business. Management meetings of Germany's Deutsche Bank and Switzerland's Credit Suisse are routinely conducted in English. Air traffic control is in English. It is usually easier to make an airline reservation in English. For that matter, the aircraft you fly in is almost always built using English. (Even Airbus, based in Toulon at the western end of the Riviera, uses English as its official language.)[54] About two-thirds of all web pages are in English. The predominance of English—especially in its American form—gives the United States influence because language incorporates—often subtly, and almost always without planning—American values and the American perspective of the world. English exports our culture, the spread of our culture gives Americans influence, and influence equals power.[55]

One can think of other dimensions of cultural influence, and the trend is not always in favor of the United States. But if you stand back and look at the total picture, the United States—at least for now—dominates more sources and channels of cultural influence than anyone else.

The problem, of course, is that no one in the U.S. government controls the media, entertainment industry, design, language, or most of the other things that make people around the world see things from our perspective, priorities, and values. Indeed, nearly three-fourths of all English speakers are foreigners who use it as a second language, including 300 million Chinese (this is correct; about as many Chinese speak

English as do Americans). This is the odd but inevitable result when your culture is so successful that it predominates.[56]

This is a core dilemma with soft power. Everyone seems to understand that it is important, but no one seems to know how to use it. Governments—the usual power wielders—have an especially hard time with this. There is probably no one as clueless about popular culture as a senior government executive, and when governments try to be a player, they are dwarfed by the private sector. The State Department's Office of Public Diplomacy, for example, has a total budget of about $500 million. By comparison, the Motion Picture Association of America reports that the annual box office receipts of the U.S. movie industry total about $25 *billion* worldwide.[57]

You can see how this plays out. The State Department spends about $50 million on its entire campaign to improve America's image in the Arab world. Meanwhile, a single major film like *True Lies* (depicting Arab terrorists plotting to explode a nuclear weapon in the United States) had a budget of about $145 million. Even more significantly, the film *earned* $250 million in box office and rental receipts because people around the world were willing to pay for the opportunity to watch it.[58]

The trends generally do not favor governments. Until the 1980s, for example, broadcast organizations were operated by government or party authorities (as in the case of Radio Moscow), or indirectly owned by a government-chartered corporation (Britain's BBC), or regulated by a government body in the public interest (our own NBC, ABC, and CBS, regulated by the Federal Communications Commission). Now, not only is the media out of the control of government; it is often not under the control of *anyone*.

Recall how Iraqi and U.S. officials wanted to shape the message conveyed by Saddam Hussein's execution. The official recording used angles and editing that portrayed a somber proceeding, presided over by responsible officials representing a stable government. The recording tastefully ended before the fatal instant. But, as in the case of the Abu Ghraib prison torture photographs, it took just one person with a camera-equipped cellphone to capture an entirely different story: officials not quite in control, with a rabble of Moqtada al-Sadr's supporters beneath the gallows taunting Saddam with chants of "Moqtada! Moqtada!" The raw version—complete with Saddam dropping through the trap door and dead an instant later—appeared on YouTube in a matter of hours. Millions viewed it around the world. It changed the appearance—and impact—of the event completely, and there was not a thing any U.S. official could do about it. It is even harder to control the influence of something like language (the French government has been trying for years to eliminate Americanisms from their mother tongue, with little to show for it).

Even so, there are ways to improve the odds of success. Some are straight from the memorandum Neil McElroy wrote more than eighty years ago:

- Make someone responsible for the brand—the equivalent of a brand manager. Even if you cannot control all the levers, someone needs to be raising the problem as it affects all aspects of government policy. This problem of responsibility and control, as we shall see later in the book, is common to many national security activities.
- Have a clear idea of what the brand is supposed to achieve, and make sure that everyone involved has a common understanding of the objective—to curry favor, intimidate, attract people or resources, or simply provide a lower profile. Everyone also needs a common understanding of who the target is for the brand's message.
- Take the target's perspective—in U.S. military terminology this is called "assessing Red's view of Blue," or how they see us. (In the Cold War, the Soviet adversary was the "Red forces," for obvious reasons, so we referred to ourselves as "Blue"; the convention has since become generic.) Focusing on how the *opponent* sees the situation is essential for crafting an effective message.
- Understand your resources and the constraints under which you must operate. This eliminates options that are desirable but unfeasible and concentrates effort where it is more likely to have some effect, if not the full effect that one might want. Generally, the

greater the effect of a brand, the less control a brand holder will be able to exert over it.

Finally, when it comes to a nation's brand influence, remember that size matters, and it may often be the only thing we can really control. It is inherently hard—especially for government officials—to manage soft power. Most of the connections are too indirect for anyone to manipulate them on a large scale. The most important decision in wielding soft power occurs when one creates the economic conditions required for the media, entertainment, design, education, and other "industries of influence" to prosper within one's territory and extended culture. Critical mass, once lost, is hard to regain.

Today and the Future

In sum, one can quibble about one measure or another, but the overall picture is clear: The United States currently has a remarkable edge in power, no matter how you define it. The question is, will we have this edge in the future?

Organski did not have it quite right. True, the demographics are against us, and we cannot reverse the sheer numbers and the basic principles of a modernizing world. But we can concentrate on those areas of national power in which we enjoy special strengths in a strategy that provides us with enough influence to protect our interests—perhaps even more influence than any other power.

Success will require some changes in how we organize and operate for national security—issues to which we will turn later in the book. For now, however, we must focus on the even larger problem of pacing, because even though the United States has unmatched power today and could even remain predominant in the future, power is never unlimited. If we run out of gas before the finish line, we lose. So we need to be mindful of our constraints. If we understand these constraints, they will not simply limit American options; they will also help us choose them more wisely—so we can win.

CHAPTER FOUR

Pacing

AS WE HAVE SEEN, one of the defining features of the threats the United States faces today is that they are likely to be with us for a long time—in many cases, indefinitely. No country has unlimited capacity, and that, combined with the resilient threats, is why pacing is so important. Especially in making decisions about national security—and especially in using military force—we need a level of effort for national security that does not exceed our long-run capacity. There are three main constraints.

The first constraint is the total size of the national economy. This determines the total resources we can devote to national security. In practice the real limit is significantly smaller, because no modern country can devote its entire productive capacity to national security (though some might say the Soviet Union gave it a good try, and paid the price). But the national economy does begin to draw a line around what a country can spend on security.

The second constraint is public opinion and competing demands. Government decisions are not directly tied to the polls, but elections— and the specter of the next election—do have influence both on how much money gets spent and on what. As a practical matter, it is simply a fact that national security must compete with other interests. Past experience tells us a lot about how all these competing interests will play out, and, thus, how much we are likely to have available to spend on national security.

The third constraint is real costs. At some point technological and economic realities kick in. A modern jet fighter might not need to cost $200 million, but it will never cost $2 million either. Similarly, we can probably improve energy efficiency by 1 or 2 percent annually for the next decade or so, but it is unlikely that it will improve by 5 to 10 percent annually over the same period. These realities shape the available options, and ignoring them inevitably sets us up for the kind of profound failures that reduce our ability to compete over the long haul.

The Cost of Defense

Let us look again at the defense budget, because that is the largest expense, and usually the most contentious part of federal spending on national security. Any enterprise involving about 2 million people and annual spending of more than $500 billion is complex. But keep in mind five facts about U.S. military forces that frame most issues that get raised.

First, U.S. armed forces are uniquely powerful. No one else comes close. A few countries and terrorist organizations can—and will—challenge us in specific situations. Sometimes these are critical. Even so, no one can match us across the board. Because it will take time for any potential adversary to make the investment needed to overtake our lead, this fact will not change for many years.

Second, America's enemies will do their best to evade our strength and hit us where we are weak. The infrastructure and trust on which American society depends are fragile and easily targeted. This is the essential paradox of defense today: We are incredibly powerful yet surprisingly vulnerable. So we will constantly be challenged to look for those vulnerabilities and to either fix them or mitigate the cost of an attack.

Third, the United States can afford its military power. We spend an enormous amount of money on our military forces, but defense spending at current levels—or even somewhat higher—will not drive the country into the poorhouse or break the national economy.

Fourth, even though America could afford to buy "more defense," it probably will not. Experience says Americans will support the current *big* defense budget but not a *bigger* one—at least not for long. More on this just below, too.

And, fifth, though the United States is uniquely powerful, it does not have *unlimited* power. So we have to size our policies to our capabilities. Forget that, and you are likely to end up in a bad situation. Once again, consider Iraq.

Can We Afford It? Will We Support It?

America did not always have this kind of military edge; in fact, for most of its history the United States hardly counted as a military power of any kind. Look at Figure 4.1, which shows U.S. defense spending in inflation-adjusted dollars since the country was founded. (The shaded bands mark major wars.)[1]

The United States spent little on defense before World War II, with the exception of blips coinciding with the Civil War and World War I. Even then, the costs of those wars were miniscule compared with today's peacetime defense budgets. The expenditures of our army and navy together totaled less than $15 billion per year, a figure today roughly equal to what Brazil or India spends on defense.

During World War II defense spending rose to levels we have not seen since. We then demobilized until the Cold War began. Defense spending spiked again for the Korean War. Since then, it has leveled off at a level that is historically high but with a trend that is, overall, flat—yes, flat. This fact often gets lost in the hurly-burly politics of the annual debates over defense spending. Look at Figures 4.2 and 4.3, which help explain why the defense budget does not stray much higher or lower than its long-term post–World War II norm.

Figure 4.2 tracks U.S. defense spending since 1945. (Again, the shaded areas are war years.) It also tracks public opinion on defense

FIGURE 4.1
U.S. Defense Spending, 1787–2007

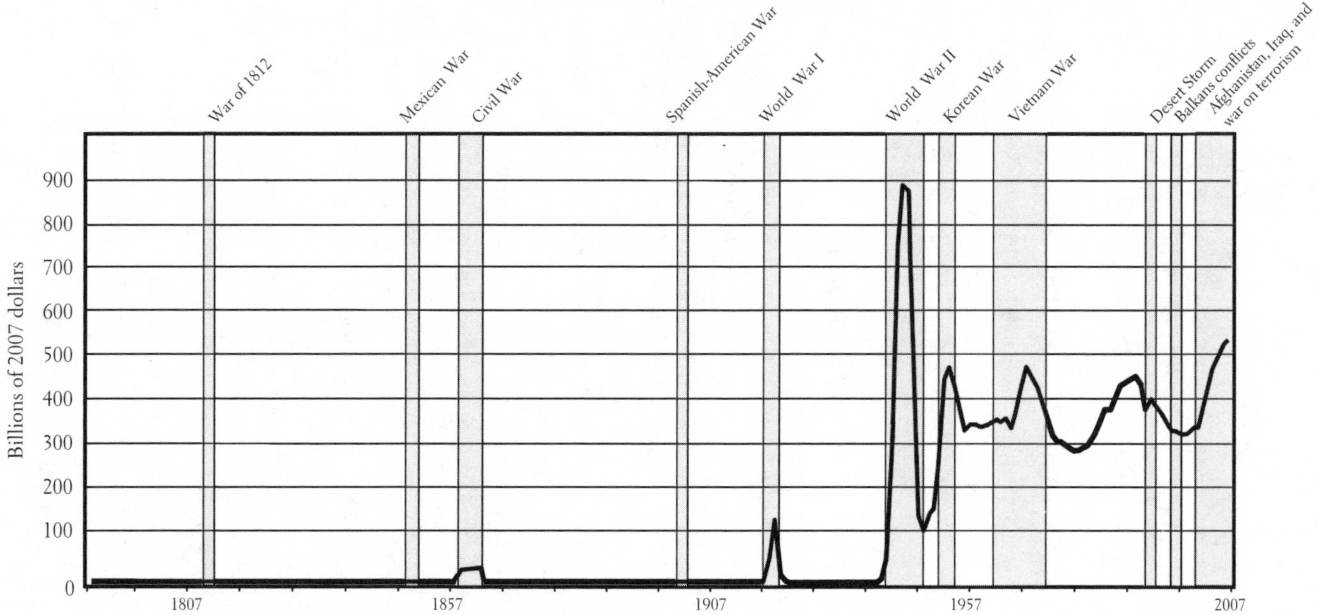

Sources: Correlates of War Project and *U.S. Statistical Abstract.*

Defense Spending and Public Opinion, 1945–2007

Percent favoring spending less on defense

100   80   60   40   20   0

Afghanistan, Iraq, and war on terrorism

Balkans conflicts

Desert Storm

Vietnam War

Korean War

Gallup Poll respondents favoring spending less on defense

Defense spending

Billions of 2007 dollars

900   800   700   600   500   400   300   200   100

1950   1960   1970   1980   1990   2000

Sources: Gallup Organization, Congressional Budget Office, and *U.S. Statistical Abstract.*

spending. As can be seen, the defense budget has seen significant swings. It rose by a third during the Korean, Vietnam, and Gulf wars and during the buildup under Ronald Reagan, and now is rising similarly again, with the recent actions in Afghanistan and Iraq. It fell by about a quarter during the 1970s and 1990s. But the long-term trend is flat—an average of about $380 billion per year.

To understand why, note the dotted line in Figure 4.2, tracking public attitudes toward defense spending. Since the mid-1940s, the Gallup Organization has surveyed Americans about once a year, asking whether they think the United States is spending too much on defense, not enough, or about the right amount.[2] As the figure shows, whenever defense spending rose, the percentage of Americans who said we were spending too much on defense also rose. Opposition to defense spending even took off when we were in the middle of a war. Conversely, when defense spending dropped off, so did public resistance.[3]

These attitudes shape elections. Recall 1952, when Dwight D. Eisenhower, campaigning for the presidency, pledged to end the Korean War. We forget today, but at the time the Korean conflict was the most expensive war the United States had ever fought other than World War II—four times costlier than even World War I. It was quite controversial at the time. Or recall the election of 2006, when the public soured on the war in Iraq, in large part because of the cost. The Democrats won majorities in both the House and Senate, and they promptly sought to tighten the purse strings on military spending. The linkage between popular attitudes and defense spending is not one-to-one, but the effects are clear, and it works in the other direction, too. The public will not let defense spending drop too far below the norm, either.

After the failed hostage Iranian rescue mission and the Soviet invasion of Afghanistan, people began to worry whether several years of declining defense budgets had "hollowed out" the American military. Public resistance to bigger defense budgets dwindled. Even before the 1980 presidential election really got under way, Jimmy Carter began to submit larger defense budgets to Congress. Reagan had been promising to rebuild the U.S. military, and Carter and Congress, which was controlled by the Democrats at the time, could sense which way the public was turning.

Reagan won the presidency and the Republicans won the Senate, and Reagan kept his promise with defense budgets even bigger than what Carter had planned. But after six years of rising defense budgets, opinion turned yet again and helped the Democrats win the Senate, and defense spending first leveled off and then began to fall. Attitudes shaped elections, elections shaped policy, and policy set spending levels.

Now look at Figure 4.3, which provides another piece of the picture. It shows government spending as a percentage of the national economy, using four major categories: domestic entitlements (mainly Social Security and Medicare); defense; discretionary domestic spending (on roads,

FIGURE 4.3
U.S. Government Spending as a Share of the National Economy, 1952–2007

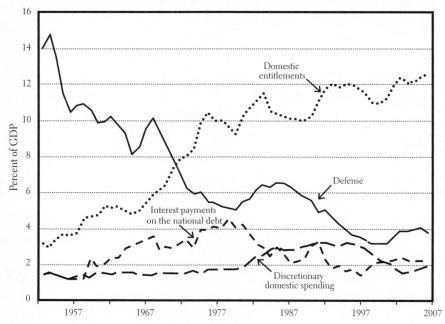

Source: Congressional Budget Office.

research, regulatory agencies, educational grants, farm subsidies, and the like); and interest payments on the national debt. Overall government spending has run steady during the past fifty years, at about 18 to 20 percent of the nation's total gross domestic product. This is, in effect, the "burden" government activities put on the economy. But look inside the trend.

The mix has shifted steadily. More of the government's share of the economy goes to Social Security and Medicare, less to defense. The burden from the other two components, interest on the national debt and domestic spending, has remained about the same. (For the record, foreign aid is so small that it does not even show in Figure 4.3.) In effect, the overall burden of government spending has remained constant as a percentage of the overall U.S. economy. As the economy has grown, the tax base has also grown, and that has supported a bigger federal budget. It is just that we have put almost all the new revenues into Social Security and Medicare—big, expensive programs that have been hugely popular with most Americans.

Now, for a sense of what the future holds, look at Figure 4.4. The lower line, gross domestic product, is the rate at which most economists think the national economy is going to grow. The two lines above it show the rates at which the costs of Social Security and Medicare are projected to grow. (We can forecast Social Security and Medicare costs by extrapolating the age distribution of the U.S. population, life expectancies, and the benefits Americans are entitled to by law.)

As Figure 4.4 shows, the growth rate in the benefits we have promised outstrips the growth we expect in the economy—by a wide margin. Determining how to pay for Social Security and Medicare is going to be one of the biggest issues of the next decade. There are really only three options: raise taxes, reduce benefits, or make the economy grow faster. But the impact on the American military ought to be clear. There is not going to be much room for growth in the defense budget. In fact, the pressures that have always eventually pulled defense spending back to its "normal" level will be stronger than ever.

FIGURE 4.4
Projected Spending on U.S. Entitlement Programs, 2007–17

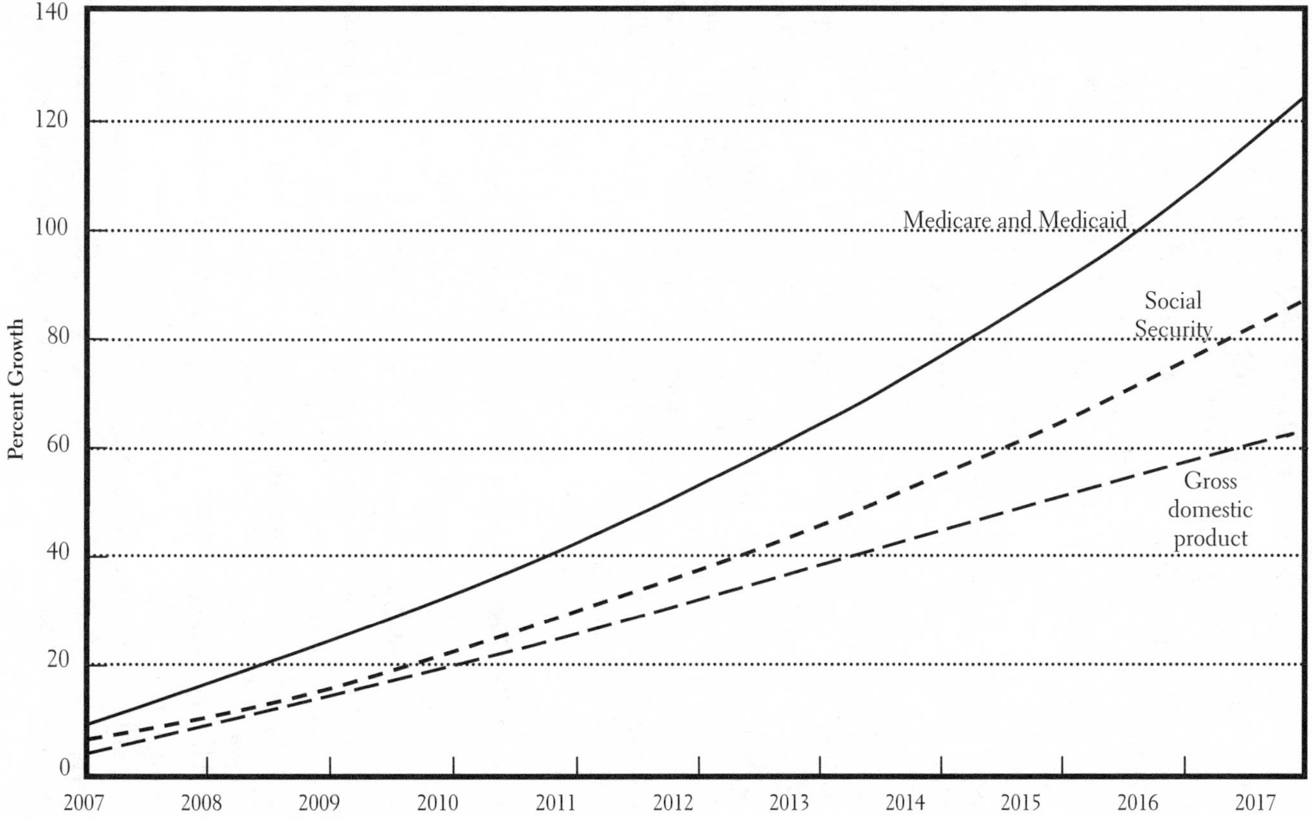

Percent Growth
140
120
100
80
60
40
20
0
2007
2008
2009
2010
2011
2012
2013
2014
2015
2016
2017
Medicare and Medicaid
Social Security
Gross domestic product

Source: Congressional Budget Office.

So, one can argue that we *should* spend more on defense, and one can even make a case that the United States *could*. But if history is any guide, it is imprudent to assume that it *will*. There are too many other interests competing for a slice of the budget pie, and enthusiasm for beefing up U.S. forces is fleeting at best. If history is any guide, five or six years from now the defense budget will be 10 to 15 percent smaller than currently.

Figure 4.4 also shows why economic growth is essential to military power, and how the two go hand in hand. We will not be able to sustain U.S. military power without an expanding economy. Even with a 10 to 15 percent reduction in real spending, the United States will still be spending more on defense than any other country, and the United States will still have more military capability than any other nation. It just will not be *unlimited* power, and that is the kind of constraint we need to keep in mind if we hope to maintain American predominance.

The decision to go to war in Iraq is exactly the case that illustrates the need to match capabilities with objectives. Because the war in Iraq will have such an effect on U.S. policy in the years ahead, it is worth dissecting this issue in some detail.

How Many Troops Did the United States Need in Iraq?

The question "How many troops did the United States need in Iraq?" is destined to become an iconic foreign policy tagline, like "Who lost China?" Today the conventional wisdom is that civilian officials rejected requests from uniformed officers for additional forces, and the resulting troop shortage led to the insurgency. In reality, the issue is much more complex.

The relevant question was not "How many troops do we need?" The more important question was always "How many troops do we have?" If we—meaning both government officials and the public as a whole—had focused on this question, we might have viewed the problem differently and realized that, whatever our goals might be, there were critical constraints to deal with.

To fully understand what happened, one must recall the situation at specific points in time, how specific officials responded, and what motivated them. As will be seen, the issue evolved in three distinct phases—the run-up to war, combat, and the postwar insurgency—and often took separate tracks in the military, political, and public arenas. As will also be seen, the more important issue is not about the past; it is about the future. Specifically: How can the United States respond to conflicts in the post–Cold War, post–September 11, post-Iraq world? And what are the implications for U.S. strategy?

Phase One: What Will the War Cost?

By early 2003 most people who were following events probably assumed the United States would launch military operations against Iraq. Congress had passed its resolution authorizing military force in October 2002. President George W. Bush had said he would not wait indefinitely for Iraq to comply with UN resolutions requiring it to disarm. U.S. Central Command had conducted exercises in the theater, and troops were assembling for deployment.

During this period, public discussions about force levels were mainly linked to the cost of the impending war. The reason was that opponents of the war were working in a difficult political environment. Surveys in January and February 2003 reported that two-thirds or more of the public favored military action of some kind.[4] Opponents needed to reframe the issue to gain political traction. One way was to highlight the potential costs of a war, which were directly linked to the number of troops required.

Sen. Carl Levin (D-MI) raised the cost issue in a Senate Armed Services Committee hearing on February 25, 2003. General Eric Shinseki was testifying. Levin asked him how many troops he thought were needed for the impending operation. Shinseki answered, "Something on the order of several hundred thousand soldiers."[5] Critics have since enshrined this estimate—"several hundred thousand"—as the number of forces that should have been provided for the war and occupation.

But to fully understand this exchange, it is important to remember who was asking and who was answering. Levin was one of twenty-three senators who had voted *against* the resolution authorizing the use of military force. As Chief of Staff of the Army, Shinseki had no direct responsibility for planning the pending operation; that belonged to General Tommy Franks, head of Central Command. Levin's question was designed to produce an estimate of war costs from a military expert that would raise concerns about the risks of the operation, not to give the Defense Department an opportunity to ask for more troops.

The Levin–Shinseki exchange triggered a debate that played out largely in the media. The debate was fueled by the reluctance of administration officials to provide their own estimate for the cost of the impending war. Hard figures might portray a worst-case scenario, and that would make it harder to muster support for a war they believed was necessary. Two days later, a reporter asked Defense Secretary Donald Rumsfeld about Shinseki's comment. "There are so many variables," he said, "that it is not knowable. However, I will say this. What is, I think reasonably certain is, the idea that it would take several hundred thousand U.S. forces, I think, is far from the mark."[6]

Few administration officials would engage opponents by hazarding an estimate. The most notable exception was Lawrence Lindsey, head of the White House's National Economic Council. Lindsey told a *Wall Street Journal* reporter that projected war costs had an "upper bound" of 1 to 2 percent of the U.S. annual gross domestic product, which the reporter translated into $100 billion to $200 billion.[7] Even this rough, implied estimate was reported to have displeased administration officials.[8]

Opponents of the war made clear their frustration in not getting a more specific estimate from the administration. Representative James Moran (D-VA) told Deputy Secretary of Defense Paul Wolfowitz at the House Budget Committee hearing, "I think you're deliberately keeping us in the dark." He continued by questioning Wolfowitz's candor, saying, "We're not so naïve as to think that you don't know more than you're revealing."[9]

For his part, Shinseki appears to have understood the link between troop levels and costs. A few days before, when Shinseki was preparing to testify before the Senate Appropriations Committee, he cut off an aide who tried to remind him of the administration's position that costs were uncertain. "We know how many troops are there now, and the projected numbers," he said. "We know how much it costs to feed them every day. We know how much it cost to send the force there. We know what we have spent already to prepare the force and how much it would cost to bring them back."[10]

So, when the war was being planned, debates over troop numbers were not just about how to ensure a successful operation. To the contrary; the opponents of the war who raised the issue wanted to reframe the debate to derail a war they believed was ill advised. They wanted to highlight the potential cost of a war, but administration officials would not give them hard estimates. So instead the opponents focused on how many troops were needed, which were in effect a proxy for costs, and that was how the troop issue was first raised.

But whatever their motivation for asking Shinseki, should elected officials have deferred to his professional judgment in any case? By the spring and summer of 2006, when it was clear how badly the insurgency in Iraq was going, several retired generals—Major General John Batiste and Major General Paul Eaton of the Army, and General Anthony Zinni and Lieutenant General Gregory Newbold of the Marine Corps—went public to criticize Secretary of Defense Donald Rumsfeld. These generals said that Rumsfeld had ignored their professional advice and had invaded Iraq with too light a force, and the insurgency was the result.

"I think the current administration repeatedly ignored sound military advice and counsel with respect to the war plans," Batiste told PBS's Jim Lehrer. "I think that the principles of war are fundamental, and we violate those at our own peril." Zinni said, "I believe the civilian leadership in the Pentagon ignored the advice. This advice was not just coming from me, these warnings, but other former commanders at U.S. Central Command."[11]

Would the war have gone better if civilians had deferred to the flag officers? Perhaps, but perhaps not. Recall the planning that led up to Operation Desert Storm twelve years before. The commanding officer, General Norman Schwarzkopf, originally proposed defeating the Iraq forces that had occupied Kuwait with a massive head-on attack. Civilian officials—Secretary of Defense Dick Cheney, Assistant Secretary of Defense Henry Rowen, and others—believed this was wrongheaded, because it played into Iraq's strengths.

The President's National Security Adviser, Brent Scowcroft, thought that Central Command was proposing a hard operation because they really did not want to go to war. "It sounded to me like a briefing by people who did not want to do it," Scowcroft (himself a retired Air Force lieutenant general) recalled.[12]

Scowcroft also recalled that "the preferred option that they presented was frankly a poor option and my first question is 'Why don't you go round to the west,' and the answer was 'Well, we don't have enough gas trucks for it, running out of gas when we're up there on the shoulder, we can't do that, it's not a feasible option.' I was pretty appalled."

The back and forth between the civilians and the generals in 1991 resembled exactly the give and take that was later labeled civilian "pressure" to attack Iraq in 2003 with too few troops. In the case of Operation Desert Storm, the solution was essentially a compromise: The military planners accepted what became famously known as the "Left Hook," and the civilians tacitly agreed to give the planners as many troops as they requested.

"Gradually we got the Command to change its view and whenever they asked for additional forces or would take more forces, the President said 'Fine, you've got them,'" Scowcroft recalled. "And I don't think he turned down a single request for additional forces." Nevertheless, civilian officials had redirected how the war would be fought, and history says that we were better off for it. This is worth keeping in mind because, though it is important to include professional military officers in the decision process, relying on them totally is a mistake and certainly does not guarantee success.

Phase Two: Defeating the Iraqi Army

Once the war began, the troop issue shifted to whether the United States had enough forces to defeat the Iraqi army. It is often forgotten today, but in March 2003 many experts worried that U.S. forces were inadequate for defeating the Iraqi army, which was supposedly among the best in building prepared defenses (Iran discovered this in its war with Iraq in the 1980s). Also, Saddam Hussein had saved his best troops for defending Baghdad, and U.S. military planners still believed that Iraq might use chemical or biological weapons.

This criticism peaked in the last week of March, when a dust storm slowed the ground offensive and Iraqi irregulars attacked the Coalition's supply lines. Reporters embedded with the troops covered these developments firsthand. Soon, media experts and retired military officers began to fault the war plan in newspapers and on television, charging that U.S. planners had not provided enough troops.

Retired General Barry McCaffrey was one of the most visible critics. McCaffrey had been a successful commander in the 1991 Gulf War and was greatly respected in the Army, so his comments carried special weight. "In my judgment," he told a reporter, "there should have been a minimum of two heavy divisions and an armored cavalry regiment on the ground—that's how our doctrine reads."[13]

"We face a war of maneuver in the coming days to destroy five Iraqi armor divisions with only one U.S. armored unit," McCaffrey wrote in an op-ed a few days later, "supported by the modest armor forces of the First Marine Division and the Apache attack helicopters of the 101st Airborne." He also warned U.S. forces had "inadequate tube and rocket artillery to provide needed suppressive fires."[14] In the event, of course, there was no war of maneuver for Baghdad. The Iraqi army collapsed, U.S. casualties were light, and most of the media quickly forgot about the controversy over the war plan.

This phase of the "how many troops" controversy was really just the latest round in a long-standing debate between military experts. Some advocate speed and agility. Others favor mass and firepower. Franks, favoring the former, used a "rolling start," sending units into battle as they arrived in theater, rather than wait until he could concentrate them. One can point to cases in which either approach has worked, but, as McCaffrey implied, Army doctrine has generally favored mass and firepower, and Franks was operating contrary to doctrine.

But to fully understand the criticism of the U.S. strategy (and later criticism of Rumsfeld by the retired generals who went public), one must consider the larger picture and Rumsfeld's desire to "transform" the U.S. military into a faster, more agile force—in other words, one that emphasized speed and agility over mass and firepower. The more orthodox officers resisted these reforms from the time he entered office. This resistance was so intense that in the summer of 2001 some press reports speculated that he would resign.

Rumsfeld had some recent history on his side. During the conflict in the Balkans, the American commander, General Wesley Clark, wanted to rush Apache helicopters to Kosovo in 1999 to protect ethnic Albanians from Serbian death squads. In that case, Army doctrine said an Apache squadron requires 5,000 support personnel, plus their tanks, fighting vehicles, and missile launchers for self-defense and support. It took two months to get everything in place. By then the war was over, and the Apaches never got off a shot. Rumsfeld (like many others) believed that the United States might need to respond to similar situations in the future, and "transformation" was partly a program of developing forces that could deploy more rapidly.[15]

Much of the controversy over Rumsfeld's plans for lighter forces that could deploy faster abated after the September 11 terrorist attacks and the mainly successful campaign in Afghanistan, but the underlying opposition remained. It resurfaced when the Iraq offensive slowed in March and subsided after Coalition forces captured Baghdad. It resurfaced again as the insurgency became a major problem. In each case, it was inevitable that anyone favoring larger forces would claim vindication whenever U.S. forces appeared inadequate—which is to say whenever they ran into difficulty.

Critics argue that civilian leaders pressured Franks to use fewer troops than he wanted. The evidence does not support this. Franks's war plan was consistent with Rumsfeld's desire for transformation, but in his memoir, Franks claims this strategy as his own; this was how *he* wanted to carry out the operation.[16] According to Franks, there were arguments for both an even smaller force than he proposed and a larger force. Franks recalls that some Pentagon civilians floated the idea of taking Iraq with just a few special operations forces, air strikes, and Iraqi opponents of Saddam. Retired General Wayne Downing, Deputy National Security Adviser in 2001 and 2002 and former head of U.S. Special Operations Command, also reportedly favored this approach.[17] But Franks says he rejected their proposals—just as he rejected proposals from others for a larger force.

Franks recalls that Secretary of State Colin Powell, himself a retired general who has favored large forces, argued for more troops. Franks says that Powell made his case to President Bush but that Bush supported Franks. Three years after the war Powell recalled in a television interview, "I made the case to General Franks and Secretary Rumsfeld before the President that I was not sure we had enough troops." He said, though, that "a judgment was made by those responsible that the troop strength was adequate."[18]

The issue for Franks was not simply whether more troops were desirable. For him, the issue was that a bigger force would have compromised his basic concept of attack, which was to strike quickly, prevent damage to the oil fields (believed essential to financing Iraq's recovery), and minimize losses to both Coalition forces and Iraqi civilians. Adding troops would have slowed the attack, especially if they were provided a support tail of traditional size. In other words, the desire for speed dictated leanness, and this was reflected in the overall troop levels. As General William Wallace, who had commanded V Corps, explained to a reporter after the operation, "I don't know any commander who would refuse additional troops. But I didn't request more troops because the support structure might have been inadequate."[19]

In their history of the run-up to the Iraq war, *Cobra II*, Michael Gordon and Bernard Trainor make much of the fact that Lieutenant General David McKiernan added more troops to Central Command's initial plans after joining Franks's staff in September 2002.[20] But this is really no surprise. Plans change as they get "chopped" in coordination. Franks oversaw the plan's evolution as his staff made additions and modification, and the final plan remained true to his initial concept of using a light force to strike rapidly and then to keep the enemy off balance by attacking continuously.

One question that is sometimes raised is whether defeating the Iraqi army more decisively might have averted the insurgency that took hold later. Some experts—including McCaffrey—had warned that a guerilla war was possible and that additional conventional forces were needed for a decisive "takedown."

The problem with this argument is that additional combat forces would not have been able to eliminate the insurgents because, for the most part, the insurgents did not yet exist. According to analysts who interviewed former Iraqi leaders for the Iraqi Perspectives Project (a study commissioned by the Defense Department after the war to interview former Iraqi leaders and understand their thinking prior to the conflict), "Since the end of the war one question that has come up regularly is whether the regime made plans to continue the conflict through the insurgency the United States is currently combating. As far as can be determined through interviews . . . and the tens of thousands of records reviewed so far, there were no national plans to transition to a guerilla war in the event of defeat. . . . Nor, as their world crumbled around them, did the regime appear to cobble together such plans."[21]

Iraqi paramilitary forces, like al-Qud and Fadayyen Saddam, were established to protect the regime from *internal* enemies, namely, the Shia and Kurds, who had rebelled after the 1991 war. When pressed into battle against Coalition forces, these groups were sometimes fanatical but almost entirely ineffective. According to Franks, when he encountered these paramilitaries, his forces would track them back to their staging points (typically, a regional Ba'ath Party headquarters) and destroy them en masse.

But if the paramilitaries (and regular troops who shed their uniforms) decided to blend into the population, it was impossible to target them, and making the rubble bounce with more tanks, rockets, and tube artillery would not have helped. Indeed, such tactics would have killed even more civilians, making a counterinsurgency campaign even harder. Recall that McCaffrey specifically recommended armored and mechanized forces, *not* dismounted soldiers—as one requires in counterinsurgency operations.

Phase Three: Occupying Iraq

It is clear now that the United States was inadequately prepared for the occupation. But the main problem was not just troop numbers; it was more fundamental. There was simply a lack of planning for postwar stabilization. Without such a plan, it was impossible to know how many troops were needed.

Some critics claim that plans for a potential occupation were available but that the Defense Department ignored them. The evidence does not support this. To the contrary; not only did the Defense Department fail to plan systematically for an occupation; no one else did, either. For example, the State Department's "Future of Iraq Project"—often cited as a blueprint for reconstruction—said nothing about how many troops would be needed to secure the country. The project report consisted mainly of policy papers outlining broad goals for the postwar period, like eliminating the Iraqi army as a threat to neighbors and democratizing the Iraqi government. It did not define requirements, plans for achieving them—or how many troops would be needed.[22]

Another study that is sometimes cited as a "plan not followed" was prepared by a team headed by Conrad Crane and W. Andrew Terrill at the Strategic Studies Institute of the U.S. Army War College. This report,

Reconstructing Iraq, accurately anticipated the situation Coalition forces later faced. It even included a detailed analysis of the major groups and factions likely to compete for power after Saddam fell and provided a checklist of activities needed for an occupation. But it, too, stopped short of translating general objectives (e.g., securing borders, protecting infrastructure) into specific plans with requirements for troops.[23]

The occupation needed the kind of planning that the combat phases of the operation received—where goals were used to identify missions, missions were analyzed to define requirements, and requirements were matched to assignments for specific units. In such a process, it soon becomes clear if there is a mismatch between objectives and the resources provided to achieve them. It was this kind of systematic planning for the postwar environment that was absent.

This lack of planning for the postcombat phases was evident in briefings Central Command prepared in May through August 2002. (The Defense Department declassified slides for the briefings three years later.)[24] The briefings posit several different possible war scenarios and present detailed plans under each for the first three phases of the war—preparation, attack, and completing the destruction of the regime. For example, the briefings identified specific units that were to arrive at specific times.[25]

By comparison, the slides describing "Phase IV" in all the scenarios—post-hostility activities—are much less detailed For example, the Phase IV slides provide only rough timelines indicating when the planners hoped to complete activities like "stabilization," "recovery," and "transition to security cooperation"—obvious things an army would do after a war. Unlike the slides describing the combat phases of the operation, the Phase IV slides do not assign responsibilities to specific units or identify operational objectives.

In short, the briefing confirms what later became clear: There was no coherent plan. So Central Command projected that U.S. forces would peak at 270,000 at the end of combat operations and the initiation of Phase IV. With no particular basis after that, it planned to draw down these forces to 165,000 within two to three months, and 25,000 within eighteen to twenty-four months after that. Three years after the end of combat operations, there were to be no more than 5,000 troops, consisting of an office for military cooperation, a security element, special operations forces, and security assistance teams.

One reason no one planned for an occupation was that no one—the White House, the Defense Department, the State Department, Central Command—*wanted* an occupation. Desire became an assumption, and assumption became the plan. This reluctance to even consider the possibility of an occupation had a ripple effect. For effective planning to have occurred, someone would have had to have fought for the money, people, and equipment needed for an occupation. With no advocate, planning for a long occupation simply did not happen. And with no planning, there was no detailed set of requirements for troops.

To be sure, before the war some experts not involved in policy or operational planning did offer estimates of how many troops would be needed to occupy Iraq. There was a sizable range of views. Yet, ironically, of those experts who hazarded an opinion in early 2003, most offered estimated troop requirements for the occupation that were close to the number of troops that were in fact deployed. So, if U.S. planners *had* consulted experts and gone with the consensus, the number of troops deployed might well have changed little, if at all.

For example, Crane and Terrill wrote in February 2003 that past U.S. military occupations suggested that "the number of troops that may be needed for an occupation of Iraq are somewhere around 100,000."[26] Philip Gordon and Michael O'Hanlon of the Brookings Institution wrote in April 2003 that "about 100,000 to 200,000 troops may be needed to police the country, find and destroy weapons of mass destruction, prevent remnants of Hussein's loyalists from regrouping, maintain a northern presence to deter conflict among Kurds, Arabs and Turks, and train a new Iraqi military."[27]

At about the same time, Scott Feil, a retired Army colonel experienced in peacekeeping operations, advised the Senate Foreign Relations Committee that 75,000 troops would be needed. The Army History Center estimated that 100,000 troops would be needed, based on past experience. The nonpartisan Center for Strategic and Budgetary Assessments said that 20,000 to 90,000 troops was a "reasonable estimate" for occupation and peacekeeping duties.[28]

These were all top-level, seat-of-the-pants "WAGs" based on experience and instinct, not rigorous analysis. But, in reality, there was considerable room for legitimate disagreement. Different people drew on different personal experiences. Shinseki, for example, had served in the Balkans peacekeeping operations during the 1990s and was extrapolating from his experience there. Officials such as Wolfowitz, conversely, had just seen the Taliban regime fall in Afghanistan in 2002, and that occupation, though incurring casualties, was achieving its objectives with a very small force.

Moreover, the history of military occupations was not of much help in resolving these questions definitively. James Dobbins of the RAND Corporation directed a study of past occupations that was completed just before the Iraq war, and drafts of this report circulated at the time the occupation was being considered. Dobbins himself had taken part in recent Haiti, Somalia, Bosnia, Kosovo, and Afghanistan occupations.[29] He found that whether a peacekeeping operation succeeds and how many casualties it incurs depend on factors that are, to say the least, complex. In addition to the size of the occupying force, one needs at least a half dozen variables to capture all the differences among the cases Dobbins studied:

- Was the adversary totally defeated, or did an organized resistance remain?
- Was the occupied territory ethnically homogeneous or diverse?
- Was the desired goal to simply displace a dictator or to create a functioning democracy?
- Was partition an option? A federation? Or was the desired goal a unitary state with a strong central authority?
- Was the environment rural or urban? Distant, or close to the United States?

- How large was the population? How large was the occupied territory? How long were the borders, and were the neighboring countries hostile or cooperative?
- Could the United States exit quickly if necessary, or did circumstances oblige it to stay, casualties notwithstanding?

Most of these factors did not favor an easy occupation in Iraq—with its multiethnic, large territory and population, hostile neighbors, and distance from the United States, and with little opportunity for an early exit if things went bad. But it was difficult to extrapolate from this experience to a hard number of required troops. The range of uncertainty is significant. For example, after World War II U.S. forces had a hundred soldiers for each thousand Germans but just five soldiers for each thousand Japanese. Both occupations were successful. Replicating the German ratio in Iraq would require 2.6 million soldiers—an impossible goal—but replicating the Japanese ratio would require only about 130,000 soldiers, about the number of troops that were deployed.

Similarly, both the Balkans and Afghanistan are ethnically diverse and have Muslim populations, and the occupations of both went well (at least at first, in the case of Afghanistan). But the ratio of troops to population in the Balkans operations was twenty to a thousand; in Afghanistan it was less than one to a thousand—a broad range that accommodates many views on the required number of forces. Moreover, to complicate matters further, Iraq resembles Bosnia and Kosovo in the degree to which each is urbanized; but it much more closely resembles Afghanistan in the size of its territory and population.

The more important factor is that U.S. military officials planned on the Iraqi government capitulating, remaining intact, and then cooperating in managing affairs during the occupation. Gordon and Trainor observe that U.S. postwar planning hinged on this key premise and remark critically that "rarely has a military plan depended on such a bold assumption."[30] But however bold this assumption might have been, there was significant evidence—even experience—to support it. During the first Gulf War, the Iraqi army capitulated in droves, with 85,000 Iraqi soldiers surrendering to become prisoners of war. Large numbers of both Shia and Kurds rebelled against the Ba'athist regime. It was at least plausible to believe that events would follow the same course in 2003.

Indeed, it was not just American officials who thought the Iraqi regime would capitulate; many Iraqi officers did, too. After the war they told American military interviewers that they had believed the war would be short and the Coalition would quickly win. Their war plan consisted mainly of avoiding getting killed. According to one colonel, "We wanted the Americans to come quickly and finish the war rapidly."[31]

Even Saddam Hussein thought collapse was possible. According to the Iraqi Perspectives Project, he feared his regime coming apart more than he feared a military defeat by Coalition forces. That was why he focused so much on internal controls—he worried about a Shia and Kurdish rebellion or a plot by the army. This was understandable; as noted, the Shia and Kurds revolted following the 1991 war, and there had been multiple plots against him during the 1980s and 1990s.

In effect, everyone agreed: Iraqi capitulation was plausible or even likely. It was just that U.S. planners were counting on it, Saddam was afraid of it, and Iraqi officers just wanted to get it over with as quickly as possible. Alas, it did not happen. Instead of capitulating, the regime just came apart. U.S. officials responsible for Iraq then compounded the problem by disbanding the Iraqi army and banning Ba'athists from the civil service, thus eliminating whatever structures might have held the government together.

In adopting "de-Ba'athification," U.S. policymakers were using the German and Japanese occupations as models. Paul Bremer, the head of the Coalition Provisional Authority in Iraq from 2003 to 2004, recalled later: "The concept behind the de-Baathification decree was that the Baath Party had been one of the primary instruments of Saddam's control and tyranny over the Iraqi people for decades. Saddam Hussein himself openly acknowledged that he modeled the Baath Party on the Nazi Party because he admired the way in which Hitler was able to use the Nazi Party to control the German people. Just as in our occupation of Germany we had passed what were called 'de-Nazification decrees' and prosecuted senior Nazi officials, the model for the de-Baathification was to look back at that de-Nazification."[32]

In that context it seemed entirely logical to eliminate the counterpart of the Nazi Party. Unfortunately, there were significant differences between Germany and Japan in 1945 and Iraq in 2003. Germans and Japanese citizens cooperated with Allied occupiers because their countries were utterly devastated. Recall photographs of Berlin or Tokyo in 1945. They were entirely dependent on their occupiers for basic survival. But it did not matter if the United States deployed 100,000 troops or 500,000 troops; no American leader was going to allow U.S. forces to inflict that kind of death and destruction on Iraq.

In addition, Germany and Japan each had a regime that—evil or not—commanded the allegiance of most citizens. After the bombing of Hiroshima and Nagasaki, Emperor Hirohito instructed his subjects "to endure the unendurable and bear the unbearable." There was no Iraqi leader who could have delivered a similar message to Iraqis, and especially to Shia and Kurds, who saw themselves as oppressed by a regime not of their choosing.

But to be clear: There was little, if any, systematic U.S. planning for Phase IV, and such planning that was carried out was based— critically—on the assumption that the Iraqi army and civil service would remain intact. And U.S. actions ensured that exactly the opposite would happen. U.S. officials effectively shot themselves in the gut, in part because organizations within the government were unable or unwilling to work together, or were simply unaware of what their counterparts were doing or planning.

One piece of evidence that illustrates this disconnect is the briefing slides that Central Command prepared in August 2002. The slides listed the command's assumptions for the postcombat phases, and stated: "Coopted Iraqi units will occupy garrisons and not fight either U.S. force or other Iraqi units."[33] In other words, the decision to disband the Iraqi army was a direct contradiction of the conditions that the commander of the operation had assumed were necessary for success. Bremer insists that the decision to disband the Iraqi army was a Bush administration decision, not just his own. But that misses the point: The concept of the military operation was based on the assumption that some parts of the Iraqi regime would remain intact to maintain order and provide services, yet those responsible for the occupation ensured that this assumption would not hold.[34]

Similarly, the briefing slides said that "DoS [Department of State] will promote creation of a broad-based, credible provisional government— prior to D-day." But even though Central Command assumed that the State Department would take the lead in setting up a provisional government, the Defense Department in Washington did not permit the State Department to do so.[35] One can argue over who was better suited for this task; but once again, the fact remains that the government's actions were internally inconsistent. Wherever the orders for excluding the State Department from participation originated, and whatever their rationale, they constituted a fundamental breakdown in the chain of thinking on which the operation had been predicated.

If officials had been faced squarely with the prospect of creating a government from scratch in a volatile, segmented society, the deliberations in the administration, the Pentagon, and Congress over whether to attack and how to prepare might have gone differently. But more important, it might have raised the most important question of all: Even if U.S. officials believed they needed more troops on the ground, where would they have found them?

How Many Troops Did We Have?

Disagreements over how many troops the United States needed in Iraq almost always miss the crux of the problem: It is hard for even a superpower like America to depose a government and occupy a distant, politically unstable, hostile territory the size of Iraq located on the other side of world.

Hard numbers make this clear. Consider the situation in 2003 facing the Army, which, along with the Marines, bore the brunt of the occupation. The Army had just over a million soldiers. Of these, 340,000 were in combat units; the other 700,000 were in support units, in training, or between assignments. Half of the combat units—170,000 soldiers—were active Army divisions and brigades. Under Army guidelines, these units were to deploy no more than one year out of three. The other 170,000 soldiers assigned to combat units were in the National Guard, which were supposed to deploy no more than one year out of six.

This rotation is important partly because it is an integral part of a soldier's career development, and partly because it is the deal soldiers accept when they make the Army their career. Active soldiers are expected to deploy more frequently because this rounds out their experience, and because "active" units are exactly that—they are the force that is supposed to be readily available for military operations. National Guard soldiers (and Army Reservists, who primarily provide support and logistics) are expected to deploy less often because, though they want a part-time military career, both they and the Army understand that their primary commitment is to their civilian jobs and that they plan to lead a civilian life.

In any case, the mathematics of manpower says that if the Army kept to its planned rotation rates, we could, on average, maintain an overseas force of 85,000 soldiers in combat units indefinitely as the soldiers cycle through their normal deployment rates. This may seem like a poor tooth-to-tail ratio, but keep in mind that no other country in the world has such a capability to deploy such a force to take and hold foreign territory far from its borders. It is unique.

But it is not *unlimited*, and to deploy more soldiers, just four variables are at play: stretch the time each soldier deploys, cut the time each has to train and reset, increase the frequency a soldier rotates onto deployment, or enlarge the total size of the force. Each comes at a cost; each presents its own problems.

Deploying troops longer and giving them less time at home wears out both the equipment and the soldiers. Recruitment and reenlistments will suffer. One can temporarily limit the problem with "stop-loss" orders and enlistment bonuses (as we did), but eventually it will be harder to attract people to an Army career if it means spending years overseas separated from family and, in the case of reservists and Guards, their jobs. Alternatively, one could enlarge the deployable Army—and this is the current plan, by about 5,000 soldiers per year. But, according to the Congressional Budget Office, adding just 18,000 to 23,000 troops would cost $18 billion to $19 billion up front and $23 billion to $29 billion annually— equal to about a 5 percent increase in the total defense budget.[37]

To appreciate the scale of this problem and the basic math that is involved, recall that the United States deployed 550,000 troops in Operation Desert Storm. Yet that was for an operation that required only seven months. It would have been impossible to sustain that kind of deployment much longer. The limited time frame for the deployment went hand in hand with the nation's limited goal: liberating Kuwait. Indeed, one of the reasons U.S. military leaders in 1991 were eager to terminate the war when they did—and forgo advancing on Baghdad—was that they knew they were bumping against the limits of their rotation rates.

One alternative might have been to assemble a larger coalition or extract more assistance from the nations that agreed to help. That was, in fact, how the United States mustered the required forces for the 1991 Gulf War. The problem in 2003 was that the operation had fundamentally different objectives. In 1991, Coalition partners provided 400,000 troops for Desert Storm. Most were from Muslim nations (118,000 Saudis, 100,000 Turks, 40,000 Egyptians, 40,000 Emiratis, 25,000 Omanis, etc.). The objective was to liberate an Arab Muslim state that had been invaded and occupied. There was little chance that such nations would provide such a force to displace an Arab Muslim government that was only in violation of UN resolutions requiring it to eliminate its weapons of mass destruction (WMD) programs.

Another alternative might have been to use surrogates, proxies, or local allies. This worked well in the Balkans during the 1990s. The Dayton Accords that settled the conflict in Bosnia were possible largely because Croatian and Muslim forces were able to secure parts of the country from ethnic Serbs. Similarly, during the conflict in Kosovo, ethnic Albanians effectively served as the ground forces that complemented the U.S.-led air campaign against Serbia. The post–September 11 operation in Afghanistan also fit this mold; the United States provided air power, and local groups that opposed the Taliban provided most of the ground forces.

The disadvantage of using allies or surrogates is that the United States usually has to crank back its goals (as in the case of Desert Storm) or align with a group that has a less-than-perfect record on democracy or human rights (as in the case of the Balkans and Afghanistan). These compromises are actually just a recognition of reality. It is better to face these limitations explicitly.

In short, the plan for overthrowing the regime in Iraq with military force was based on assumptions that were plausible but crucial. Despite concerns at the time by many about the combat phases of the war, that part of the operation went extraordinarily well. The issue was always the "war after the war," and U.S. officials seemed determined not to delve into the true nature of the risks the nation was assuming. To the degree that anyone did any planning, U.S. actions contradicted the very conditions that were assumed to be necessary for success.

Lessons for the Future

Probably the main lesson of the war in Iraq is that Americans need to make clear in their own minds what kind of military we want, and what we expect it to be able to do. As we have seen, the essential reality today is that U.S. military forces are uniquely powerful but not unlimited, and none of the nostrums proposed to avoid this reality offers a true solution.

What about a Draft?

For example, some officials think our experience in Iraq is proof that America needs to reinstate the draft, partly to make sure everyone bears their fair share of the burden of war, partly to improve the public's involvement in military affairs, and partly because we cannot afford the number of volunteers we need. But a draft will not solve these problems, and it would leave most U.S. military forces less able to perform the missions we expect of them, not more.

One reason a draft would not work is because of the basic arithmetic of the American population, the requirements of the armed services, and some paradoxes that result. Though the military must compete hard for potential recruits who meet their standards, there are, ironically, far too many people in that pool for the services to possibly use.

Today there are approximately 31 million people in the United States of draft age (i.e., eighteen to twenty-five years old). The law does not authorize drafting women, so the total eligible population is about half that. According to the Selective Service System, 95 percent of men eligible for the draft actually register, leaving a pool of eligible registrants totaling about 15 million men.[38] Approximately 2 million Americans become eligible for the draft each year. As we saw in Chapter 3, the larger problem for the military today is not simply finding recruits but also finding recruits who meet the mental, physical, and moral criteria. Just under 30 percent meet current military standards. So the annual pool of men newly available for military service is about 600,000.

The Army typically has an annual goal of 100,000 recruits (about 80,000 active and 20,000 reserve), meaning that the pool is six times larger than the number of soldiers the Army needs. Or, to put it another way, if the Army were obliged to consider drafting every qualified man when he became of age for military service, it would have to find a reason *not* to induct five of every six—and that is after it eliminated those who are unsuited for military service.

Experience from the Vietnam era suggests that the ones who get the exemptions or deferments will be upper income, well connected, or clever. Because we know that three-quarters of the population is unsuited for military service, it would not be that hard to "game" the system, especially because the services would be looking for grounds to exclude a large number of would-be draftees. (This was also typical during Vietnam.)

Even assuming we had a fair lottery to select one out of six draftees, this is simply not a rational way to staff an organization. In effect, we would be making military service undesirable for those who want to serve and forcing people into the service who do not want to serve. We would also likely leave the military services with recruits who are less qualified than the above-average personnel who currently serve.

Which brings us to the second reason a draft is not a solution: We would have to change the "business model" that has made the U.S. military uniquely powerful. In the process, we would reduce its effectiveness, and we would have to adopt a military doctrine that would make wars even more costly for the Americans who fight in them.

To see why, one needs to recall how the draft came to be.[39] The modern system of universal conscription in which all males are obligated to serve in the armed forces upon reaching adulthood dates to the late eighteenth century. Before that, officers inherited or purchased their commissions, and armies were manned either by hiring mercenaries or employing press gangs. Most colonies raised local militia for self-protection, and these were almost always considered inferior. (George Washington, who was commissioned a colonel in the Virginia militia, wanted to be made an officer in the British regular army. He was turned down.)

The first country to draft en masse was France, which adopted conscription in 1793 during the French Revolution; other governments followed. The United States introduced conscription by the federal government during the Civil War, but fewer than 10 percent of the soldiers in the Union Army were draftees or substitutes that would-be draftees hired to take their place. The vast majority of soldiers who fought in the Civil War were volunteers.

Yet the more important rationale for the draft, and the reason it emerged when it did, was closely linked not to the French Revolution but to the Industrial Revolution. Industrialization made the mass production of firearms possible. Previously it required an armorer or gunsmith to handcraft a sword or musket. Industrialization led to assembly lines that could crank out cheap, easy-to-use weapons in huge quantities.

Indeed, one of the very first items to be manufactured using standardized, interchangeable parts were muskets that Eli Whitney made for the U.S. Army in 1798. The idea had been rattling around for several decades in Europe, but Whitney, better known as the inventor of the cotton gin, used it in a contract to make guns for the Army, mainly because he needed to deliver a lot of weapons and it simply seemed the best way to use the machinery he had available.[40] Whatever the exact origins, conscription supplied mass-produced soldiers to use the mass-produced weapons. Once the French set the precedent, other countries followed suit.

Under this new approach—which, as we can see, is only about two hundred years old and was not really adopted in the United States until the 1940s—every male served one or two years in the Army. Then they rotated into the reserves, and their weapons were put in storage, making room for the next cohort of eighteen- and nineteen-year-olds and a new generation of weapons. Soldiers entering the reserves would attend drills for a few years to keep up their proficiency.

In wartime, armies using the conscript model immediately sent the active troops to the front. They then began calling up reservists, got their weapons out of storage, trained them to be soldiers again, and then sent them to the front, too. Armies would work backward through the rolls to mobilize the most recently active reservists, then the next, and so on. In other words, it was an assembly line approach—exactly what one would expect in the nineteenth and early twentieth centuries. The objective was to keep feeding wave after wave of soldiers to the front; the side that could do it most efficiently would overwhelm its opponent and win.

But for this approach to work, one had to keep drafting men not *into* the Army but *through* the army. The objective was to get as many men trained as possible, with their weapons on standby. It was not enough just to draft and induct them; it was equally important to muster them out, to make room for the next cohort. So one did not *want* to make military service too attractive. No one wanted the conscripts to be eager to stick around. The goal was to build up the pool of reserves.

As a result, draftees do not serve long enough to become masters of their trade. Also, because the objective was to get all men trained, virtually *all* nineteen- and twenty-year-olds served. To afford that, armies had to pay them below-market wages—not exactly the best way to motivate young men eager to get on with their lives.

Every country that has a military requiring a modicum of skill has wrestled with this same problem. Some, like France and Germany, kept conscription much longer than any military rationale would justify because the draft was a national tradition and a social integrator. But they could not afford the flood of recruits any more than the United States could, so they devised ways to reduce the actual number who served— women were automatically exempted, it was easy to get deferments, enlistment terms got progressively shorter, and, for those who still managed to get drafted, there were ample provisions for "early out."[41]

Some supporters of a draft understand this, and they propose that a draft just be part of mandatory national service. Representative Charles Rangel (D-NY), for example, proposed the Universal National Service Act of 2007, which would "require all persons in the United States between the ages of 18 and 42 to perform national service, either as a member of the uniformed services or in civilian service in furtherance of the national defense and homeland security."[42]

Rangel (who served in the Korean War, receiving a Purple Heart and Bronze Star in the process) believes the current system makes a few assume an unfair share of supporting the nation's defense. In his proposal, young Americans not needed for military service would instead serve in the Peace Corps, AmeriCorps, or a modern version of the Civilian Conservation Corps. Yet this would still leave the problem of choosing who spends the springtime building riprap on streams in Yosemite, and who deploys to a forward operating base in Fallujah. And, if we are considering truly "universal" national service, there is the additional problem of what to do with the millions of Americans unfit for military duty but still fit for other service.

Proposals for national service also confuse two issues: whether Americans want young people to work for the government for some period in their lives, and whether they are willing to pay them a fair wage. If Americans truly want young people to serve in the military, the Foreign Service, schools, hospitals, or the Park Service, they should be prepared to pay market prices. Otherwise, they are, in effect, levying a special tax on the young people who must bear the cost. One might just as easily ask why other Americans—doctors, teachers, lawyers, engineers, journalists, or members of Congress from New York—should not be required to serve the government for free or at reduced wages for three or four weeks of the year.

The reason we do not is because most people agree that the market, as imperfect as it may be, is the best mechanism for both getting the best talent and offering the greatest opportunity. It may be harder to recruit personnel during wartime. But we will still get a better soldier through an all-professional force than with a draft, and one who truly wants to make a career out of the military, rather than one who just wants to do his time and get out. This is what we mean when we say conscript armies were based on an entirely different business model—it was a fundamentally different idea of what soldiering was about and a different set of assumptions about why people join the Army, how they view their jobs, and what you can expect of them. Once adopted, a draft commits a nation and its army to the low-proficiency, high-quantity military model.

The all-professional force allows the United States to use one of its special strengths. Many Americans want to serve in the military services as a matter of principle, culture, and tradition. It makes sense—and results in a better military—to make the most of their ambitions and values. Other Americans may be just as patriotic, but everyone is better off if they stay where they are.

Prepare Better for "Small Wars"?

The United States has fought many so-called small wars against pirates, insurgents, and guerillas. Examples include the wars along the Barbary

Coast; the Indian wars; naval operations against African slave traders; expeditions to Korea, China, Russia; and interventions in Haiti, Central America, Cuba, Grenada, the Philippines.[43] These small wars have varied greatly and have included counterinsurgency operations, supporting friendly insurgents, peacekeeping missions, and providing on-the-job training to allies. Small wars require special tactics, but they cannot avoid the basic issues of how many troops are needed and how many can be afforded.

In a conventional war, troop requirements depend mainly on the equation between offense and defense: how many soldiers are needed to overrun a prepared defense or, if you are trying to protect something, how many soldiers are needed to prevent this from happening. The conventional wisdom is that, however you happen to measure forces, the offense needs between a four-to-one and five-to-one advantage to win. During the Cold War, defense analysts used models to simulate how this ratio between Warsaw Pact and NATO forces would fluctuate over the course of several weeks, as each side mobilized and delivered troops to the Central Front in Germany. Most experts assumed NATO would be at a disadvantage and would give up sizable pieces of West Germany until American reinforcements arrived. Then the U.S. forces would tilt the ratio in the favor of NATO and slow the Soviet offensive. For example, this was the story line Sir John Hackett used in his 1978 novel *The Third World War: August 1985.*[44]

As we saw above, it is harder to model insurgencies, but one can look at past occupations and calculate a broad estimate of the ratio of forces an occupier needs to control a population. In 1995 James Quinlivan (like Dobbins, now a RAND analyst), did just such a hypothetical exercise, and he published the results in an often-cited article in *Parameters*, the journal of the Army War College. Experience suggests that when the terrain is favorable and the locals are cooperative, one needs four soldiers per thousand inhabitants to maintain order. When the terrain is less favorable and the locals are shooting at you, each other, or everyone in sight, you would need at least ten soldiers per thousand inhabitants. With this rule of thumb, one can posit, hypothetically, which countries the U.S. Army has a reasonable chance of securing without assistance.[45]

Suppose we updated Quinlivan's analysis and assumed that we currently have an Army that can deploy about 85,000 combat troops using its normal rotation rates, and can sustain a prolonged surge of twice that. One can then get a sense of the U.S. Army's capabilities to occupy a country. An optimist using the best-case assumptions—peaceful conditions, maximum surge—would say we can occupy a country of 45 million (e.g., Columbia, Ukraine). A pessimist using worst-case assumptions would say the limit is about 8 million (e.g., Switzerland, Honduras). It also suggests how an occupation of Iraq (population: 28 million) just *might* have succeeded, if we had been able to preempt the insurgency.

Of course, we are not planning to occupy Switzerland anytime soon, but going through the exercise gives one a real, concrete sense of what the Army can do—and, despite its best determination, probably cannot. Iraq was quite a stretch, and it depended on everything going right— which of course, it did not, and partly because of our own actions. A unilateral occupation of Iran (population: 65 million) is not even on the table.

And expanding our capability for occupations is tough. Because of the need to rotate troops, one would need to increase the size of the Army by three or four soldiers for each soldier one is able to continuously deploy. Moreover, besides sheer numbers, small wars and counterinsurgency require special skills: policing, civil affairs, public outreach, and special operations. Unfortunately, at the time the operation to overthrow Saddam was launched, most American soldiers with these specializations were reservists—97 percent of the Army's civil affairs specialists, 82 percent of its public affairs specialists, and similar proportions of the military police, intelligence operatives, and special forces.

This reliance on reserves for after-combat operations was a legacy of Cold War–era planning. The NATO plan was to repel a Warsaw Pact assault and push the attackers back into Eastern Europe. U.S. planners envisioned a brief, intense war—perhaps a month or two. Then NATO would restore order in the Low Countries, Germany, and perhaps parts of France—friendly, familiar territory—using the reservists specializing in civil affairs, policing, and so on. This would take only a few weeks or months, and then everyone would go home. Now, unfortunately, we face situations in which a combat phase can be even shorter than what was envisioned in a European war, but peacekeeping and counterinsurgency operations can go on for years—long enough to put a self-employed professional or small company owner serving in the reserves out of business.

But even if America did gear up a gendarmerie for extended occupations, there is a more fundamental problem when preparing for small wars: Americans have little taste for them. When a small war has gone badly—like Vietnam or Korea—we have effectively tried to avoid them in the years that followed by not maintaining a capability to wage them. The "Powell Doctrine," which argued for not deploying U.S. forces except in overwhelming numbers to achieve clear-cut objectives that are supported by a majority of the American public, was named for Colin Powell, a veteran of Vietnam, which had begun as a so-called small war. Powell had seen how costly it had been for the Army and the nation as a whole, and as a senior officer, he was determined not to repeat it. Small wars require the proverbial "fighting with one arm tied behind one's back" and often require long deployments and exposure to the enemy.

General David Petraeus told an interviewer after taking command of U.S. forces in Iraq that "in fact, typically, I think historically, counterinsurgency operations have gone at least nine or ten years."[46] Patraeus was given command partly because he was seen as one of the Army's experts in counterinsurgency and had directed the team that had just written a new field manual on the topic. But while Americans have been willing to base military personnel overseas for very long periods (U.S. forces have been in Japan and Germany since World War II, and in Korea since the 1950s), popular resistance quickly mounts if it means exposing U.S. forces to fire and taking casualties. So U.S. forces will prepare for small wars and will undertake them when directed, but many officers are skeptical of their viability, and public support, which is often critical to success, has been thin.

Diplomacy and Strategy

One way the United States might have finessed the military problem in Iraq would have been to stabilize the country with a political settlement. Unfortunately, the prospects for success, based on past historical experience, were not promising. Iraq is a segmented society, divided along ethnic lines (75 to 80 percent Arab, 15 to 20 percent Kurd) and sectarian lines (60 to 65 percent Shia Muslim, 35 to 40 percent Sunni Muslim, with a handful of Christians and others). Politically, the situation in Iraq had many of the features of the Balkans in the 1990s, when Yugoslavia splintered following the collapse of the Soviet Union and the death of Josip Broz Tito, who had ruled Yugoslavia since World War II.

Like Tito in Yugoslavia, Saddam had kept the lid on sectarian violence with a combination of using terror to control outright opposition and doling out benefits to keep each sectarian group quiescent. Like Saddam, Tito was a member of a minority (his father was Croatian and mother Slovenian; the largest group in Yugoslavia were the Serbs; other groups included Montenegrins, Albanian Kosovars, and Macedonians). Also like Tito, Saddam (at least at first) had tried to portray himself to the West as an "enlightened" despot, moderate enough to be acceptable. Both also portrayed themselves as essential as a counterbalance to a regional adversary that concerned U.S. leaders even more than they—the Soviets, in the case of Tito; the Iranians, in the case of Saddam.

Both Tito and Saddam had tried to control ethnic tensions, but in the end each created more problems than he solved. Both forced migration in the hope of diluting sectarian concentrations. Tito subsidized Serbian migration to Croatia, Bosnia, and Kosovo. Saddam forced Kurds out of the northern city of Kirkuk, forced thousands of Shia "Marsh Arabs" from their homes along the lower reaches of the Tigris and Euphrates rivers, and generally tried to mix populations in Baghdad. But, in both cases, the main result was only to create pockets of minorities that would later be the fodder for ethnic cleansing. When Saddam fell, the United States had a choice: facilitate a process of reseparation, or try to hold together a centralized state with artificially redistributed ethnic populations.

The Bush administration chose to attempt to keep the Iraq government centralized and leave populations as they were; and, to complicate matters further, it sought to create a secular, Western-style democracy. The common wisdom before the war among U.S. officials was that Iraq was secular, urban, and nationalistic, but events proved otherwise. Sectarian and religious sentiments may have been submerged, but they did not disappear. (This also was true in Yugoslavia; national identities were strong even after more than four decades under Tito.) So as the central regime crumbled, sectarian rivalries came roaring back, and the three major groups all had aspirations that were mutually exclusive. The Shi'ites wanted to assume power; the Sunnis wanted to regain power; and the Kurds wanted to be left alone. The challenge was to get each to accept a settlement that was no better than its second choice—federation—and to believe that the alternative of civil war was hopeless.

The United States might have averted some of the conflict that followed by resolving some of the most contentious issues before it transferred power back to the Iraqis—in particular, oil rights and the future of the Iraqi army. The United States could have assigned Iraq's oil to a national corporation and allocated the shares of the corporation to all Iraqis on a per capita basis. This would have guaranteed Sunnis a share of oil revenues and, given their eagerness to take power, the Shia leaders might have accepted this if it had been presented as a fait accompli.[47] Similarly, if the Transitional Authority had kept most of the Iraqi army intact and paid its salaries for a period, it might have kept its members off the streets and out of the insurgency. The officer corps was disproportionately Sunni; by retaining officers below, say, brigadier general or colonel, the army might have prevented looting, while U.S. forces supervised it to protect the Shia population from abuse. Admittedly, even then, the occupation might have been a long shot—but success might have been possible with some diplomatic deftness, and this was lacking.

Ironically, at the time the military situation had reached its nadir in early 2007, the ethnic conflict had been resolved—unfortunately, at tremendous cost. The Defense Department reported at the time that 80 percent of the attacks by insurgents and terrorists were occurring in just four provinces, which accounted for 37 percent of the Iraqi population—or about 8 million people. One reason was that by then 4 million Iraqis (about 15 percent of the country's prewar population) were refugees, having left their homes. About half had relocated within Iraq, and about half had fled to neighboring countries. Per capita, this was about the same percentage of Yugoslavs who had become refugees when that conflict settled down. Baghdad itself, which before the war had a heterogeneous population, had separated out into well-defined Sunni and Shia neighborhoods.

In effect, the feared ethnic cleansing had taken place, intended or not, and the hot spots in the war were limited to a size that U.S. forces could control. In the areas where fighting was under way, the United States had close to the same ratio of troops to population that it had in Bosnia. Also, by that time the Iraqis were more willing to cooperate because they were themselves weary of war and each ethnic group wanted stability and order in the areas it now dominated. The "surge" of approximately 30,000 troops in 2007 was, for all the controversy it generated, just a 20 to 25 percent increase in soldiers. Better counterinsurgency tactics also helped. But it is also unlikely that the surge or better tactics would have been sufficient to change the course of the war if the facts on the ground—ethnic cleansing, the marginalization of extremists by the Shi'ite mainstream, and the weariness of Sunni leaders of the war and the foreign al-Qaeda interlopers—had not changed.

Partly because of the experience of Iraq, in November 2005 the Defense Department adopted a new policy to improve its capabilities for postwar stabilization.[48] Under this policy, stability operations are to be "given priority comparable to combat operations." But this does not escape the larger issue: Where do the soldiers come from? And what about the fact that long wars have never enjoyed the public support they require?

One purpose of strategy is to gain a favorable tactical position—that is, one that plays to your strengths and avoids your weaknesses. Preparing

U.S. forces to fight insurgencies more effectively is not a strategy; it is at best a plan for salvaging a situation when strategy fails.

A Strategic Critique

From a strategic perspective, there were problems with U.S. policy throughout the period from 1993 to 2003. The policy of the Clinton administration was to "keep Saddam in his box." Its approach was to work through the United Nations to disarm Iraq. This was, in part, a legacy of the fact that the 1991 cease-fire, sanctions, and inspections process were all based on UN resolutions.

But it also reflected the Clinton administration's "enlargement" doctrine—building institutions and working through international organizations, except when vital U.S. interests seemed at stake. This policy obliged us to work with countries whose goals were at odds with our own, whether or not their support was essential. It also made the diplomacy as public as one could imagine and constrained any action we might try.

U.S. policy also tried to pressure Saddam with sanctions and "no-fly zones"—which exposed a second conceptual problem in the strategy. Whenever Iraqi radar "painted" an aircraft patrolling the no-fly zones, our forces would bomb the offending transmitter. The Iraqis, knowing this, often placed their radar transmitters near schools, hospitals, and mosques, and, inevitably, some of the bombs would go astray. As more innocent civilians were killed or injured, the Iraqis rallied behind Saddam, and the other countries that we needed to maintain the sanctions were alienated. Meanwhile, Saddam offered bounties to any missile crew that shot down one of our aircraft. It was only a matter of time before an Iraqi missile crew would get lucky and a U.S. pilot would be taken hostage; *that* would have been a real problem.

So Saddam could bide his time. The now-infamous Oil for Food Program provided his regime with ample revenues. Indeed, it gave him *greater* control over Iraq, because it was the main source of food and other necessities. The program also garnered support for Saddam from officials in France, Russia, and the UN itself who personally benefited from the program.

As the Iraqi Survey Group, a team investigating Iraqi weapons programs for the Director of Central Intelligence after the war, reported, "The introduction of the Oil-For-Food program (OFF) in late 1996 was a key turning point. . . . OFF rescued Baghdad's economy from a terminal decline created by sanctions. The Regime quickly came to see that OFF could be corrupted to acquire foreign exchange both to further undermine sanctions and to provide the means to enhance dual-use infrastructure and potential WMD-related development."[49]

The fact that most Iraqis suffered during this period was, for Saddam, a strategic bonus. Journalists—especially from the Middle East and Europe—regularly reported the worsening conditions within Iraq. This eroded public support and isolated the United States. According to the Iraqi Study Group, "By 2000, the erosion of sanctions accelerated. The semi-annual debates over the renewal of sanctions in the Security Council became the forum for Iraqi proponents to argue the case for relaxing sanctions further." Thus it may have seemed that Saddam was "in a box," but in fact it was America that had lost the strategic advantage—the ability to dictate when and how we would engage the enemy, and the general course of events. As a result, the most fundamental flaw in the U.S. strategy before 2001 was simply that it would eventually *fail* and it offered no plausible story for how the United States could ever win.

The problem with the decision to intervene with a full-scale military invasion, conversely, was that it did not adequately consider all the possible outcomes and potential costs. As we have seen, Bush administration officials were adamant in avoiding speculation about the war's potential costs. Strategically speaking, though, that was *exactly* what they should have been most concerned about. They should have tried to estimate the possible downside of a military strike and entertained scenarios so they could at least consider the plausibility of each.

There were some warnings before the U.S. attack on Iraq that its sectarian groups might begin fighting each other; these were not seriously considered, as the lack of postcombat planning revealed. Beyond that, hardly anyone seemed to think systematically about how a war in Iraq might trigger other events in the region and beyond. There was some talk about how democracy, once established in Iraq, would spread through the region. But there was never a cause-and-effect explanation of how overthrowing Saddam would, say, push Hosni Mubarak to risk greater reforms in Egypt, or how events in Baghdad might shape events in Lebanon or the Occupied Territories. Indeed, logically, removing Saddam—the main regional counterbalance to Iran—was bound to give the Iranians *greater* freedom to support clients like Hezbollah; and this has proven to be the case.

Another problem with the decision to invade Iraq was that American officials not only failed to consider all the possible alternatives to an invasion; U.S. actions progressively *reduced* their options, exactly when they could have used more. U.S. forces began to deploy in December 2002. The largest wave was ordered to mobilize in mid-January, and the force was "cocked and ready to fire" by the first week of February, when there were a total of 140,000 personnel in theater.

Once the forces were staged, it was impossible to sustain them in the field indefinitely. The troops would lose their edge. Supplies would run down. Iraqi forces would "read" the preparations and get better prepared. There was also the Iraqi summer to consider. Few wanted to launch an invasion in protective gear when temperatures exceeded 120 degrees Fahrenheit. In sum, by deciding to prepare for a full-scale invasion to pressure Saddam, U.S. leaders effectively put themselves on a course where they had fewer and fewer alternatives. Burning bridges behind oneself is sometimes a useful tactic to convince an adversary that one is serious. But before using this tactic, one must decide if it really is a good idea to eliminate all other options.

The ironic thing was that, by pulling U.S. forces out of Afghanistan and preparing to attack Iraq in 2002, we transformed the regional situation from one in which we had the upper hand to one in which our adversaries did. When we pursued al-Qaeda in Afghanistan, we had the support of Sunni allies in the region. Many of them feared the extremist group. Indeed, Osama bin Laden had been exiled by Saudi Arabia, and Ayman al-Zawahiri had fled Egypt. The government of Iran was also an arm's-length ally of the United States, because Iran is predominantly Shia and al-Qaeda considered Shia Muslims to be apostates. It was a strong hand to play.

But by striking Iraq, the United States broke up much of this alliance. Many of our Sunni allies either provided quiet support to Sunni insurgents or just tried to keep out of the conflict completely. By late 2003, virtually the entire deployable force of the U.S. Army was in Iraq, en route to Iraq, or returning from action in Iraq. The U.S. armed forces that were committed to Iraq became unavailable for use elsewhere. The clock worked against us as the finite capacity of the Army and Marines was expended. Effectively, we disarmed ourselves. The U.S. military had much more influence on world affairs before Iraq, when it was a *potential* force to be used. That is one of the ironic features of American military power. Once deployed, it cannot be used elsewhere, and thus has less influence.

In short, again, America lost the strategic advantage. The international squash master Hashim Khan once explained his secret for controlling the tempo and course of a game. It was not in *taking* the "kill" shot but in constantly being in position to take it, with his racquet cocked and ready to swing. As he put it: "Impossible to slam shut door."[50] By committing so many of its military forces in Iraq and having them pinned down there for so long, the United States effectively slammed that door.

In retrospect, the reasons for the troubles of the United States in Iraq are clear. The public supported intervention because the September 11 attacks made Americans acutely aware of our vulnerability, and because nearly all experts believed Iraq had some WMD capabilities. If we had found WMD in Iraq, Americans might still believe intervention was the right decision, no matter how difficult the occupation turned out to be.

Overthrowing Saddam and establishing a new government in Iraq was never going to be a "cakewalk," no matter what some pundits argued. In 1991 U.S. leaders decided not to proceed to Baghdad during Operation

Desert Storm because occupying Iraq would be like trying to occupy a country the size of California with the population of Canada.[51] These facts had not changed; it was just that the threat of Saddam appearing to be on course to acquire WMD made the situation seem more dire.

In the event, the occupation of Iraq turned out to be as difficult as past experience and the mathematics suggested, and mistakes made the situation even worse. Because there were no WMD, as the situation deteriorated, the public experienced "buyer's regret" even faster than it might have otherwise. By not acknowledging that the situation was worsening, administration officials made it even harder to fix. Its credibility suffered as conditions failed to improve. This also made it harder to rally political support.

The Iraqi insurgents, once organized, were able to define the pace of the war — where and when to attack, engage, and withdraw. They initially gained the strategic advantage. U.S. forces had the logistical challenge of having to support a war on the other side of the world, and the insurgents had the home turf advantages — understanding the local languages, tribal structure, terrain, and so on, all of which were unfamiliar to our troops. With these factors in place, events unfolded as one might expect. Popular support diminished at historical rates once U.S. forces began to take casualties. Support for defense spending sank as annual expenditures rose — again, as past history would have anticipated.

The United States' best chance for a military victory in 2003 hinged on quickly stabilizing the situation in Iraq. It had to maintain order, protect property, and ensure the continuation of services at least at the level Iraqis had enjoyed under Saddam. There might have been a brief window of opportunity to achieve this in the months following the capture of Baghdad. Once this window was missed, we were constantly playing catch-up, ensnared in a situation that was costly to sustain but even more costly to withdraw from. It took years for the situation to reach a new equilibrium as ethnic populations separated, local leaders consolidated power in their own regions, U.S. forces adopted better tactics, and U.S. leaders lowered their expectations for the government in Baghdad.

Yet, whatever the reasons for launching the U.S. military operation against Iraq and whatever the breakdown in planning combat operations and planning the occupation, a critical question remains: Why were the White House staff, the military services, the State Department, and the intelligence community so slow to respond once the situation began to go sour? This question relates directly to the other quality America needs if it hopes to be secure and retain predominance: agility. And that is the issue we examine next.

CHAPTER FIVE

Agility

IN MODERN COMBAT, whoever gains a step on their opponent usually wins. The same rule applies to government organizations, corporations, and political systems. With the world moving so much faster, making decisions quickly and taking action can offer a decisive advantage.

So how is America doing? Let us look at a recent competition between al-Qaeda and the United States. Here is the question: Who has the more agile organization? Al-Qaeda, in planning, developing and executing a terrorist attack? Or the United States, in planning, developing, and executing the measures to stop one?

Consider the record. Sometime in the spring of 1999, Khalid Sheikh Mohammed, the mastermind behind the plot for the September 11 terrorist attacks, visited Osama bin Laden at his camp in Afghanistan and asked if al-Qaeda would fund the "planes operation"—the suicide attack plan using commercial airliners. Bin Laden agreed, and a few months later selected four al-Qaeda members—Khalid al Mihdhar, Nawaf al Hazmi, Khallad bin Attash, and Abu Bara al Yemeni—as team leaders.[1]

The team leaders began to enter the United States in early 2000 and started taking flying lessons in the summer of 2000. The so-called muscle hijackers, the fifteen terrorists who planned to overpower the crews on the targeted flights, began arriving in April 2001. The teams spent the summer preparing for the attack, which, of course, took place on September 11. In other words, from what a government contracting official would call "authority to proceed" to completion, the operation took approximately twenty-seven months.

Compare that to the U.S. response. U.S. officials began debating options for preventing future terrorist attacks immediately following the strike. Congress took a year to debate the bill establishing the Department of Homeland Security; George W. Bush, who originally opposed creating the department, changed his mind and signed the bill into law on November 25, 2002.

A joint House-Senate committee finished the first investigation of the attack in December 2002. The 9/11 Commission issued its own report on July 22, 2004, recommending, among other things, establishing a National Intelligence Director and a new National Counterterrorism Center. President Bush established the center by executive order on August 27. Adoption of the Intelligence Reform and Terrorism Prevention Act, which embodied most of the commission's other proposals, took three more months. The measures it authorized—including appointing what was then being called a "Director of National Intelligence"—sat until after a second commission, investigating intelligence prior to the war in Iraq, issued its own report. That was four months later. The new Director was sworn in on April 21, 2005.

So, total response time, charitably defined: about forty-four months. Implementation continues today. True, the two tasks are not completely comparable. But, looking at the big picture, it seems clear that al-Qaeda has an agility advantage. The terrorists are sizing up the situation, making decisions, and acting faster than we are. Indeed, since September 11 al-Qaeda has been moving faster than ever. British authorities investigating the July 2005 London bombings (which destroyed three subway trains and a double-decker bus, killing fifty-three people) concluded that the terrorists first visited Pakistan in July 2003 and returned in the winter of 2005—suggesting that the attack was proposed two years earlier and planned in detail six months prior to the strike.[2]

It may seem unfair to compare a government bureaucracy and the legislative process with a network of small terrorist cells. But that is precisely the point. Terrorists will *always* make the war as "unfair" as possible. So will insurgents, rogue states, and proliferators. That is what asymmetric warfare is all about: avoiding our strengths and exploiting our vulnerabilities. They will use their agility to gain any advantage they can. We simply will not win if our adversaries consistently make decisions and act faster than we do.

The idea of a "decision cycle" and the need to stay a step ahead of your adversary is an old one, but its modern incarnation can be traced to John Boyd, a fighter pilot who famously applied the principle to combat tactics. He realized that the aircraft with better "transients" (the ability to change speed, direction, or attitude faster) usually won. He applied the idea to tactics, and then organizations, coining the term "OODA loop" to capture the entire process to "observe, orientate, decide, and act." Like fighter aircraft and fighter pilots, organizations also compete against each other and the environment. Whoever had the edge in completing the process, he said, would win.[3]

The problem today is that we are taking too long to respond to threats and changes in the environment. Reading the 9/11 Commission report, for example, one cannot help but be struck by how often delay and slowness led to failure. For example, President Bill Clinton said he requested military options to eliminate bin Laden in late 1999. But General Hugh Shelton, Chairman of the Joint Chiefs of Staff, was reluctant. Secretary of Defense William Cohen thought the President was speaking hypothetically. And the one person who could have given everyone a direct order, Clinton himself, believed raising his temper would not accomplish anything. So the issue dragged on.[4]

Meanwhile, organizations further down the line also moved sluggishly. One case, now notorious, involved the Predator, a robotic aircraft originally built for battlefield reconnaissance and later modified to carry missiles. The Air Force had flown the Predator in the Balkans since 1996, but it had to be modified to operate over Afghanistan and carry missiles. The Air Force continued the Predator's development and testing throughout the spring and summer of 2000. It took until July 2000 to work out all the details, and two more months to deploy the Predator over Afghanistan. Predator operators thought they spotted bin Laden during tests that began in September 2000.

Then a new problem emerged: Officials disagreed over the rules of engagement. Clinton's National Security Adviser, Sandy Burger, wanted greater confidence in bin Laden's location before he would approve a strike and was worried about civilian casualties. Air Force officials were reluctant to carry out what looked like a covert operation. But the Central Intelligence Agency (CIA) was reluctant to get directly involved in a combat operation—or violate the legal ban on assassination. These disagreements dragged into 2001, as the Bush administration took office. Then President Bush put the matter on hold while his National Security Adviser, Condoleezza Rice, directed a new, comprehensive plan to eliminate al-Qaeda. George Tenet, the Director of Central Intelligence, in turn, deferred resolving the legal issues over whether the CIA could take part in an attack until the administration had its new strategy. So it went, until the clock ran out and the terrorists struck.

Although the events leading up to September 11 are now familiar, almost everyone seems to miss the core problem from which all others followed: There was always time for another meeting, another study, or another round of coordination. No one, it seems, was worrying about the clock—*whether time itself mattered.* It is not that every concern raised did not have some legitimate rationale (at least within the legalistic, bureaucratic culture that characterizes the U.S. government). Yet the fact is that while U.S. officials were working out legal issues, al-Qaeda was developing and executing its plan.

This same problem surfaced again just a year later, and it was a reason why the war in Iraq did not go better. Just about everyone agrees now that the United States was unprepared for the insurgency in Iraq. But they overlook that someone else was also unprepared: *the insurgents.* As we saw in the preceding chapter, captured Iraqi officials and military officers claim that they were not planning a guerilla war.[5] No one was prepared for an insurgency. Everyone—the United States, its coalition partners, Ba'athists leaders on the lam, tribal leaders, religious authorities, and foreign fighters—were all starting from scratch.

So, when Saddam Hussein's statue came down in Baghdad's Firdos Square on April 9, 2003, the question that mattered most was who could organize and execute faster, the would-be insurgents or America? Alas, we were left in the starting blocks. The insurgents organized faster than U.S. officials could recognize the situation and respond. So we were playing catch-up from the beginning, which is another way of saying we were behind—which is another way of saying we were losing.

Once, When We Were Fast

The war on al-Qaeda and the war in Iraq are not exceptional. The problem of a lack of speed seems to plague almost all government organizations with national security responsibilities. It has been developing for some time. And it is getting worse. For example, though it has become fashionable to recall how much the Greatest Generation accomplished in winning World War II, we often forget how fast they accomplished it. The Japanese attacked Pearl Harbor on December 7, 1941. The Battle of the Coral Sea was fought in May 1942, and the Battle of Midway in June. In effect, the U.S. Navy destroyed most of Japan's naval aviation and reversed the flow of the conflict in just six months. Indeed, the entire war in the Pacific took just forty-six months—or about the time today's officials required just to agree to a plan to rebuild the World Trade Center.

Or consider the atom bomb. Albert Einstein first wrote to Franklin Delano Roosevelt on August 2, 1939, to alert him to the possibilities of nuclear weapons. Roosevelt established the U.S. nuclear fission research program a month later. The effort to build a nuclear weapon really got under way, however, in September 1942, when Leslie Groves was appointed director of what became known as the Manhattan Project. The first nuclear device was tested less than three years later, on July 16, 1945. Hiroshima was bombed three weeks after that. The entire project under Groves cost $21 billion in today's dollars, and yielded two bomb designs, three different means of producing fissile material, and three actual nuclear devices.[6]

Or consider the Office of Strategic Services (OSS), the predecessor of today's CIA. Roosevelt appointed William Donovan as his Coordinator of Information in July 1941. The OSS was itself established in June 1942. Harry Truman disbanded it in September 1945. In other words, the entire history of the OSS—what many consider the golden age of American intelligence—spanned just thirty-seven months.

During this period, the OSS recruited, trained, and deployed a workforce that totaled up to 13,000 people. William Casey, directing OSS espionage in Europe, stood up his entire network in eighteen months.[7] By comparison, after September 11, U.S. intelligence officials said on several occasions that the CIA would require five years to rebuild its clandestine service.[8]

The United States was also able to adapt and make course corrections faster. U.S. forces performed poorly in early campaigns. The Battle of the Kasserine Pass in February 1943 has become synonymous with bad planning and inept command. General Dwight D. Eisenhower sacked the commander and made it clear that he wanted change—and quickly.

Compare this to how slowly the United States moved when the Iraq insurgency began to gain steam in the summer of 2003—even as many analysts and journalists reported the developments were moving in the wrong direction.[9] But this, though ironic, is not unusual. While jet airliners, Interstate highways, the computer, and the Internet are making just about everything else in modern life move faster, government, including the parts responsible for national security, is generally slowing down.

Consider this example. Everyone knows the cost of military aircraft has been rising. But they are taking much longer to develop, too. Observe Figure 5.1. In the early 1940s it took twenty-five months to get a new

FIGURE 9.1

Time Required for U.S. Fighter Aircraft Development, 1930–2007

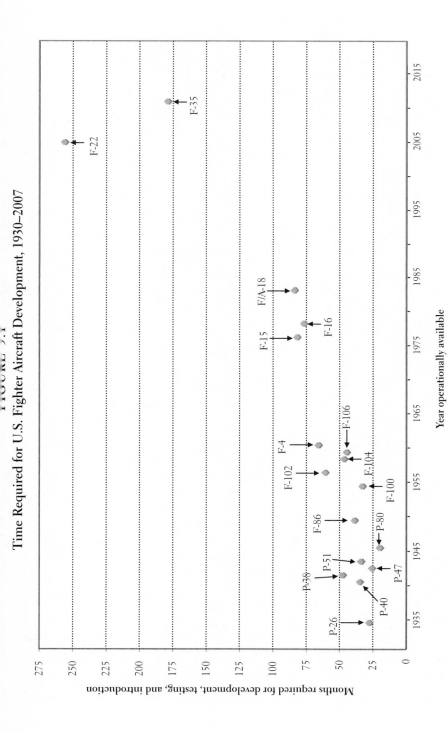

Sources: U.S. Air Force; industry references.

fighter like the P-47 Thunderbolt into service, from when the government signed a contract for a prototype to when the aircraft entered action. In the late 1940s, the time grew to about forty-three months for an early jet fighter like the F-86 Sabre. By the 1960s, the F-4 Phantom required sixty-six months.

The Phantom's replacement, the F-15 Eagle, took 82 months. Today's newest fighter, the F-22 Raptor, traces its development to a prototype built under a contract signed in October 1986. That prototype first flew in September 1990. The production model entered service in December 2005—a total of 230 months, or about nineteen years or, to put it another way, slightly longer than the typical career of an officer in the U.S. Air Force. The new F-35 Lightning II, which will replace the F-16, is slated to require "just" fifteen years from signing the contract for the prototype to when it enters service. We shall see.

When weapons take this long to develop, there are all kinds of other pernicious effects. A twenty-year program simply does not feel like an attack on an urgent objective. Rather, it resembles cathedral building—a never-ending public works project, part of the day-to-day life of a quiet village, where participants come and go, newcomers stop by, work on a piece, and then move on.

One might think the ever-lengthening development time fighter aircraft require is because of their unique complexity. Not so. Government aircraft of *all* kinds take longer to develop, and longer than their commercial counterparts. Compare a military transport, like the C-17 Globemaster III, with the new Boeing 787 Dreamliner. The C-17 required twelve years to enter service, while the 787—more complex than the C-17 in many respects— will require less than half the time, even with its much-publicized delivery delays.

There are other examples that suggest defense acquisition is dysfunctional. Automobiles, for instance, are more complex than ever. Like jet fighters, cars today go faster and handle better. They also require less maintenance, tell you how to reach your destination, surround you in sound rivaling a good recording studio—all while meeting ever-tougher safety, pollution, and fuel economy standards. Yet the time required to develop a car and get it into the showroom is getting shorter all the time. Toyota currently is best; it can get a new model into production in about two years, and it is trying to cut this to twelve months. Ford and GM are trying hard to improve, but they still take one to two years longer, which is one reason they have been suffering in the market.[10]

The development of the F-22 illustrates some of the penalties from the lack of organizational speed: built-in obsolescence. Military hardware has the reputation for being at technology's cutting edge, but that is really the exception, not the rule. More often military technology lags its commercial counterpart, largely because it takes so long to deliver. The F-22's avionics use the Intel i960, a microprocessor comparable to the chips used in IBM personal computers in the mid-1980s, when the fighter's design was frozen, and now so old that it is no longer in production. When offered for sale on eBay, Intel i960s are typically described as "rare," "vintage," "hard to find," or "collectable." To ensure a supply for the F-22, the Defense Department had to arrange for a special production run. Long development times, almost by definition, leave military systems stuck with old technology.

Government programs suffer all the obstacles of their commercial counterparts—technical glitches, financing—plus some of their own, like the lockstep pace of the annual federal budget cycle and the requirements for documentation and review to ensure that the taxpayer's money is well-spent. The most important difference, however, seems to be the lack of market pressure. Boeing's commercial aircraft division could go out of business if it did not deliver new airliners fast and on time. (Witness what happened to the stock price of its rival, Airbus, when its new A380 superjumbo jet slipped, and, to a lesser extent, Boeing when the 787 was delayed.) It would be much harder for that to happen to Boeing's military division.

The problem is not just aircraft. Military ships, tanks, and electronic systems all take longer to deliver than before, and longer than their commercial counterparts. The result: threats change faster than we can develop the means to counter them. This is why some officials occasionally say we have to anticipate requirements further into the future. But that is unrealistic. When you try to forecast threats two decades ahead because your weapon takes twenty years to develop, it is not analysis. It is fortune telling.

Staffing Up

The ever-slowing pace of government appears in other ways as well. Take the matter of getting a new administration up and running. As Figure 5.2 shows, every administration since John F. Kennedy's has taken longer than the one preceding it to fill the top five hundred appointed jobs in government. In the early 1960s it took just over two months; now it takes more than eight. A new administration is not up and running until almost a year after the election that put it in office. How can you win the big game if your team does not show up until the end of the first quarter?

That is what happened in 2001, as al-Qaeda was preparing its September 11 strike. The Bush administration's Cabinet secretaries were confirmed and ready to go when the new President was sworn in on January 20, 2001. But that was about it. The administration did not nominate Paul Wolfowitz for Deputy Secretary of Defense until February 5. In other words, it took the administration almost two months (starting on December 13, when Al Gore conceded the election) just to sort out who was going to fill the second-ranking position at the Defense Department.

Wolfowitz had to wait until February 27 for his confirmation hearing; this was for Wolfowitz to make the rounds of the Armed Services Committee members and allow their staff an opportunity to review his files. He was finally confirmed and sworn in on March 2. But his wait was, in fact, comparatively short. Richard Armitage, nominated for Deputy Secretary of State, was not sworn in until March 23. Six months passed before the top Defense Department leadership was in place; Douglas Feith, the Under Secretary of Defense for Policy—as in "policy for combating terrorists"—was the last to be sworn in, in July 2001.

What is really troubling is that *every* administration took longer than its predecessor. There is no improvement. The problem never gets better;

Time Required to Staff Incoming U.S. Administrations

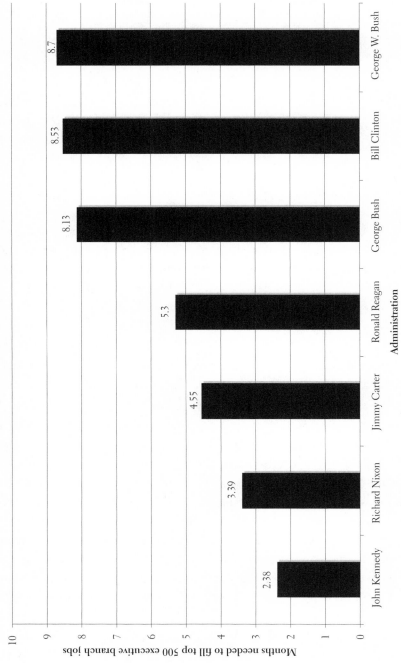

Source: National Academies Committee on Science, Engineering, and Public Policy, *Science and Technology in the National Interest* (Washington, DC: National Academies, 2005). The committee based its work on earlier studies by Paul C. Light, who headed the President Appointee Initiative at the Brookings Institution from 2000 to 2003.

it just gets worse. And the government gets slower and less agile. Indeed, a top official entering at the beginning of an administration is a best-case scenario. Candidates selected for Assistant Secretary in the middle of a term can often wait six months or more. Further down the ranks, bringing on new staff is paced largely by how long it takes to obtain a security clearance. For civil servants, this can take almost a year; for contractors, the average is about 450 days.[11]

Why Is Everything So Slow?

There have been countless studies on streamlining contracting, speeding up background investigations, shortening the process of nominating and confirming appointees, and so on. But the underlying problem that must be solved is that *when balancing risk with speed, there is rarely a champion for speed, and usually no advocate for accommodating more risk.*

The risks that worry people take many forms: the risk that some group will be underrepresented in a decision, the risk that a design will not work properly, the risk that a secret will be compromised, the risk that someone will cheat the government, or the risk that an official will have a conflict of interest. Whatever the specifics, the loss of speed is almost always the result of someone trying to manage risk by adding measures to reduce the probability of "something bad" happening. And the process of government and administration steadily grows.

Congress is responsible for part of this problem. The Kennedy administration could get up and running in one-third of the time administrations require today partly because three times as many officials today require Senate confirmation. Committees take more time today to review a nominee's materials. Senators can put "holds" on a nomination, often delaying a vote to gain concessions from an administration on issues they believe are important but that are often unrelated to the qualifications of the nominee.

Yet, to be fair, about half the time required for confirmation is internal vetting within the executive branch. In recent administrations—both

Democratic and Republican—the White House personnel office has gotten more deeply involved to make sure that the nominee is not only capable but also politically correct. More people get involved, and the process bogs down further, even when nominees are well known among their peers, have held office previously, or are even currently serving in lower-ranking positions when they are nominated.

All these delays in getting appointees into place have ripple effects that slow things down even more. "Acting" heads defer decisions until permanent appointees are in place. The appointees, meanwhile, make it a point not to have contact with the organization they may eventually head, for fear of getting ahead of the confirmation process and offending a legislator. The interesting thing is that about the same number of nominees are eventually approved as before; we are not discovering that more candidates are unsuitable. It just takes a lot longer to get them through the process.

It is a classic example of Parkinson's Law: Work expands to fill the time available. Officials, in effect, are defining the "time available" by the annual budget cycle, the congressional calendar, or the next election. Yet in reality, when it comes to national security, the time available is the time an adversary requires to act.[12]

Examples of Speed

There is no single answer that says when speed should be the highest priority. But if we do not at least have a mechanism for weighing the potential costs of delay with risks of speed, then government will always become slower. Worse, we will not have the option to act fast even when it is critical.

Lest we seem *too* pessimistic, there are cases—including some fairly recent ones—in which government organizations moved out smartly on national security missions. These cases show us what we need to do if we want organizations to move faster—for example:

- *The U-2 aircraft*: In the 1950s the United States needed a higher-flying airplane to take pictures of Soviet military facilities. The CIA gave Lockheed authority to proceed in December 1954; the aircraft flew its first reconnaissance mission over the Soviet Union in July 1956. Total time required: eighteen months.[13]
- *The Explorer 1 satellite*: Determined to match the Soviet's Sputnik I, which was launched in September 1957, the Defense Department authorized the Army Ballistic Missile Agency to prepare a satellite for launch on November 8, 1957, and Werner von Braun's team launched it three months later on January 31, 1958.
- *U.S. ballistic missile programs*: Studies in early 1954 said that the United States could build an intercontinental ballistic missile (ICBM) in four to five years if performance requirements were not too demanding and the program was given adequate funding. The first Atlas ICBM was operational in September 1959. The Polaris submarine-launched ballistic missile (SLBM) was operational in late 1960.
- *The F-117A Nighthawk*: In the mid-1970s, U.S Air Force officials became concerned about the steady improvements the Soviets were making in air defense systems. In response, they developed the F-117A—the first aircraft designed specifically for stealth—in about four and a half years.
- *The GBU-28*: At the start of Operation Desert Storm in 1991, the Air Force did not have a bomb that could penetrate Iraq's deepest underground shelters. The Air Force Research Laboratory cobbled together an effective bomb in twenty-seven days.
- *Clementine*: In 1992 the Ballistic Missile Defense Organization (BMDO) had to test some miniature sensors in a deep space environment, far from Earth. The Naval Research Laboratory (NRL) conducted the tests by building a space probe that would survey the Moon and an asteroid. At the time, building space probes typically required five to ten years. NRL built Clementine in twenty-two months.

- *JAWBREAKER*: George W. Bush asked for options to respond to the
  September 11 attacks; the CIA presented its plan two days later to
  use Northern Alliance forces as a surrogate army. The CIA units,
  operating under the designation "JAWBREAKER," arrived in weeks
  and Kabul was taken on November 14.[14]

All these programs are related to national security, but they are as
different from one another as anyone might imagine. Two are aircraft
development programs, two are space research missions, one is a family
of weapon systems, one is a munition, and one is a covert paramilitary
operation. The Army, Navy, Air Force, and CIA are all represented. Two
were in wartime, four in peacetime. Yet, as different as they were, they
share some common features.

At the most general level, all five involved someone bending the rules
and taking responsibility for doing so. This is a logical — even *necessary* —
condition for speed. Every organization has a "natural" rate of operation
defined by its standard operating procedures. Some rules are formal and
documented; others are implicit or part of the organization's culture. In
either case, these rules define who must consult with whom, who can
approve what, how much supporting documentation must be prepared,
and so on. This rate can be speeded up some, but when organizations
have moved significantly faster, it is almost always because someone
either bent the rules or managed to evade them. Consider the cases cited
above.

In each case, someone bent, broke, or just finessed the normal rules.
For example, in developing the U-2, the CIA avoided the constraining
pace of the federal calendar that most agencies and departments must
operate under by using its special authority to spend money without a
specific appropriation. Congress had given the CIA this authority to use
"unvouchered funds" so that it could carry out intelligence operations
without revealing the operation in public budget documents. No one,
however, had ever used this authority to develop a major system, like an
aircraft. By using the CIA's special funding authority, the U-2 program
could leapfrog the annual budget cycle. Also, because the CIA was not

bound by the Defense Department's acquisition regulations, the program avoided the military's arduous contractor selection process. Instead, it simply chose Lockheed.[15]

Notice the key point: The authority the CIA used for the U-2 already existed, although Congress had created it for a different purpose. A handful of officials and contractors had a vision for a radically new kind of aircraft—one that could fly so high it would be invisible to radar and beyond the range of Soviet interceptors. They first pitched the idea to the Air Force. Its leadership was uninterested. They then shopped it to the CIA. Its chief, Allen Dulles, was also skeptical, but other officials thought the idea was promising. Making do with this level of support, the U-2's supporters then looked for ways to build the aircraft as quickly as possible. That is how they found the CIA's funding authority. All these steps were within the law, but it required advocates who would stretch this existing authority in an unprecedented, creative—but legal—application.

Lockheed's "Skunk Works," in turn, shortened or eliminated many steps a military contractor would ordinarily take. By having all its people work together in one location, an engineer could ask a worker to adjust the design on the spot with a conversation instead of a meeting and follow up with documentation later. Normal Defense Department procedures would usually not permit this. It could even constitute a serious contract violation.

The Army also broke rules in building the Explorer 1 satellite— specifically, the rule that said that the Army was not supposed to build satellites. The Defense Department and White House had given the Navy that mission. Major General John Medaris, at the time the Army Ballistic Missile Agency's Director, "went out on a limb," as he later put it. He set aside some extra hardware, and when the White House gave the go-ahead after the Soviets launched Sputnik, the Army cobbled together a satellite and launch vehicle for a quick shot. (Medaris was a lifelong risk taker, having learned to fly at twelve by lying about his age and joined the Marines at sixteen.)[16]

The U-2 and Explorer 1 also shared something in common: they "stole" a lot of technology from other programs, using them in ways no one had originally intended but that sped up the process. The U-2 was, in many ways, the F-104 Starfighter that Lockheed had designed earlier for the Air Force but with longer wings and a lot of weight removed. The rocket that launched Explorer 1 was based on an Army Redstone ballistic missile, which in turn was an updated and improved V-2 that the Army's German engineers had developed in World War II.

There was also a synergetic effect, where one fast-paced program accelerated another. The early U.S. satellite and ballistic missile programs were, for all practical purposes, one and the same, and launching a satellite was really just an incremental step beyond launching a long-range ballistic missile. The Army, Navy, and Air Force were all developing their first generation of ballistic missiles. These programs were moving at a remarkably fast pace, and, though different in specifics, they all shared some common technologies and hardware. Moreover, they were all headed by strong-minded leaders determined to achieve success quickly—Medaris and von Braun, as noted, at the Army; General Bernard Schriever at the Air Force, and Rear Admiral William Raborn at the Navy.[17]

The Army's approach in launching Explorer 1 set the mold for the Clementine space probe the Navy built almost four decades later. In 1992 BMDO was planning a constellation of small satellites to detect missile launches. The satellites would use a new family of minisensors developed by Lawrence Livermore Laboratory, so BMDO had to test them beyond earth orbit to make sure they would not fry when subjected to the heat and radiation of deep space.

The Naval Research Laboratory proposed putting the sensors on a small space probe and testing them by taking pictures of two targets: the Moon, and Geographos, an asteroid due to pass within 3.1 million miles of Earth in 1994. This plan threaded the eyes of several bureaucratic needles. By designing the sensor trials as a scientific mission, BMDO avoided the time-consuming controversy that testing them against a missile would create. By choosing the Moon as a target, NRL avoided a time-consuming turf war with the National Aeronautics and Space Administration (NASA); the space agency had turned its attention to planets. By including Geographos as a target, everyone committed to a launch date that could not be moved; the asteroid was going to arrive on schedule, no matter what.

NASA space probes had become bigger and more complex, and had taken longer and longer to build. Some, like the Cassini-Huygens mission to Saturn, had taken more than ten years to build and launch, and had cost more than $3 billion. By scaling the mission's goals to what could be easily achieved with the hardware at hand, and by using a much simpler design, the Clementine team built its spacecraft in under two years.

Ironically, Clementine never got to Geographos; a thruster malfunctioned as it was leaving the Moon, exhausting the probe's fuel supply. But by then the sensor tests were completed—and Clementine had made a complete map of the Moon, which had not been surveyed since the 1960s. More important, by showing what could be accomplished with "good enough" technology and a firm deadline, Clementine changed the way the space community thought about probes and satellites. The trend since then has been toward smaller, more frequent missions, such as Sojourner, NASA's own Mars rover.[18]

In the case of JAWBREAKER, CIA officers like Gary Schroen acted largely on their own initiative in the 1990s when they kept up contacts with Northern Alliance figures like Ahmed Massoud. The CIA had turned its interest elsewhere after the Soviets left in 1989. These contacts greased the process of reestablishing the relationship when the United States decided to retaliate against al-Qaeda and the Taliban after the September 11 attacks. As Henry ("Hank") Crumpton, who managed the operations in Afghanistan from CIA Headquarters, later recalled, "The CIA did not start from scratch in Afghanistan. On the contrary, HUM-INT [human intelligence] networks with roots in covert action against the USSR and its puppet Afghan government from 1980 to 1992 provided continuity in intelligence collection. Although the networks deteriorated as the U.S. government lost interest in Afghanistan and the CIA lost funding and support in the 1990s, CIA officers maintained sufficient links for regeneration."[19]

As in the case of the U-2 and Explorer 1, JAWBREAKER's speed was only partly the result of someone deciding to move fast. It also took advantage of opportunities and groundwork. It is also notable that Crumpton was familiar with John Boyd, OODA loops, and the need to gain a step on your opponent. So he understood the need for speed, and he was largely responsible for breaking through the organizational red tape that would ordinarily slow an operation. He succeeded by using his supervisors' names for "top cover," and partly by just constantly making everyone involved understand that delay was not an option.

After the fighting started, the CIA turned to officers known for their inclination to focus more on results than procedures. For example, Gary Berntsen, who took over command from Schroen in the field as the fighting began, described himself as a "bad kid" from Long Island who graduated second from the bottom in his high school. He bragged about his "grab-them-by-the-collar" approach at the CIA.

"Hank had chosen me in part because he knew that I was the kind of officer who was wired to push the envelope," Berntsen recalled. "He liked the fact that I took charge and pressed forward aggressively without stopping every five minutes to ask permission."[20] This is a common feature in government organizations that move fast: There is usually someone—often a misfit in routine times—who spurs the organization to go faster. As Admiral Ernest King supposedly said in the early months of World War II, "When they get in trouble, they send for the sons of bitches."[21] But if you do not have SOBs on staff and the means to put them in charge when you need them, organizations will continue to run at their normal pace. There needs to be someone to throw the switch marked "FASTER."

In the case of the GBU-28 bomb, it was Al Weimorts.[22] In autumn 1990 the United States was preparing its first war against Iraq, which had just invaded Kuwait. Air Force planners realized they did not have a weapon that could destroy some of Iraq's command bunkers. At least one, the bunker under the presidential palace, had a steel-reinforced concrete roof over six feet thick, buried under another hundred feet of earth.

No existing nonnuclear weapon could destroy such a target, so Lieutenant General Thomas Ferguson told his staff to find a new approach. Ferguson headed the Air Force's Aeronautical Systems Center in Dayton, which was responsible for developing new bombs. Word went out down the chain and soon reached Eglin Air Force Base in the Florida panhandle. Eglin is home to the Air Force Research Lab's Munitions Directorate, where Weimorts was chief engineer.

Weimorts and his team, in effect, resurrected the Tallboy, a bomb Sir Barnes Neville Wallis developed for the Royal Air Force (RAF) to use against Germany in World War II. In 1944 the RAF faced the same problem the U.S. Air Force faced in 1991: how to destroy deeply buried, hardened underground shelters. (Ironically, some of the shelters the British targeted were built by Boswau & Knauer, the same German engineering firm that later built the Iraqi shelters.) Wallis's idea was a 21-foot, 12,000-pound, finned, streamlined projectile built of high-grade steel and packed with two and a half tons of explosive.

Dropped from a Lancaster bomber at 25,000 feet, the Tallboy would reach a velocity of over two thousand miles per hour before it plunged a hundred feet into the earth. There its mass, velocity, and high explosive would combine to send a shockwave through the ground that would destroy anything in its path.[23] The British used Tallboys against railroad tunnels, submarine pens, underground missile factories, and the *Tirpitz*, the sister of the infamous battleship *Bismarck*. Having proven the concept, Wallis followed with a bomb almost twice the size, dubbed Grand Slam, which the RAF used to generate artificial earthquakes to topple reinforced concrete railroad viaducts.

After Hiroshima most people forgot about big conventional explosive bombs, assuming that, if you needed a big bomb, you would go nuclear. This was not an option for the United States in Desert Storm, and Weimorts recalled the Tallboy. The question was whether his team could design, build, and test a new bomb in ten weeks, which was all the time they had before the Coalition forces gathering in Saudi Arabia were scheduled to strike. "This was a very intense time because we knew we had a time limit," Weimorts recalled later. Ordinarily delivering a new bomb takes about two or three years.[24]

Lockheed Martin already had a contract with the Air Force to do munitions research and development and, with some liberal interpretation, everyone agreed that this contract would cover the new bomb. The toughest part was finding a casing. One retired Army officer who worked for Lockheed recalled that the Army had stockpiled some worn 8-inch howitzer barrels at the Letterkenney Arsenal in Pennsylvania. On January 25 Weimorts requested that the Army ship the gun barrels to its Watervliet Arsenal in New York, which had equipment to machine them to the required dimensions for the casings. Two weeks later Weimorts received formal approval for the project. He, his team, the contractors, and everyone else had been working on spec. "I didn't have to ask anybody to do anything," Weimorts recalled later. "People were volunteering left and right. Everybody was anxious to contribute."

Meanwhile, the Eglin team manufactured the Tritonal explosive for the weapon and worked with Texas Instruments to modify an existing laser-seeking guidance system, taken from the GBU-24 smart bomb, which had been developed a few years earlier. Watervliet shipped the new casings to Eglin on February 16, and Texas Instruments shipped the modified laser seekers four days later. With all the parts at Eglin, Weimorts and his team treated the inside of the casings to prevent static discharge. They then buried the 13-foot long casings upright in the ground outside their shop so they could ladle the required 630 pounds of molten explosive into each.

As Weimorts's staff was loading the explosives into the bomb, a captain at Eglin called a technician at the Tonopah Test Range in New Mexico to ask if they could test it the next weekend, February 15. Usually getting a date for a test drop takes months because of the safety analyses that are required, and in this case there were special issues. Tonopah uses optical tacking systems, and a laser-guided bomb could blind anyone looking through a scope at the wrong moment. Nonetheless, they were ready to go by the time the explosive in the first bomb had cured.[25]

Weimorts's team fabricated a dummy bomb for flight tests to see if it would fit properly on an F-111. Then on February 24, they used the first bomb in their only test drop (typically a new bomb gets thirty), hitting a target from 20,000 feet. To see if it would penetrate the intended target in Iraq, they mounted another bomb on a rocket sled and fired it through a 22-foot concrete barrier. (The bomb went through the barrier and continued on its trajectory for an additional half mile beyond.) The third and fourth bombs were loaded on a C-141 aircraft back at Eglin, so new that their explosive was still warm. The bombs arrived in theater on February 27 for a mission that night. The target was a pair of bunkers near Al Taji Air Base. The first bomb missed. The second hit.

In sum, Weimorts made at least a half dozen decisions that did not follow the letter of the rules, regulations, or chain of command. Rather, he used his best professional judgment and took responsibility for his actions. One reason we do not see this kind of initiative more often is because our military, diplomatic, and intelligence organizations are all showing the classic symptoms of "organizational aging"—a problem of bureaucracies that the economist Anthony Downs once described.[26]

When organizations are first established, they have few rules—written or unwritten—and, because new organizations tend to be small, they have a flat, short chain of command and little hierarchy. But as time goes by, organizations add personnel. Because a manager can oversee only a limited number of people—the familiar span-of-control problem—organizations adopt a reporting hierarchy. This adds to the time and difficulty of making a decision. More officials are in a position to say no, and the joint probability of yes diminishes. The fact that people expect promotion to positions with greater responsibility (and pay) also encourages the establishment of more management slots.

Moreover, as organizations mature, they develop dogma—some written, some simply part of the organization's culture. This is, of course, exactly what bureaucracies are supposed to do: Simplify decisions and improve efficiency by adopting rules—which is fine, until the rules are cumbersome or inappropriate to the situation, which is what is happening all too often today.

But the most insidious problem of all is that, as organizations mature, their character changes, too, and that slows things down even further. New organizations with few rules offer lots of challenge and risk. So they attract, naturally enough, "risk-taking cowboys" who want to make their own rules. Conversely, mature organizations with well-defined rules and missions attract—by definition—"organization men," people who want to plug themselves in and carry out a job as set forth in an official, approved position description.

So when critics complain that this or that long-established government organization should innovate, show initiative, and take more risks, they are usually speaking to people who, by natural selection and self-selection, have arrived where they are precisely because they are risk-averse. They like the way things are now; otherwise they would not have joined the organization and stayed with it. Organization men are no less patriotic, dedicated, or capable than the cowboys, but they are very different by temperament. This is why, if you are really serious about agility, you almost always have to break some china. Rearranging boxes on an organization chart is not enough. You need a new mix of people who can develop new ways of doing things and attract the kinds of recruits who thrive on doing just that.

One way to create such a "forcing function" is to establish a new organization under some pretext, such as exploiting some new technology, or to protect the secrecy of a new technology. The program to develop the F-117A Nighthawk used both these rationales. The F-117A "Stealth Fighter" came about because of a combination of necessity— the need for a means to overcome improved Soviet air defenses—and opportunity—the advancements in computers that had occurred all through the 1970s.

In the 1973 Yom Kippur War, Egypt shot down almost a hundred Israeli fighters in a few short weeks. Egypt used Soviet air defense missiles (the SA-6 was especially lethal); Israel relied mainly on American aircraft. U.S. planners became concerned because the Soviet Union and its allies used essentially the same missile systems in Europe. So they needed a solution.

Meanwhile, computers were steadily improving, and this was important to the F-117A in two respects. Computer modeling made it easier to design a stealth aircraft. "Stealth" is not a single technology. Rather, it is a multipart problem of reducing all the things that an adversary might use to detect an aircraft—sight, sound, heat, and radar reflection. Tackling the radar part of the problem is partly a matter of using radar-absorbing or diffusing materials, but it depends at least as much on shaping the aircraft so it reflects the signal in directions away from the enemy. For example, the F-117A was shaped to reflect radar in an up or down direction, rather than back to the enemy, who most likely is illuminating the aircraft from the front or sides. Better computers made it easier to design the best shape.

The other way in which computers were critical to the F-117A is in the aircraft's "fly-by-wire" control system. The best aerodynamic shapes often reflect a lot of radar; the most stealthy shapes are unstable in flight. Fly-by-wire systems make minute corrections automatically, faster than a pilot would realize he is losing control. This technology let the designers of the F-117 concentrate on making the aircraft stealthy; its odd "faceted" shape was a technique they used to simplify the stealth calculations, knowing that the software developers would fix the stability problems.

This technology was all very secret in the 1970s, and it thus served as the rationale for setting up a restricted program with limited access. That, in turn, served as the justification for a remarkably small program office. In the 1970s, a typical program office for a military aircraft had a staff of 250 to 350 people. The F-117 program office had about 50.[27] In Congress, a smaller number of legislators and staff than usual reviewed the program.

This secrecy proved both a boon and a burden. The most frequent cause of delays in the program was the time required to get people cleared. Also, because the F-117A was so secret, it was never fully integrated into the Air Force's plans and culture. It was expensive to maintain and, in its early years, had a low availability rate. The aircraft's specialization eventually pushed it into a backwater, where it was not upgraded and was often left out of routine planning. It was, in effect, *too* special and, like fine china, often got left on the shelf. Nevertheless, the technology and lessons learned from the F-117A were picked up by other aircraft. This shows how speed is not a cure-all, though the option for speed and risk taking can benefit U.S. national security capabilities as a whole.[28]

How to Get Faster

Government organizations will not become fast and agile until speed and agility become considerations in the design of organizations and procedures. In the private sector, market forces push management to at least consider removing excess "process." Government officials must do likewise by understanding that risk-reducing documentation, coordination, and review are not free. Their price is often speed, and today especially the lack of speed in war and diplomacy can mean failure or defeat.

Agility depends on whether organizations can shift gears from their normal rate of operation to a higher speed by readjusting the balance between speed and limiting risks. This balance is always a matter of judgment; there will never be a single correct answer for all situations. But the United States can do at least four things that would improve its agility and ability to keep up with its adversaries.

First, it helps to be aware that there is an unavoidable trade between speed and risk so we all know that this is, in fact, what we are doing—using our best judgment to make a trade between two desirable goals that are, to some degree, mutually exclusive. Currently officials, analysts, the media all tend to imply that we are "solving" problems of corruption, safety, or reliability when we impose requirements for greater oversight, review, or documentation. In reality, we are not *solving*, we are *choosing*—that is, choosing one priority (risk) over another (speed). There is no rule that prescribes how to always make the best choice. But by being conscious of the fact that a choice is being made, one can at least focus on achieving the best compromise.

Second, to have speed as an option, there must be a "switch" so that organizations can opt for more speed rather than reducing risk. This requires, at a minimum, an official with the responsibility and authority to make the choice, and a point in the routine processes of government and the bureaucracy at which they can act or intervene. Recent history suggests that we lack such a switch, and the overall tendency is to increase "process" at the expense of speed.

Third, there are some general principles or lessons that one can draw on if one wants to act fast or set up an organization that has speed—for example:

- Keep staffs of new organizations small, and shed people in existing organizations to reach an optimal size. There is a sweet spot between having enough people to get essential work done and not having so many people that they get in each other's way. A management structure that is too large divides authority too thinly.
- Reach an agreement with Congress that appointees are not to be held hostage. Appointees should be quickly confirmed or rejected on their own merits. Congress can withhold funds or deauthorize activities to exercise clout, but it should not undercut the structure of government.
- For its part, a new administration has a responsibility to organize itself before it assumes office. It should meet a "three-levels down" standard—that is, it should have appointees lined up three levels down, to the Deputy Under Secretary or Deputy Assistant Secretary level, *before* the President is sworn in.
- In general, organizations get slower with age. If one wants speed, one usually must start with a new organization or replace so many people that the old organization (or the part that must be fast) is no longer recognizable. Sack enough people to break up existing procedures, rules, and culture; keep just enough veterans to preserve institutional memory.

Fourth, and finally, speed has to become a valued trait in the national security bureaucracy. This is almost an oxymoron; but if no one values speed and protects those officials who favor getting things done fast, then there will be no one to push organizations into a faster pace when we need them.

Speed is not always the right choice, and it is easy to find cases in which staffs were stretched too thin, budgets were too tight, and schedules too short—and the results were dismal. In many cases, shaking up an organization was not a forcing function that improved speed but merely a misguided exercise that frittered away institutional memory. Making cuts and ladling resources randomly can both lead to failure. And as the F-117A illustrates, sometimes the very features that make a program fast and spectacularly successful can also make it short-lived. The most troubling thing about those times when America has acted too slowly is that it often seems we have lost the option to go fast, even when it is critical. That is because the lack of speed today is a symptom of an even larger problem.

It is hard to find anyone—even the President—who can "throw the big switch" to put national security organizations and the government as a whole on a more risk-accepting footing. The controls for most national security matters are unclear and ineffective. If we ever hope the government will gain speed, or will be effective as a whole, we need to fix this problem, and that is what we will consider next.

CHAPTER SIX

Command

No MILITARY COMMANDER would direct forces the way the President of the United States tries to direct the executive branch in national security affairs. No corporation would make decisions the way the executive branch does. Departments and agencies do not work effectively together. Turf and stovepipes get in the way. Organizations negotiate with each other over policies as though they were sovereign states. Often no one other than the President can direct a department head to act, and this creates a chokepoint.

The frequent result is that the government is ineffective or too slow in responding to events. The disconnects we described earlier in Chapter 4 for the war in Iraq and the delays we described in Chapter 5 in responding to al-Qaeda before the September 11, 2001, terrorist attacks were examples of the problem, but only two of the most extreme and costly ones.

The Evolution of a Process and a Problem

One way to illustrate the problem, its dimensions, and how it has evolved is by looking at how Washington and the national security bureaucracy have changed over the course of two centuries. Hard as it may seem to imagine today, there was once a time when every top official in the U.S. government responsible for national security worked within shouting distance of the President. It may have been a hands-cupped-around-the-month shout, but a shout nevertheless. When the federal government moved from Philadelphia to Washington in 1800, the entire executive branch occupied just three buildings: the President's House and two small executive offices, each providing about 4,000 square feet each — about the size of a present-day McMansion. One was home to the Department of the Treasury. The Department of State, the Department of War, and the Department of the Navy shared the other. (The President's House was not officially known as the White House until Theodore Roosevelt took office in 1901.)[1]

British troops essentially destroyed all three buildings when they sacked Washington in 1814. After the war, the government built four new identical executive offices, each resembling a two-story Georgian house. Treasury returned to its site southeast of the President's House, and the Navy returned to the site at the southwest. The State Department and War Department moved into the new buildings, which were located to the northeast and northwest, respectively. So the national security bureaucracy's footprint doubled in just two decades, although all employees still shared a single title — "clerk." The Treasury Department building burned down again in 1833, and a new, larger office was built on the site, which it occupied in 1839. (Fire was a frequent problem; a serious fire had also burned much of the Treasury Department in 1801.) The federal professional workforce at this point consisted of 336 employees.

The Treasury Building evolved into its present complex over the next thirty years, occupying the entire block east of the President's House. The building we see today on the back of the ten-dollar bill was completed in 1869, overrunning the site of the State Department's offices, which were demolished. From 1866 to 1875 the Secretary of State worked out of a converted orphanage at the corner of S and 14th streets, NW, about a dozen blocks away. Congress supplemented the title of "clerk" with a subclerical job category to cover laborers, messengers, and watchmen.

Meanwhile, the War Department building was so convenient to the President's House that Abraham Lincoln used it as his second office during the Civil War. The Army had its main telegraph terminals there, and Lincoln kept tight control on the Union forces by cabling his generals directly. He checked on dispatches from the front personally, often stopping in the telegraph office several times a day.[2] After the Civil War, the State, War, and Navy departments were all moved again into a single large building that required seventeen years to complete; this was the State, War, and Navy Building (the "SWN"), directly to the west of the White House. All three departments were in their new home by 1888, so that the national security bureaucracy's footprint had grown to fill three full city blocks.

Even so, the Navy moved out of the SWN across Constitution Avenue to a "temporary" concrete building in 1918, Main Navy, a structure that stretched about a third of a mile, from 17th Street to 21st Street, NW.[3] The Army, which had been planning its own headquarters for many years, built a new building at 21st Street and Virginia Avenue, about a half mile west of the White House, which it occupied in 1938. The State Department remained in the SWN, which it naturally renamed the Department of State Building.

The Army had barely moved into its new headquarters when World War II began, and the government began to mobilize. Army officials believed they needed a building that could hold 30,000 workers. There was no longer enough vacant land near the White House for such an enormous structure. So the War Department staked out a site across the Potomac in Virginia at the foot of the Memorial Bridge. The lot was originally part of Robert E. Lee's estate and was bordered by five roads. To fit all the required floor space into the site, the designers came up with an irregular, five-sided building.

Critics complained that the building would spoil the view from Washington. President Franklin Roosevelt agreed, and ordered the Army to move to an open, but swampy spot three-quarters of a mile down the river. The site presented more of an engineering challenge, but it gave the planners the opportunity to give the 6.5-million-square-foot building a more symmetrical shape, and this, of course, became the present-day Pentagon.[4]

The War Department moved to the Pentagon, and the State Department moved into the vacated Army headquarters building in 1947 (today this is the Harry S Truman Building). The building next door to the White House then became the Executive Office Building, housing the Executive Office of the President. But just as every other occupant had, the President's staff outgrew the building, and the government built Federal Office Building No. 7 around the corner at 17th Street and H Street, NW. This building became known as the New Executive Office Building, so, naturally, the building that had been built back in 1888 became known as the Old Executive Office Building. In 2002 it was renamed the Dwight D. Eisenhower Building.

The final component in this ever-expanding map was the intelligence community. The Central Intelligence Agency (CIA), which had been established in 1947, originally was headquartered in a red brick building located at 2430 E Street, NW, a site just beyond the current State Department. William Donovan, the Director of the CIA's predecessor, the Office of Strategic Services, had used the building during World War II. The CIA, along with the Director of Central Intelligence, moved to its current facility in 1961, about seven miles up the Potomac River. But the Intelligence Reform and Terrorism Prevention Act of 2004 said that the new Director of National Intelligence could not also be the CIA Director, nor have his office at Langley. So, when the new Office of the Director of National Intelligence was organized, it first took up offices in the New Executive Office Building. As it grew, it first moved in 2007 into a new wing that was being built onto the Defense Intelligence Agency's building at Bolling Air Force Base—about four miles down the river, southeast of the White House. In the spring of 2008 it moved again, this time to the Northern Virginia suburbs.[5]

So, from a small group of five men (six if you count the Vice President) all within an easy walk of each other, the modern leadership of the national security community has evolved into a body consisting of the corporate heads of a constellation of organizations whose collective footprint extends across a ten-mile circle.

This tale of geography gives a sense of how the sheer physical size of the government has expanded, but it is even more interesting because it illustrates a problem of how the government is organized for national security. Department heads today are expected to perform two very different functions: adviser to the President, and chief executive officer of organizations, each with annual budgets between $30 billion and $400 billion. These two jobs are too much for one person, and they contain built-in conflicts of interest. An adviser needs to be close to his or her boss, and he or she has to be agnostic when it comes to proposing one organization or another for a task. A department head, conversely, needs to lead his or her organization and argue for his or her department's interests and priorities. In short, it is hard to be a fiduciary to national security as a whole and a single government department simultaneously.

Meanwhile, the President has similar problems under the current arrangement. He needs department heads that lead their organizations, promote their programs, and maintain their cultures. But he also needs "his guys" who do *not* have any particular loyalty to a department but can grab whatever capabilities the country needs to accomplish a mission, regardless of where they some from. The notion that a department head should also be an adviser to the President might have made sense in the nineteenth century. As we have seen, these heads worked close to the President. Now their organizations have grown and require all their attention to manage.

Meanwhile, national security issues have also become more complex. They are more likely to exceed the focus of any single department head, and they may even require the participation of nongovernmental organizations as well. The officials who see the President every day—the National Security Adviser and the National Security Council (NSC) staff members—can propose options without worrying about the stake one department or another may have in the decision. But currently they lack the stature or the authority to make departments do anything.

Bob Woodward, in his account of the war in Iraq, *State of Denial*, describes an episode where Condoleezza Rice, at the time Assistant to the President for National Security Affairs, wanted to know more about the Defense Department's plans for the Iraq war. Donald Rumsfeld would not return her call. When Rice complained, Rumsfeld reminded her that the military chain of command went from him to the President—and not through her. (The President declined to fix the problem, or perhaps did not see one.)[6]

To an outsider this all may sound silly. But if Woodward was correct, in the spring of 2003, nothing short of a communication passed directly from the President to the Secretary of Defense would allow the U.S. government to change the course of the Department of Defense or, for that matter, make him reveal its plans to other senior members of the executive branch. And, assuming Rumsfeld's observation about the chain of command also applied to the State Department, it would have taken a three-way direct conversation between the President, the Secretary of State, and the Secretary of Defense to get State and Defense to work together. It is little wonder that they did not.

The National Security Process

The NSC traces its roots to World War II and earlier. Presidents always had advisers, confidants, kitchen cabinets, and war councils. The National Security Act of 1947 reflected Harry Truman's preference to rely on his department heads for national security advice, and so they comprise the NSC.[7] Even so—aside from saying that there would be such an NSC whose function was "to advise the President with respect to the integration of domestic, foreign, and military policies relating to the national security"—the act mandates that the President can organize his office for national security as he chooses.[8]

In practice, the roles of the NSC and its staff have evolved over the years, reflecting the personality of the President and his operating style. Some Presidents—like John F. Kennedy and Bill Clinton—were freewheeling and avoided making the NSC's operation too tidy and regimented. Other Presidents—like Eisenhower and Richard Nixon—preferred an organization with clear responsibilities and procedures. But if one insisted on identifying a specific date for the current way the NSC works today, it would probably be 1987, when the Reagan administration was trying to clean up the Iran-Contra affair.

In the 1980s Ronald Reagan was determined to support the anticommunist resistance in Nicaragua—the "Contras." Congress had, at various times and to various degrees, restricted this aid. Meanwhile, Iranian-affiliated terrorists in Lebanon had kidnapped several Americans, and the United States had an unofficial—but firm—policy against negotiating with terrorists. In November 1986 a Lebanese newsmagazine reported that NSC staffers had sold weapons to Iran in exchange for help in releasing the American hostages. It soon emerged that the CIA had supported the operation, and that the profits might have been used to fund the Contras.

Thus, it seemed that Reagan administration officials had violated several laws and policies: negotiating with terrorists, aiding the Contras, dealing with Iran, and not notifying Congress of CIA activity. To make matters worse, Reagan professed not to know fully what was going on. He appointed a commission to investigate. It included former Senator John Tower (R-TX)), former Secretary of State Edmund Muskie, and retired Lieutenant General Brent Scowcroft, who had been Gerald Ford's National Security Adviser. Scowcroft would also serve in the same post when George H. W. Bush became President in 1989.

Most Americans have probably forgotten the Iran-Contra affair; a half dozen other flaps, scandals, and investigations have occurred in the two decades that since have passed. But it remains important because the Tower Commission effectively established the procedures the NSC uses today, and that is the process through which U.S. national security policy is made. If anyone could be considered the architect of this process, it is Scowcroft, partly because he was a member of the Tower Commission, but more important because he was able to put its recommendations into practice when he again became the National Security Adviser. Also, many people who have since served on the NSC staff and upper levels of the departments have either worked for or with Scowcroft. His way of working is simply the benchmark for how work is done.[9]

In its report to the President, the Tower Commission concluded that orderly policymaking had broken down. It also concluded that NSC staffers—in particular, Vice Admiral John Poindexter, the National Security Adviser at the time, and Lieutenant Colonel Oliver North—had exceeded their authority. The members reported that the failure had occurred "in large part from the flaws in the manner in which decisions were made. Established procedures for making national security decisions were ignored. Reviews of the initiative [with Iran] by all the NSC principals were too infrequent. The initiatives were not adequately vetted below the Cabinet level. Intelligence resources were underutilized. Applicable legal constraints were not adequately addressed. The whole matter was handled too informally, without adequate written records of what had been considered, discussed, and decided."[10]

If the problem in Iran-Contra was too much informality and not enough involvement by the departments, then George H. W. Bush—who, as Vice President, saw the affair firsthand—had the opportunity to make sure that there was more formality and greater involvement when he was himself elected President. Scowcroft, recalling how he managed Bush's morning intelligence briefing and national security meeting, later wrote, "I was mindful of questions which arose during the Iran-Contra investigations about 'process' in these daily meetings, questions implying that this was the venue for secret, irregular decisions 'slipped by' the President without the knowledge of others who should have been informed. Therefore I was careful not to try to use them to seek decisions involving other national security departments or agencies. If the President indicated a policy direction he wished to take, I made sure others concerned were advised so they could provide any comments that they might wish to make."[11]

Scowcroft also said that he had Robert Gates, then the Deputy National Security Adviser, attend the meetings to "take notes and serve as the check on the proper interpretation of communications which might have taken place." Subsequent administrations have followed Scowcroft's model. The result has been that, ever sense, the executive branch has had a *very* formal, *extensively* documented process for developing policy that goes to *extraordinary* lengths to make sure all of the "principals"—meaning Cabinet officers—are involved.

In short, the current process is a classic bureaucratic process. Bureaucracies are good at dealing with some kinds of problems (in particular, those that require standard procedures and have few time constraints). But they are badly suited for others (namely, those that require redirection and speed). That is why armies have bureaucracies to develop policies, provide logistics, and even develop most weapons—but *commanders* to fight wars.

Where the Tower Commission criticized the Reagan White House for not having enough formal procedures and record keeping, now we have the opposite problem—*too much* paper and process, and too much deference to department heads and building consensus. This morass contributed to our inability to move fast enough before September 11.

During the Clinton administration, the policy process failed to crystallize the stakes and the need to take action. President Clinton recalled that he wanted to destroy Osama bin Laden but was somehow unable to get the bureaucracy to act. Below, in the bureaucracy, officials said they were unable to get the authority they needed to act. The George W. Bush administration acted no faster and no more decisively, and al-Qaeda got the jump on us. Later, during the war in Iraq, the same bureaucratic mode of operation was too slow to keep up with the insurgents.

The Bush administration had an additional problem: too much secrecy for no good reason. According to one report by Barton Gellman and Jo Becker, for example, Vice President Dick Cheney had his personal lawyer draft a directive ordering the Defense Department to establish prisons and military tribunals for suspected foreign terrorists. Cheney supposedly gave the document to the President, who signed it and then transmitted it directly to the Defense Department. Other top officials found out about it when they heard reports on CNN.[12]

The officials who gave that account to Gellman and Becker obviously had an axe to grind; they were likely among the officials cut out of the process. Yet they had at least one valid point. Even in emergencies, it is possible to act both quickly and transparently, and transparency has virtues beyond holding officials accountable and protecting civil liberties. It is good management. It gives everyone involved a common view of the problem. When things go wrong, someone gets held responsible. People know who to see to make their views known. Decisive command is completely compatible with transparent command, and unless secrecy provides specific benefits, transparency is almost always better.

Chain of Command

Ironically, no one has summed up the current problem of command—or the solution—better than Donald Rumsfeld. Just before leaving office, he put his own thoughts on paper about how to make the executive branch run better. At the time he had his own complaints. Among other things, he could not get other departments to help him in reconstructing Iraq. He might exclude others as the Defense Department ran the war, but even he could not force another department to provide people, material, or expertise.

In a memo (which inevitably found its way to Bob Woodward), Rumsfeld wrote that the country needed a "Goldwater-Nichols process for the national security portions of the U.S. Government." He continued, "Only a broad, fundamental reorganization is likely to enable federal departments and agencies to function with the speed and agility the times demand."[13]

"Goldwater-Nichols": Anyone who works in the Defense Department knew instantly what Rumsfeld was talking about—it is part of the military tongue, a single term, universally understood. Until twenty years ago the Army, Navy, and Air Force fought wars as separate, loosely linked organizations. Sometimes this did not matter; in World War II, the Japanese military services were even more disjointed than we were. Occasionally it did, as when our Army and Navy officials failed to coordinate prior to Pearl Harbor.

But when the gaps and barriers separating the services began to lead to a string of high-profile snafus, it was hard to miss that something in how the Defense Department was organized was fundamentally awry. It began in 1980 with the Iranian hostage rescue mission. The attacking force was supposed to fly from Navy ships, using Navy helicopters. It was composed mainly of Army soldiers, along with some Marines. The Air Force was to provide air cover and fly everyone out of Tehran after the hostages were freed and assembled at a staging point.

Rarely before had anyone tried to combine people and equipment from different services to work so closely together in an operation. Planners had to start from scratch to pull the pieces together. For many of the people involved, it was a tough learning experience, akin to learning a foreign language. They had spent all their careers in their own service.

Bad luck caused the plan to fail. Two helicopters broke down, and then one crashed into an aircraft during a refueling operation. It was a high-risk mission. But everyone knew that organizations did not work together as well as they might.[14] Then, in the 1982 invasion of Grenada, Army and Navy units could not communicate because they used different radio systems. The next year, after terrorists bombed the Marine Corps barracks in Beirut, it became clear that there was no common understanding of the chain of command—and responsibility for protection. And so on.

So in 1986 Senator Barry Goldwater (R-AZ) and Representative Bill Nichols (D-AL) cosponsored legislation that fundamentally changed how the Defense Department operated. Sam Nunn (D-GA) can also be considered a father of this legislation, although his name did not appear on the bill.[15] The Goldwater-Nichols Defense Reform Act was the most important change in how the United States prepares and organizes for war since World War II. Most military experts believe, on balance, that it was a success, although the provisions aimed at improving how the Defense Department fights have been much more successful than the provisions aimed at improving how the Defense Department buys weapons. It had several important effects.

First, Goldwater-Nichols put someone in charge. Someone in a military organization must be in charge or rivals for control will waste time wrestling with each other rather than fighting the enemy. In combat, the margin for success is often slim, and so such wasted effort can lead to defeat. Goldwater-Nichols designated "commanders in chief," or CINCs, four-star generals or admirals who would be in charge of all U.S. forces in an area or carrying out an operation. Later Rumsfeld changed the term to "combatant commanders," or COCOMs, to avoid confusion with the President who, under the Constitution, is Commander in Chief of all U.S. forces.

Designating a single commander forced the services to work together. It did not matter whether one was in the Army, Navy, Air Force, or Marines; at the end of the discussion, there was going to be a single person who would have the deciding say, and it would not be a surprise if that decision came from someone wearing the uniform of a different service.

The second important effect of Goldwater-Nichols is that it clarified the chain of command to everyone. It is as critical for every member of a military organization to know where to expect commands to come from as it is for commanders to agree who is in charge. Laying out the chain of command provides a common picture of where to look for direction, and who is available to be directed. This common picture also makes it clear if something is falling between the cracks.

Investigators found that when the Marines deployed to Beirut in 1983, it was not clear who beyond the immediate area of operations was responsible for directing the mission. Because responsibility for the mission was ambiguous, the mission itself became ambiguous, and the Marines unwittingly were shifted from monitoring a ceasefire to being a player in the middle of a civil war. Most important of all, no one went to bed at night knowing they were singularly responsible for the safety and success of the Marines. This kind of problem is less likely to happen today.[16]

Third, while Goldwater-Nichols cleaned up the chain of command, it also preserved the benefits of specialization within the services. This is a case in which there were benefits in separating functions and allocating them to different organizations, each with its own leader and management structure. Under Goldwater-Nichols, combatant commanders direct forces, and the services provide forces. Both functions have equal stature. A service chief (Army or Air Force Chief of Staff, Chief of Naval Operations, Commandant of the Marines) is a four-star officer. They are responsible for recruiting, training, and equipping soldiers, sailors, airmen, and Marines. They are custodians of the service's culture and institutional knowledge.

Combatant commanders have equal rank but a different job: planning and directing military operations in their area of responsibility. In many respects, the combatant commander is the counterbalance to the culture and traditions that make a service effective; part of his or her job is to break through the traditions and bridge the cultural gaps so that soldiers, sailors, airmen, and Marines all work together effectively.[17]

One can see why Rumsfeld would believe Goldwater-Nichols explains problems we have in national security—and provides the outline of a solution. The departments, whose great strength is specialization, are analogous to the military services in 1986. The State Department provides diplomatic capabilities. The Defense Department provides military capabilities. Treasury provides economic and financial capabilities. The intelligence community provides information that is unavailable otherwise, and a covert action capability that the State Department and Defense Department cannot.

What is missing in this mix, however, is someone who is analogous to a combatant commander—someone who reports to the President and works on his or her behalf but is independent of the departments and can ensure that all the resources available for a problem are focused effectively. Under the current system, the President either must do this himself or herself (which he or she cannot, any more than he or she can personally direct a combined-service military operation), or he or she can anoint one department as "lead"—in which case, they will have little success in commanding the others.

Or the departments can simply fight for control or try to evade responsibility, as is often the case today. The Defense Department and State Department competed over who would direct the reconstruction of Iraq. The Defense Department won but was unprepared. It was also unable to direct other departments to help. The results speak for themselves.

What would "Goldwater-Nichols" at the national level look like? There are many different ways of getting there (several think tanks have looked at the problem lately, as the need has become more and more apparent), but to achieve the same effects as Goldwater-Nichols, all would need the same three essential components: Have the President put someone in charge, give the President a more effective system of command, and separate the providers of capability from the commanders of policy.[18]

The President would need the equivalent of combatant commanders. For shorthand, call these deputies Presidential Policy Directors. They would be based in the White House (organizationally, if not physically) to make clear that they work for the President and act under his or her authority. These officials would organize the "attack" on each of the nation's strategic goals.

Anyone taking this job would have to be a tough political heavyweight, so he or she would not be cowed by a Secretary of Defense or Secretary of State. The Policy Directors would not micromanage. They would command—establish objectives, give general direction, make course corrections, make sure everyone worked together, and settle any disagreements. They would let the departments fill in the details.

How would these Policy Directors do this? Again, Goldwater-Nichols provides a model. Today the Secretary of Defense periodically issues his unified command plan (UCP, in the inevitable acronym), which assigns areas of responsibility (AORs; yes, another acronym) for each combatant commander. Each commander prepares operations plans (OPLANs, more Pentagon-speak) for the missions they anticipate in their area, using a range of planning scenarios. Each OPLAN identifies the forces that will be used and what they will do.

The Policy Directors would need their counterpart to the Pentagon's UCP. It could be the *National Security Strategy of the United States*, which the President issues every year or so. Currently the *Strategy* is a fluffy statement with no real teeth, aimed mainly at external public relations. It is the kind of thing on which midlevel officials spend countless meetings wordsmithing, although it does not affect anything that matters.

Under the new approach, the strategy would identify a half dozen strategic goals the United States hoped to achieve, and assign each to a Policy Director. That would be the equivalent of the UCP. The Director would develop the plans and assign tasks for each department. That would be the equivalent of a Combatant Commander's operations plan.

One can imagine the kinds of issues that such a strategy would include. They would be big, strategic goals, at a scale appropriate to a President's attention and direction, for example:

- bringing China into the world community, integrating it into accepted international economic and commercial practices, and deterring it from acting as a military threat to the United States and allies in the region;
- combatting terrorism and eliminating the use of religion and sectarianism as a vehicle for recruiting international terrorists;
- curbing the proliferation of nuclear weapons and other weapons of mass destruction through a combination of actions carried out by U.S. diplomatic, military, and intelligence organizations;
- stabilizing Iraq so as to deter adventurism on the part of Iran and to ensure that it does not become a safe haven for al-Qaeda and other international terrorist organizations;
- securing U.S. borders and protecting U.S. territory against attack while also attracting the people with the talent and willingness to take risks who are essential to sustaining American power;
- maintaining the capability to react to sudden natural emergencies or prevent genocides in cases in which doing so is consistent with

American values and presents little risk or cost; and, as noted in Chapter 3,

- integrating the statements and actions of the U.S. government with the private sector in a way that maintains the "American brand" to attract talent, capital, and maximize U.S. influence.

In a world in which threats change, one might expect these priorities to change steadily over time as well. The rate of change would likely approximate the rate threat priorities change in the annual assessment the Director of National Intelligence presents to Congress. It is clear that some of these goals compete with each other (e.g., many measures for securing borders make it harder for the United States to attract foreign talent that helps keep the U.S. economy productive and competitive). One problem with the current approach is that there is no venue for officials to articulate where these conflicts must be reconciled; they get lost in the interagency process, where the agenda is dominated by each department looking out for what it perceives as its interests.

The Policy Directors would not have to micromanage — and would not be given the staff that might tempt them to. But they would make the government move faster and shift gears when necessary. If a Policy Director has a friendly relationship with the President's budget staff (and a hand on the funding tap that goes with it), the departments would be sure to respond to direction — or at least answer phone calls. This would also link budget decisions to national strategy decisions in the White House, which would be a good thing.

There are some precedents that suggest how this new approach would work and the role the Policy Directors would have. The current Director of National Drug Control (the so-called drug czar) is organizationally in the White House and is usually a retired general, admiral, or civilian officeholder of comparable stature and experience. The main problem the drug czar encounters is that he or she lacks authority and thus cannot direct departments to do anything, and has no control over money.

The Director of National Intelligence, created under the 2004 Intelligence Reform and Terrorism Prevention Act, resembles what a Policy

Director might be. He or she has the budget authority necessary to exercise control over intelligence agencies. But the process of setting up the Office of the Director of National Intelligence got off track.

None of the commissions that proposed a Director of National Intelligence dreamed it would create such a large office or take over other organizations. In effect, it has become so big that it has not been able to focus on the main purpose it was created for: to break down the barriers that had developed among sixteen existing agencies that had grown up piecemeal over the years. Hopefully, the experience would show how *not* to establish a Policy Director.

The Director of the National Counterterrorism Center (NCTC) also has some of the features a Policy Director would need. But the idea for the NCTC also got distorted in the process of implementation. The 9/11 Commission envisioned a combined-agency team focused on combating terrorists, the way combatant commanders direct combined teams comprising units from each of the services. Instead, the NCTC became almost a new intelligence agency, complete with headquarters. The process of creating Presidential Policy Directors should not be so complex (or slow). Leave the agencies where they are, let them develop their expertise—just do what is necessary to make them work together.

Some administrations have had an especially strong National Security Council staff that made sure that that departments carried out administration policies and linked them into a coherent strategy; this kind of "loose but strong" organization closely tied to the President is close to what the U.S. executive branch needs. The Nixon administration provided an example of how such an organization might work. Nixon made clear strategy originated in the White House, and Henry Kissinger's NSC staff had strong-minded people who were not reluctant to use the President's name to get action. But Nixon's approach was never formalized, and so each administration's NSC has had to assert its own influence.

The President could put together a command system through an executive order and by making clear to his appointees when they are sworn in that his staff speaks for him. But it would be better to codify this arrangement in law, so that Congress also accepts it.

Promoting Jointness

Just as any officer or civilian official in the military knows what "Gold-water-Nichols" means, they also understand the meaning of the term "jointness." It is the Pentagon's shorthand for all the things that make it easier for the services to work together easily, and, in particular, operate effectively together under a combatant commander. At one level, joint-ness is the common specifications that allow Army, Navy, and Air Force systems to share parts. But at another level, which is at least as important, it is the idea that all military personnel know that, under law, all U.S. military operations are carried out under a combatant commander. It is so instinctive that military personnel are more apt to ask, "Who's the COCOM?" rather than "Is this an Army operation or a Navy operation?" The Defense Department spends enormous effort encouraging this mindset.

To get the kind of jointness among departments outside the Depart-ment of Defense that Rumsfeld said he wished he had, the government would have to make a similar investment—requiring tours of duty out-side one's department before one could be promoted to a flag rank or executive salary level.

These kinds of organizational issues may seem esoteric. But in an era when even military affairs are rarely just military in nature, a govern-ment-wide Goldwater-Nichols reform is critical for getting the kind of agility America needs.

CONCLUSION

Keeping the Strategic Advantage

TWENTIETH-CENTURY THREATS lent themselves to a storyline about how the world worked—and about how the United States hoped events would play out. The Soviet Union—and Nazi Germany and Imperial Japan before it—were the kind of threats that could define the world and frame debates over American national security for decades. They were singular threats that captured nearly all America's attention. And because they changed incrementally, the terms of those debates changed incrementally, too, year by year.

This kind of threat gave planners a reliable storyline that they could use to develop ideas for defense, diplomacy, intelligence, and international economics and finance. Doctrine, knowledge, technology, and tradecraft were all based on common assumptions about an adversary. The storyline served a similar purpose for an international scale for alliances and organizations. In short, twentieth-century threats were the kind that made it easier to develop grand strategy and the institutions to support it.

Since the Cold War ended, American leaders have been searching for a new storyline and trying to identify the new threat that can serve as the organizing concept for our national security policy. Yet, as we observed at the beginning of this book, if there is any lesson from recent experience, it is that there is not going to be a new storyline with a new threat. Rather, we are more likely to face a world with many storylines, all unfolding at the same time, with a continuing, never-ending stream of varied and often disconnected threats.

This kind of environment fundamentally complicates the task of national security. Ronald Reagan, for example, once famously said that his strategy for the Cold War was simple: "We win, they lose." Today, alas, it is hard even to specify who "they" are—there are too many potential adversaries. The nature of "winning" has changed, too. Few of the challengers we face today are apt to collapse like the Soviet Union. As we have seen, whereas the Soviets were brittle, these new adversaries are remarkably resilient. Indeed, many are hardly even "adversaries" in the traditional sense.

All this is why "winning" in global politics today is *staying on top*— that is, maintaining the strategic advantage, having more influence than others, and setting the agenda for global affairs—*for as long as necessary*—to avert truly bad events and generally move the world in a direction favorable to freedom, democracy, peace, and prosperity. Whether the United States can maintain the strategic advantage depends on the answers to several questions:

- Can we achieve the agility required to stay a step ahead of all the varied threats and challengers we are likely to face? National power can be irrelevant if government organizations cannot move quickly enough to develop it in time and use it when needed, or simply cannot get out of their own way.
- Can we optimally manage risk? That is, can we move aggressively enough to deal with potentially dangerous threats before they get out of hand, without acting so precipitously that mistakes become very costly? As we have seen, the September 11 terrorist attacks showed what happens when we do not move aggressively enough; the decision to strike Iraq showed what happens when we do not fully consider the downside risks.
- Can we navigate the crosscurrents under way in economic development and democracy? We favor capitalism and freedom, and both

have gained ground. Yet many democracies no longer seem to favor policies needed for growth, and many market economies are determined to stifle freedom. We often must make choices about whom we will partner with, and, despite globalization and the development of common cultures, the odds of finding partners whose interests match our own on all dimensions seem to be dwindling.

- Can we use our special strengths effectively to keep the strategic advantage? As we have seen, trends in demographics and in economic development run against us. But the United States has strengths that are unique, and that other countries will be hard pressed to match. Staying on top depends on our being able to make the most of our special assets—our culture, our legal and economic traditions, and our brand—to maintain the military power, commercial clout, and cultural influence that allow us to set the agenda for events and shape the world's progress.

An à la Carte World

One of the difficulties in developing strategy in such a complex world is that, just as there is no single storyline that explains events, there is also usually no one solution to a problem. Rather, there are often many solutions to many problems, and each competes for priority. The solution one needs to deal with one problem is likely to be ill suited or even completely incompatible for dealing with another.

Consider the military dimension, for example, and recall the different kinds of military operations U.S. forces have been required to carry out since the end of the Cold War:

- nuclear deterrent patrols by Navy ballistic missile submarines and Air Force missile crews standing on alert;
- conventional ground combat with infantry, armor, and artillery, like Operation Desert Storm in 1991 and the initial phases of Operation Iraqi Freedom in 2003;

- quick reaction, precision strikes, like the cruise strikes against suspected al-Qaeda camps in Afghanistan in 1998;
- small-scale direct action raids by special operations forces against "high-value targets" in Iraq, Afghanistan, and elsewhere;
- air patrols to monitor "no-fly zones" over Iraq in the late 1990s;
- counterinsurgency operations in Iraq, Afghanistan, the Philippines, and Colombia;
- peacekeeping operations in the Balkans, Africa, and the Middle East, and policing actions to restore the government in Haiti;
- "show of force" operations, like the deployment of aircraft carriers to the Taiwan Strait in 1995 and 1996;
- maritime interdiction, like those carried out by the Navy and Coast Guard to stop illegal trafficking in drugs, weapons, and people;
- training exercises on land, air, and sea with U.S. allies; and
- humanitarian relief and disaster response in Pakistan, Indonesia, and elsewhere.

During the Cold War, the working assumption was that the forces we trained and equipped for a conventional war in Europe could be adapted for the "lesser included threat." Some thought it was a questionable assumption even at the time; but, as this list of operations, shows, it is clearly not true today. Fighting conventional forces and fighting insurgents require different skills and equipment, and it is hard to think of many roles for heavy artillery in peacekeeping operations. Hedging against all the different military contingencies we might face requires options, and options result in additional costs.

The situation on the diplomatic front is similar. Cold War diplomacy was usually a global confrontation between the United States and our allies versus the Soviet Union and its allies, or, if not, then a regional confrontation between predictable opponents. Today, in contrast, there are so many more players and crosscutting interests that it is hard to develop a consensus among a given set of nations across very many issues. Consider some of the conflicting goals and priorities America currently must deal with among its potential partners:

- All NATO members are democracies. But, as we have seen, the United States places a higher priority on economic growth than other NATO members, or is at least less willing to reduce growth for the sake of the environment, in part because our geography and growing population make that trade-off much more costly for us.
- For their part, our NATO partners are much less willing to spend the money necessary for military forces, and most are less willing to deploy forces far from Europe or into actual combat.
- The United States, India, and China all share an interest in promoting growth to accommodate expanding populations, and all would be reluctant in varying degrees to risk growth for the sake of the environment. But whereas America and India are both committed to democracy, China's political leaders are resolved to limit democracy for the foreseeable future. That complicates cooperation.
- Few countries are as determined as Russia to combat militant Islamic terrorist organizations, and Russia will cooperate with almost any country that shares that interest. Yet Russia's leaders are almost as resolved in restricting democracy as China's and are even more sophisticated in the tactics they use. They also seem determined to reassert control or influence over neighbors like Ukraine, Georgia, Belarus, and the states along Russia's southern border.
- Even if major reductions in energy consumption were economically possible, few serious thinkers believe we can reduce oil imports significantly in, say, the next five to ten years. This implies that we will need working relationships with the governments of countries like Venezuela, Saudi Arabia, Nigeria, and Indonesia—all of which have proven problematic in one way or another in the past.
- The United States has special interests with Israel and Taiwan, yet both are pariahs to most world organizations. Even today, Japan has a stigma in much of Asia, which limits, for example, the military support it can provide to the United States in the region.

You can see the dilemma: Do we align with the democratic governments that are reluctant to bear the cost of economic growth? Do we align with the authoritarian governments that share our interest in economic growth? And, if a problem requires a military solution, is there anyone to align with at all?

One might think that with the growing acceptance of capitalism, governments might at least agree on rules for governing world markets. Indeed, that was the goal of the World Trade Organization (WTO). Yet even the WTO has difficulty achieving a consensus. Members of the European Union try to constrain American companies like Microsoft through antitrust litigation. Within the WTO, countries try to carve out exceptions for their individual benefit. The United States and the EU retain farm subsidies (to the detriment of Africa), and China still fails to protect foreign intellectual property effectively, knowing that companies will risk their intellectual property to get access to the Chinese market.

In the past, the assumption was that diplomatic success depended on building a broad consensus for joint action; that was the basic concept underpinning the United Nations, as well as international conventions on arms control, human rights, the conduct of war, and, later, the protection of the environment. Today, in contrast, the ability of the United States to work with other countries depends at least as much on segregating issues and ignoring disagreements as on finding common ground and building a consensus. No institution—the UN, NATO, or whatever—can address all the issues we must face. Instead of building institutions to support "wholesale diplomacy," today we need to create as many opportunities for cooperation as practical by concentrating on "retail diplomacy"—being attuned to the concerns and capabilities of individual countries and finding a basis on which to work with them.

The overarching challenge is how to develop, select, and combine the various capabilities—military, economic, diplomatic, and so on—and then recombine them as conditions change—all the while avoiding becoming so overcommitted that we are unable to deal with the next challenge that comes along. It is military planning and diplomacy à la carte.

And, as anyone who dines out very often knows, à la carte almost always costs more. Developing the extra margin that gives us the flexibility to navigate in this kind of complex world carries an extra cost. For the military services, it means funding a larger force than we might think immediately necessary, and a wider range of capabilities for scenarios that, at least for the moment, might seem implausible. For diplomats, it means we cannot automatically turn to organizations just because they are established or familiar. It means studying each potential partner more closely to determine exactly what its interests and concerns might be, and, thus, the opportunities and constraints on working together.

In this kind of environment, we will face tough choices—compromise democracy for the sake of security, risk security for the sake of growth, spend taxpayer money for defense systems that may never be used. This is not new; we faced similar choices in the Cold War. But today it seems that juggling such competing interests will be significantly more complex.

Philosophers and ethicists can debate the ethics of such choices. But American officials have a more prosaic task: simply understanding what Americans will accept and support over time. Our success in winning the Cold War was in large part a result of Americans developing a core consensus on the commitments we would sustain and risks we would run—and the limits to both. There was a significant range of views within this consensus, but it was still broad enough to support several decades of defense spending, foreign aid, and diplomatic engagement. The United States faltered when it approached the limits of this consensus, either by overextending (Vietnam) or by being overly accommodating (as with the Soviet Union toward the end of the 1970s).

Americans will need to identify a similar consensus for the current era. This will undoubtedly be a contentious, untidy process—as democracy itself is—but it cannot be short-circuited with secrecy, end runs, or language that is intended more to incite than inform. Democratic politics is the only way that the United States can decide issues like how many casualties and how much expense we will accept in a military operation, how many civil liberties we will restrain for the sake of homeland defense, how many national prerogatives we will forgo for the sake of an international treaty, and so on.

National Security for the New Environment

The broad outline for a strategy for "staying on top" in the current environment can be defined by a set of six principles. The first is to try to understand as many potential scenarios for world events as practical. Identify the most important variables—demographics, technology, economics—that underlie each scenario. Identify the mileposts that might signal how events are actually unfolding. As we have seen, the realities of demography and modernization say that larger countries will eventually outpace the United States in many important dimensions of power. The diffusion of technology means that even seemingly minor adversaries can present major threats.

The second principle is to recognize the special strengths that give the United States outsized influence—and then cultivate and exploit them. These include:

- the willingness of the United States to support a large professional military force, and the tradition, culture, and inclination that lead millions of Americans to choose that profession—or a career in the diplomatic service or intelligence community—during at least some part of their lives;
- the ability of American media and culture to spread throughout the world and influence the attitudes and beliefs of people, often subtly, but usually in ways that benefit the United States;
- the ability of the United States to attract talented, risk-accepting people at all income levels because of our educational institutions, economic opportunities, and (at least compared with the rest of the world) social tolerance; and
- the "critical mass" that the United States enjoys in several economic, cultural, and technical sectors, which can be sustained, if properly tended.

In this new environment, military power will be important, and, as we have seen, when it comes to military power, no one will match the

United States for some time to come. But American culture and commerce will likely have an even greater effect. They are attractive, powerful forces that lead others to see the world from our perspective. This is all worth keeping in mind when we consider policy questions that may seem small on the geopolitical scale, like whether to grant more foreign student visas, or whether to defend American media and software companies that trade in intellectual property abroad.

The third principle is to plan knowing that that situation five or even three years from now will likely—indeed, almost inevitably—look very different from what we think it will be. The finer the detail in the forecast, the greater is the likelihood for error. Such complexity is inevitable in a faster-moving world with a greater number of players. This applies to foreign nuclear programs, the economy, climate change—just about everything. Keep in mind, too, that there are likely more "unknown unknowns," especially as one tries to see further into the future. Some uncertainty may resolve itself in our favor; some will not. Build margins into your policies and plans. But because this margin is not free, apply the same focus on balancing risks and costs in planning these margins as in making other plans.

Fourth, understand the practical constraints under which the United States will likely have to work. These constraints are partly determined by the actual availability of people, resources, and money, and partly by public opinion. Realistic planners plan accordingly.

Fifth, organize in a way that rejuvenates all organizations involved in national security. Most departments, agencies, corporations, and international bodies of all kinds tend to become ossified, bureaucratic, and averse to risk as they mature. Therefore they need a mechanism for resetting this balance. Officials need the means to accommodate more risk, quickly, when situations require. The President needs an effective means to direct the bureaucracy.

Sixth and finally, America's ability to develop all these options depends on the resources it can bring to bear or bring to the table. That is why, especially today, economic growth is so important to national security. The more growth, the more options. But with pacing, foresight, and planning, the United States can sustain its leadership for the long haul.

NOTES

Introduction

1. See *Dictionary of Military and Associated Terms*, Joint Publication 1–02 (Washington, DC: U.S. Department of Defense, 2007).

2. James Clapper, *The Worldwide Threat to U.S. Interests*, prepared statement to the Senate Armed Services Committee, January, 17, 1995; George Tenet, *National Security Threats to the United States*, testimony to the Senate Select Committee on Intelligence, February 5, 1997; George Tenet, *Statement by Director of Central Intelligence before the Senate Armed Services Committee Hearing on Current and Projected National Security Threats*, testimony to the Senate Armed Services Committee, February 2, 1997; George Tenet, *The Worldwide Threat in 2001: National Security in a Changing World*, testimony to the Senate Armed Services Committee, March 7, 2001; George Tenet, "DCI's Worldwide Threat Briefing: The Worldwide Threat in 2003: Evolving Dangers in a Complex World," testimony to the Senate Select Committee on Intelligence, February 11, 2003; Porter J. Goss, *Global Intelligence Challenges 2005: Meeting Long-Term Challenges with a Long-Term Strategy*, testimony to the Senate Select Committee on Intelligence, February 16, 2005; John D. Negroponte, *Annual Threat Assessment*, testimony to the Senate Select Committee on Intelligence, January 11, 2007.

3. George F. Kennan, "The Sources of Soviet Conduct," *Foreign Affairs*, July 1947, 556–82.

4. Some of the more vivid accounts of the racism and generally hard life in the Soviet Army were published by the former Soviet military intelligence officer who defected and wrote under the pseudonym Victor Suvorov. See his account of the invasion of Czechoslovakia, *The Liberators* (New York: W. W. Norton, 1981); and *Inside the Soviet Army* (New York: Penguin, 1982).

5. See, e.g., John Van Oudenaren, *Exploiting 'Fault Lines' in the Soviet Empire: An Overview* (Santa Monica, CA: RAND Corporation, 1984).

6. For one early report that picked up this trend, see Robert F. Worth, "Jihadists Take Stand on Web, and Some Say It's Defensive," *New York Times*, March 13, 2005. Also see Steve Coll and Susan B. Glasser, "Terrorists Move Operations to Cyberspace," *Washington Post*, August 7, 2005; and Daniel Kimmage and Kathleen Ridolfo, *Iraqi Insurgent Media: The War of Images and Ideas* (Washington, DC: Radio Free Europe / Radio Liberty, 2007).

7. Directorate of Intelligence, Central Intelligence Agency, "Soviet Economic Problems and Prospect," declassified memorandum of July 1977, in *CIA's Analysis of the Soviet Union, 1947–91*, ed. Gerald K. Haines and Robert E. Leggett (Washington, DC: Center for the Study of Intelligence, Central Intelligence Agency, 2001).

8. Presidential Directive/NSC 18, "U.S. National Strategy," White House, Washington, August 24, 1977, www.jimmycarterlibrary.org/documents/pddirectives/pd18.pdf.

9. Ronald Reagan, "Address to Members of the British Parliament," June 8, 1982; a transcript and recording are available at http://millercenter.virginia.edu/scripps/digitalarchive/speechDetail/32.

10. Craig K. Elwell, Marc Labonte, and Wayne M. Morrison, *Is China a Threat to the U.S. Economy?* CRS Report for Congress RL33604 (Washington, DC: Congressional Research Service, 2007); and U.S. Treasury International Capital System Statistics, available at www.ustreas.gov.

11. Henry S. Rowen, "When Will the Chinese People Be Free?" *Journal of Democracy*, July 2007, 38–52.

12. See the article and analysis by Edward Cody, "Communist Party Cautions Reformers in China," *Washington Post*, February 27, 2007.

13. See Office of the Secretary of Defense, *Annual Report to Congress: Military Power of the People's Republic of China 2007* (Washington, DC: U.S. Department of Defense, 2007), 1.

14. See Peter Finn, "In Russia, a Secretive Force Widens; Putin Led Regrouping of Security Services" *Washington Post*, December 12, 2006. Finn quotes Olga Kryshtanovskaya, Director of the Center for the Study of Elites, a Moscow think tank.

15. World Bank, *Dying Too Young: Addressing Premature Mortality and Ill Health Due to Non-Communicable Diseases and Injuries in the Russian Federation* (Washington, DC: World Bank, 2005). Also see Francis C. Notzon, Yuri M. Komarov, Sergei P. Ermakov, Christopher T. Sempos, James S. Marks, and Elena V. Sempos, "Causes of Declining Life Expectancy in Russia," *Journal of the American Medical Association*, March 11, 1998, 793–800.

16. Peter Baker, "Putin Moves to Centralize Authority; Plan Would Restrict Elections in Russia," *Washington Post*, September 14, 2004.

17. Peter Finn, "Russia Halts Activities of Many Groups from Abroad," *Washington Post*, October 20, 2006.

18. See the assessment by the Committee to Protect Journalists in *Special Report 2007: Backsliders—The 10 Countries Where Press Freedom Has Most Deteriorated*, www.cpj.org/backsliders/index.html. Russia is ranked third.

Chapter One

1. Gordon E. Moore, "Cramming More Components onto Integrated Circuits," *Electronics*, April 19, 1965.

2. See Andrew Kohut, Richard Wike, and Nicole Speulda, *Truly a World Wide Web: Globe Going Digital* (Washington, DC: Pew Research Center, 2005).

3. See John B. Horrigan, *A Typology of Information and Communication Technology Users* (Washington, DC: Pew Internet and American Life Project, 2007).

4. See David Pogue, "Laptop with a Mission Widens Its Audience," *New York Times*, October 4, 2007; and John Markoff, "Intel, in Shift, Joins Project on Education," *New York Times*, July 14, 2007. For an overview of One Laptop per Child, see the organization's website at http://laptop.org. For Intel's competitor, the Classmate, see the company's website at www.intel.com/intel/world ahead/classmatepc/.

5. Testimony by Donald Rumsfeld to the Committee on Armed Services, U.S. Senate, May 7, 2004; transcript published by Associated Press, May 8, 2004.

6. Xeni Jardin, "Wartime Wireless Worries Pentagon," *Wired*, May 26, 2004, www.wired.com/politics/law/news/2004/05/63604. For Rumsfeld's comments, see Ann Scott Tyson, "Rumsfeld Discussess Successes, Failures," *Washington Post*, December 9, 2006.

7. See the account by the photojournalist Horst Faas, "The Saigon Execution," *Digital Journalist*, October 2004, http://digitaljournalist.org/issue0410/faas.html.

8. For the official assessment of the Abu Ghraib incident, see *Final Report of the Independent Panel to Review DoD Detention Operations* (Washington, DC: U.S. Department of Defense, 2004). Joseph Darby, the soldier who reported the abuses and provided the images to his superiors, gave his account to Wil S. Hylton, "Prisoner of Conscience," *GQ*, September, 2006, http://men.style.com/gq/features/full?id=content_4785.

9. Douglas Macgregor, *Breaking the Phalanx: A New Design for Landpower in the 21st Century* (New York: Praeger, 1997); John Arquilla and David Ronfeldt, *The Advent of Netwar* (Santa Monica, CA: RAND Corporation, 1996); and Bruce Berkowitz, *The New Face of War: How War Will Be Fought in the Twenty-First Century* (New York: Free Press, 2003).

10. In the autumn of 2004 the media reported the capture of Muhammed Naeem Noor Khan, said to have been an al-Qaeda communications specialist who had been captured by Pakistani authorities. Khan, according to the reports, described how messages were ferried from al-Qaeda leaders hiding in the Afghanistan-Pakistan border region to Lahore in eastern Pakistan, and then posted in code on websites or transmitted via e-mail. See Douglas Jehl and David Rhode, "Captured Qaeda Figure Led Way to Information behind Warning," *New York Times*, August 2, 2004.

11. Nevil Shute, *On the Beach* (New York: William Morrow, 1957), 39.

12. E.g., Terry N. Meyer, *Biological Weapons: The Poor Man's Nuke* (Maxwell Air Force Base, AL: Air War College, 1995).

13. Though, to be sure, there is enough general information about centrifuges available that a good engineer can design his own version—which is what the Iraqis did. Mahdi Obeidi, who later headed Iraq's uranium enrichment program, recalled a conversation he had in 1987 with Hussein Kamel, then son-in-law to Saddam Hussein and head of Iraq's military industries. Obeidi told Kamel that Brazil and Pakistan had experimented with centrifuges. "The Pakistanis!" Obeidi recalls Hussein Kamel exclaiming. "Surely, if the Pakistanis can develop such a thing, then so can we."

14. Before the strike on Iraq, David Albright, a former UN arms inspector who has a record of nonpartisanship, wrote, "Based on the available information, the intercepted aluminum tubing could have been intended for use in a centrifuge. It is far harder to confirm the Administration's view that the tubes were specifically intended for use in a centrifuge." So it was at least plausible, and illustrates the difficulty of controlling the technology. See his "Aluminum Tubing Is an Indicator of an Iraqi Gas Centrifuge Program: But Is the Tubing Specifically for Centrifuges?" October 9, 2002. For an analysis of the issue and erroneous assessment by U.S. intelligence, see the declassified "Key Judgments from the October 2002 National Intelligence Estimate, Iraq's Continuing Programs for Weapons of Mass Destruction," National Intelligence Council, Washington, 2003; and *Report of the Commission on the Intelligence Capabilities of the United States regarding Weapons of Mass Destruction* (Washington, DC: U.S. Government Printing Office, 2005).

15. For Zippe's role, see Jack Boureston, "Tracking the Technology," *Nuclear Engineering International*, August 31, 2004. For Khan's role in getting the technology from Urenco to Pakistan, see William Langewiesch, "The Wrath of Khan," *Atlantic Monthly*, November 2005. For an account of the Iraqi centrifuge program, see Mahdi Obeidi, *The Bomb in My Garden: The Secrets of Saddam's Nuclear Mastermind* (New York: Wiley, 2004); the quotation is on 62. Currently the only uranium enrichment facility in the United States is the gaseous diffusion plant operated by the United States Enrichment Corporation (USEC) in Paducah, KY. In 2007 USEC applied for a license from the Nuclear Regulatory Commission (NRC) to build a new centrifuge-based facility in Kentucky. The NRC had already licensed a Urenco subsidiary in 2006 to build a new commercial gas centrifuge facility in New Mexico.

16. Richard Butler, *The Greatest Threat: Iraq, Weapons of Mass Destruction, and the Crisis of Global Security* (New York: PublicAffairs, 2001); also see the interview he gave to PBS's *Frontline*, October 2001, www.pbs.org/wgbh/pages/frontline/shows/gunning/interviews/butler.html.

17. Cyber Defense Systems has sold UAVs like this to several Defense Department organizations, who use it for tactical reconnaissance. It carries 12 pounds of payload; for a sense of scale, a standard block of C-4 explosive weighs about 1.25 pounds. A demolition team would use about eight pounds of it to destroy a structural beam. Cyber Defense Systems is careful to whom it sells its aircraft, but the basic technology is generally available, so a less scrupulous oganization could probably build a similar system.

18. Robert A. Pape, *Dying to Win: The Strategic Logic of Suicide Terrorism* (New York: Random House, 2005). For a critique of Pape's argument, see Assaf Moghadam, "Suicide Terrorism, Occupation, and the Globalization of Martyrdom: A Critique of Dying to Win,"*Studies in Conflict & Terrorism*, December 2006, 707–29. Pape argues that nationalism is a more important factor in motivating suicide bombers than religion, but Moghadam argues that suicide bombing is mainly a globalized phenomenon of radical Islam. Also see Scott Atran, *The Strategic Threat from Suicide Terror* (Washington, DC: American Enterprise Institute–Brookings Institution Joint Center for Regulatory Studies, 2003).

19. See Andrew Kohut, Richard Wike, and Juliana Horowitz, *A Rising Tide Lifts Mood in the Developing World: Sharp Decline in Support for Suicide Bombing in Muslim Countries* (Washington, DC: Pew Research Center, 2007).

20. See the analysis by Daniel Yergin and Joseph Stanislaw, *The Commanding Heights: The Battle for the World Economy* (New York: Simon & Schuster, 1998).

21. Samuel Huntington, *Political Order in Changing Societies* (New Haven, CT: Yale University Press, 1968).

22. David Ronfeldt, *In Search of How Societies Work: Tribes—the First and Forcever Form*, RAND Working Paper WR-433-RPC (Santa Monica, CA: RAND Corporation, 2006). Ronfeldt notes that the study of social evolution extends over at least two centuries—e.g., dating back to Herbert Spencer and Karl Marx—and continuing through to today, with Benjamin Barber, Francis Fukuyama, and many others.

23. George Field, a self-taught man of letters who bounced around jobs in radio and advertising in the 1920s and 1930s, founded Freedom House in 1941. The war in Europe was going badly, and Field was incensed by isolationists who were determined to keep the United States out of the conflict. He launched Freedom House to make the public more aware of the stakes. Field, who had a knack for promotion, assembled a high-visibility Board of Directors that included newspaper columnists, Hollywood stars, and socialites, like Herbert Agar, Burgess Meredith, and Tallulah Bankhead (at the time, the approximate counterparts of, say, Nicholas Kristof, Richard Gere, and Candice Bergen today.) Field was a one-time socialist who idolized Eugene Debs, but he made Freedom House strictly nonpartisan. Franklin Roosevelt and Wendell Willkie were both supporters.

Field retired in 1967 and had a parting of the ways with his successors. He wanted Freedom House to be literally that—a house. The organization's headquarters, the Willkie Memorial Building at 20 West 40th Street, was an elegant clubhouse dating from 1909 that once was home to the New York Club. Under Field, several nonprofits, like the NAACP, the Anti-Defamation League, and B'nai B'rith shared the building as a home for the politically active. Freedom House's annual program was highlighted by an annual dinner that honored Presidents, civil rights leaders, and foreign leaders, among other luminaries. The new managers wanted to sell the building to fund a bigger research program, which they did. The funds from the sale paid for an expanded, more systematic version of the freedom assessments the organization had published since the 1950s. These annual ratings became a staple of research on democracy. After some litigation, the tenants were compensated, and 20 West 40th Street became a parking lot. Field died in 2006 at the age of 101. See "Freedom House Records," George Field Files, 1933–1990, Seeley G. Mudd Manuscript Library, Princeton University. A summary is available at http://infoshare1.princeton.edu/libraries/firestone/rbsc/finding_aids/field. html.

24. See Eric A. Nordlinger, *Conflict Regulation in Divided Societies* (Cambridge, MA: Center for International Affairs, Harvard University, 1972); and

Arend Lijphart, *Democracy in Plural Societies: A Comparative Exploration* (New Haven, CT: Yale University Press, 1977).

25. E.g., see Alvin Rabushka and Kenneth Shepsle, *Politics in Plural Societies* (Columbus: Charles E. Merrill, 1972). Rabushka and Shepsle examined about a dozen cases in which segmented societies tried to achieve democratic rule, and concluded the probability for success was generally low. For a more recent study of five conflicts with an analysis of strategies and their potential use, see Daniel L. Byman, *Keeping the Peace: Lasting Solutions to Ethnic Conflicts* (Baltimore: Johns Hopkins University Press, 2002).

26. See Adam Przeworski and Fernando Limongi, "Political Regimes and Economic Growth," *Journal of Economic Perspectives* 7, no. 3 (Summer 1993): 51–69; they argue that the often-noted pattern for rich countries being more likely to be democratic than poor countries is not through a maturing of traditional political structures but through the collapse of traditional systems. Also see Douglass C. North, John Joseph Wallis, and Barry R. Weingast, *A Conceptual Framework for Interpreting Recorded Human History*, NBER Working Paper 12795 (Cambridge, MA: National Bureau of Economic Research, 2006); they argue that only eight countries have evolved into stable democracies since World War II. And see G. Bingham Powell Jr. and Eleanor N. Powell, "Democratization: A Briefing Paper for AP Comparative Government and Politics," unpublished manuscript, September 2004.

27. That is the view of the International Climate Change Panel (ICCP), which has been chartered by the UN to look at the issue. See S. Solomon, D. Qin, M. Manning, Z. Chen, M. Marquis, K. B. Averyt, M. Tignor, and H. L. Miller, eds., "Summary for Policymakers," in *Climate Change 2007: The Physical Science Basis: Contribution of Working Group I to the Fourth Assessment Report of the Intergovernmental Panel on Climate Change* (Cambridge: Cambridge University Press, 2007). The National Oceanic and Atmospheric Administration has measured the concentration of carbon dioxide in the atmosphere at its observatory at Mauna Loa in Hawaii since 1959; the concentration has tracked steadily upward for almost fifty years. It is now 20 percent higher than when the observatory first started keeping records.

28. See Council of the European Union, *Brussels European Council: Presidency Conclusions*, March 8–9, 2007; and Dan Bilefsky, "Europe Sets Ambitious Limits on Greenhouse Gases, and Challenges Others to Match It," *New York Times*, March 10, 2007.

The most prominent critic of the ICCP and those who believe human activities are causing climate change is probably Richard Lindzen, a professor of meteorology at the Massachusetts Institute of Technology. Lindzen, who is a "dynamical meteorologist," or one specializing in the application of fluid dynamics to climate, participated in some of the global warming studies and has written several articles and op eds disputing their conclusions and how they have been reported. See, e.g., his "Climate of Fear," *Wall Street Journal*, April 12, 2006. Lindzen argues that there are insufficient data to infer statistical significance to published findings, and without statistical significance, he further argues, it is impossible to reach a scientific conclusion. See his prepared testimony before the U.S. Senate Commerce Committee, May 1, 2001. Lindzen also believes that the IPCC's summaries for policymakers misrepresent the findings of the actual reports, and that media reports misrepresent the summaries even further.

29. The Correlates of War data measure total energy consumption, which is almost entirely coal, gas, and oil; 5 percent or less is hydroelectric. After 1960, up to 5 percent is nuclear power. Geothermal, solar, and wind power account for 1 percent or less.

30. See, e.g., Jeffrey Ball, "Kyoto's Caps on Emissions Hit Snag in Marketplace," *Wall Street Journal*, September 4, 2007. The EU's "cap-and-trade" system led to companies reducing emissions related to farming and industrial production but had virtually no effect on carbon dioxide emissions, which are produced mainly by burning fossil fuels. In effect, the system proved to be a subsidy for traditional controls on pollutants, optimally distributed through a trading system, but had little effect on fuel consumption.

31. See the press release from the U.S. Census Bureau, "Americans Spend More Than 100 Hours Commuting to Work Each Year, Census Bureau Reports," March 30, 2005; and the press release from Statistics Canada, "General Social Survey: Commuting Times." Also see the BBC report "UK Commute 'Longest in Europe,'" July 22, 2003, which cites studies by the RAC Foundation. The general trend is that people in urban centers travel shorter distances but spend longer in transit. Americans in cities like New York spend about as much time getting to work as their London counterparts.

32. See the Population Database in *World Population Prospects: The 2006 Revision*, ed. United Nations Population Division, available at http://esa.un.org/unpp/.

33. Board on Energy and Environmental Systems, *Effectiveness and Impact of Corporate Average Fuel Economy (CAFE) Standards* (Washington, DC: National Academies Press, 2002). Also see the information sheet from the National Highway Transportation Safety Administration, "CAFE," www.nhtsa.dot.gov/cars/rules/cafe/overview.htm.

34. "China Ready to Fight Global Warming, but Not at Any Cost," *Thompson Financial Re*port, June 4, 2007.

35. Wang Zhenghua, "China Faces Uphill Task on Job Creation in 2006," *China Daily*, February 20, 2006.

36. See the official statements by the Chinese government: "China not to Undertake Quantitative Task for Reducing Greenhouse Gas Emissions," June 4, 2007; and "China Adopts a Series of Policies to Reduce Greenhouse Gas Emissions," June 8, 2007; both are available at the official website of the People's Republic of China, www.gov.cn.

Chapter Two

1. Dominic Wilson and Roopa Purushothaman, *Dreaming with BRICs: The Path to 2050*, Global Economics Paper 99 (New York: Goldman Sachs, 2003).

2. Much of this section is based on the work of Charles Adams, a historian and tax lawyer, and the leading expert on the history of taxes. See his *For Good and Evil: The Impact of Taxes on the Course of Civilization* (New York: Madison Books, 1993); and *Fight, Flight, and Fraud: The Story of Taxation* (Buffalo: Euro-Dutch Publishers, 1982).

3. Numbers 1:1–54, *New American Standard Bible*.

4. Luke 2:1–5, *New American Standard Bible*.

5. Quoted by Elizabeth M. Hallam, *Domesday Book through Nine Centuries* (New York: Thames and Hudson, 1986), 16. Hallam is a historian with the British Public Records Office and is the source for this section.

6. See Hallam, *Domesday Book*, 30.

7. See Wilson Lloyd Bevan, *Sir William Petty: A Study in English Economic Literature*, monograph based on Bevan's dissertation, published by the American Economic Association in 1894); http://socserv2.socsci.mcmaster.ca/~econ/ugcm/3ll3/petty/bevan.html. Also see Charles H. Hull, "Petty's Place in the History of Economic Theory," *Quarterly Journal of Economics*, 1900; and John Aubrey, "A Brief Life of William Petty, 1623–87," in *Aubrey's Brief Lives* (Boston: David R. Godine, 1999)

8. William Petty, *Political Arithmetick* (London: Robert Clavel, 1690). Several reproductions are available online; e.g., see http://socserv.mcmaster.ca/econ/ugcm/3ll3/petty/poliarith.html.

9. Quoted by Frans De Bruyn, "From Georgic Poetry to Statistics and Graphs: Eighteenth-Century Representations and the 'State' of British Society," *Yale Journal of Criticism*, Spring 2004, 107–39; the quotation is on 116–17.

10. See Ian Hacking, *The Emergence of Probability* (Cambridge: Cambridge University Press, 1975).

11. Petty, *Political Arithmetick*, chap. 3.

12. Ibid.

13. Ibid.

14. See James Madison, *Notes on the Debates in the Federal Convention of 1787*, entry of July 12, available at the Avalon Project's website, www.yale.edu/lawweb/avalon/ debates/712.htm. Madison reported that Charles Cotesworth Pinckney, a South Carolina delegate, "liked the idea" of proportional representation and taxation, "But foresaw that if the revision of the census was left to the discretion of the Legislature, it would never be carried into execution. The rule must be fixed, and the execution of it enforced by the Constitution."

15. See Margo J. Anderson, *The American Census: A Social History* (New Haven, CT: Yale University Press, 1988), 7–31; and James H. Cassedy, *Demography in Early America: Beginnings of the Statistical Mind, 1600–1800* (Cambridge, MA: Harvard University Press).

16. This account is taken mainly from the biography of John Sinclair by Rosalind Mitchison. See her *Agricultural Sir John: The Life of Sir John Sinclair of Ulbster, 1754–1835* (London: Geoffree Bles, 1962). Also see Sir John Sinclair, *The Statistical Account of Scotland, 1791–1799* (London: E. P. Publishing, 1977). The quotation is from "Sir John Sinclair's Vision for the Statistical Accounts of Scotland," Edinburgh University Library, http://edina.ac.uk/stat-acc-scot/reading/vision.shtml.

17. Frederick Hendricks, "On the Vital Statistics of Sweden, from 1749 to 1855," *Journal of the Statistical Society of London*, June 1862, 111–74. George Chalmers quotes from the Spanish 1787 census in *Estimate of the Comparative Strength of Great Britain during the Present and Four Preceding Reigns* (London: John Stockdale, 1794), vi.

18. From the foreword to the *Statistical Accounts*. See the website hosted by the Edinburgh University Data Library as part of EDINA, the Internet site devoted to the Statistical Accounts, http://edina.ac.uk/stat-acc-scot/reading/vision.shtml. By comparison, the Swedish information seems to have been intended just as raw data for the use of government planners. Hendricks, "On the Vital Statistics of Sweden," wrote of the Swedish census—e.g., that "there have, notwithstanding, been great difficulties in the way of its being utilized. The very copiousness of the information, and its minute detail, deters investigation. Many are content with the mere knowledge that in a certain place, if certain facts be wanted, there they can be referred to."

19. William Playfair, *The Statistical Breviary* (London: T. Bensley, 1801); and J. G. Boetticher, *Statistical Tables Exhibiting a View of All the States of Europe*, trans. William Playfair (London: John Stockdale, 1800).

20. See Michael J. Cullen, *The Statistical Movement in Early Victorian Britain: The Foundations of Empirical Social Research* (New York: Harverster Press, 1975), 12–13, 29–30.

21. The primary source of information available on Jane, on which this section is based, is the biography by Richard Brooks, *Fred T Jane: An Eccentric Visionary* (Coulsdon, U.K.: Jane's Information Group, 1997). Oddly enough for an author-illustrator with political aspirations, Jane did not leave a collection of personal or official papers. Brooks pieced together Jane's life by searching public documents and contemporary newspaper stories. Also see "A Wealth of Knowledge," *The Guardian*, October 31, 2001.

22. Edward Gibbon, *The Decline and Fall of the Roman Empire*, ed. Dero A. Saunders (New York: Penguin Books, 1985), 621.

23. Paul Kennedy, *The Rise and Decline of the Great Powers* (New York: Random House, 1990).

24. Jared Diamond, *Collapse: How Societies Choose to Fail or Succeed* (New York: Viking, 2004).

25. See Chalmers Johnson, *Nemesis: The Last Days of the American Empire* (New York: Metropolitan Books, 2007); Charles Kupchan, *The End of the American Era: U.S. Foreign Policy and the Geopolitics of the Twenty-First Century* (New York: Vintage, 2003); and Cullen Murphy, *Are We Rome? The Fall of an Empire and the Fate of America* (New York: Houghton Mifflin, 2007).

26. There are several articles from the early to middle 1900s that give the basic outline of Playfair's life. E.g., see "The Inventor of Graphic Statistics," *Bulletin of the Business Historical Society*, September 1926, 13–16; a Marxist perspective by Henryk Grossman, "W. Playfair, the Earliest Theorist of Capitalist Development," *Economic History Review* 18, no. ½ (1948); and Paul J. Fitz-Patrick, "Leading British Statisticians of the Nineteenth Century," *Journal of the American Statistical Association*, March 1960, 38–70. Also see Patricia Costigan-Eaves and Michael Macdonald-Ross, "William Playfair (1759–1823)," *Statistical Science*, August 1990, 318–26.

Edward Tufte revived interest in Playfair's work with statistical graphics with his book, *The Visual Display of Quantitative Information* (Cheshire, CT: Graphics Press, 1982). Since then, Howard Wainer and Ian Spence have published the most extensive body of work on Playfair, concentrating almost entirely on his development of graphics. See, in particular, their reprint of Playfair's *The Commercial and Political Atlas* and *Statistical Breviary* in a combined volume published by Cambridge University Press in 2005. This reprint also contains their biography of Playfair. Also see their entry in the *Oxford Dictionary of National Biography* (Oxford: Oxford University Press, 2004); and Howard

Wainer, *Graphic Discovery: A Trout in the Milk and Other Visual Adventures* (Princeton, NJ: Princeton University Press, 2005).

Wainer and Spence, along with Tufte, essentially ignore the work he published after 1801, and so they do not discuss his writings on political economy. In their Oxford biography, Spence and Wainer even say that "after the great inventions of 1786 and 1801 [the publication dates of, respectively, *The Commercial and Political Atlas and The Statistical Breviary*], Playfair introduced no further innovations of any consequence" (p. 78). This was exactly when Playfair began his main works on political economy.

In fairness, one has to keep in mind that Wainer is a statistician and Spence is a psychologist, and it can be understood if they did not appreciate the significance of Playfair's other contributions, which are outside their fields. Tufte, who is a well-known political economist, writes in a personal communication that Playfair's "political economy stuff was cranky, unanalytical, and based largely on his hatred of the French revolution," referring to Playfair's pamphleteering. In fairness to Tufte, this may reflect that he has devoted his attention to the study of graphics in recent years (indeed, becoming the leading expert in that field), and, like Wainer and Spence, appears to be unfamiliar with most of Playfair's other work. Playfair also managed to escape the attention of scholars in the field of quantitative studies of international relations; see note 41 below.

27. For a recent study of the Scottish Enlightenment and its influence, see Arthur Herman, *How the Scots Invented the Modern World: The True Story of How Western Europe's Poorest Nation Created Our World and Everything in It* (New York: Crown, 2001).

28. William Playfair, *The Increase of Manufactures, Commerce and Finance, with the Extension of Civil Liberty, Proposed in Regulations for the Interest of Money* (London: G. G. J. and J. Robinson, 1785).

29. Costigan-Eaves and Macdonald-Ross, "William Playfair (1759–1823)," 318–26.

30. William Playfair, *The Commercial and Political Atlas* (London: John Stockdale, 1787).

31. A copy of *The Columbiad* is available at the Project Gutenberg website, www.gutenberg.org/dirs/etext05/8clmb10h.htm. Strictly speaking, Barlow, who died in 1812 while traveling to an audience with Napoleon, was the second American diplomat to die in the line of duty. William Palfry was lost at sea in 1780 while sailing to France to serve as consul-general representing the Second Continental Congress.

32. See Theodore Thomas Belote, *The Scioto Speculation and the French Settlement at Gallipolis* (New York: Burt Franklin, 1907); Charles Burr Todd,

Life and Letters of Joel Barlow, LL.D. (New York: G. P. Putnam's Sons, 1886); and *Journal of the House of Representatives of the United States, 1789–1793,* February 9, 1793.

33. "English Actors in the French Revolution," *Edinburgh Review,* reprinted in *Littell's Living Age,* November 19, 1887, 387–90. Also see Ian Spence and Howard Wainer, "Who Was Playfair?" *Chance* 10, no. 1 (1997): 35–37.

34. See Jennifer Mori, "Languages of Loyalism: Patriotism, Nationhood and the State in the 1790s," *English Historical Review,* February 2003, 48. Mori writes that Playfair first began to receive payments from Windham in 1793. Playfair had also previously proposed a similar plan to the Home Office; see his letter to HM Home Office, from Knightsbridge, on April 24, 1794, reprinted by Arthur Aspinall, *Politics and the Press, c. 1780–1850* (London: Home & Van Thal, 1949), 152–53. It appears that the Home Office either rejected the proposal or referred Playfair to Windham.

35. William Playfair, *A General View of the Actual Force and Resources of France* (London: John Stockdale, 1793).

36. Sir John Swinburne, a member of Parliament, came upon the operation after hearing rumors of its existence. He described it in a memorandum recounting his visit to a paper mill in Northumberland that produced the paper for the bogus *assignats.* According to Swinburne, the operation continued from 1793 to 1795, and Playfair managed the business and met with the forgers in London. The memorandum is reproduced by John Philipson, "A Case of Economic Warfare in the Late Eighteen Century," *Archaeologia Aeliana,* vol. 18 (Newcastle upon Tyne, U.K.: Society of Antiquaries of Newcastle upon Tyne, 1990), 151–63. Further evidence of the operation is given by Isaac Espinasse, *Reports and Cases Argued in the Courts of King's Bench and Common Pleas* (London: Butterworth, 1801), 388–91. Espinasse cites the case of *Strongitherm v. Lukyn* in 1795. Strongitherm, an engraver, sued Lukyn, a stationer, for failing to pay for a copper plate Lukyn had ordered; the plate was for forging *assignats.* Lukyn tried to quash the suit by arguing that, because forgery was a crime, the contract was not binding. The court disagreed, ruling that because Strongitherm had represented that the forged *assignats* were for the British government, the illegality of forgery was no defense and the contract was enforceable. Also see the account by Thomas Doubleday, *The Political Life of Robert Peel* (London: Smith, Elder, and Co., 1856), 40–42.

37. See Adam Smith, *An Inquiry into the Nature and Causes of the Wealth of Nations,* 11th edition, ed. William Playfair (London: Cadell and Davies, 1805). Playfair makes a cameo appearance in one of the first full-length scholarly biographies of Smith, in which he meets Smith upon his return to London in 1787.

See John Rae, *Life of Adam Smith* (London: Macmillan, 1895). Rae mentions the meeting at the beginning of Chapter 23. Playfair himself included a biographical essay on Smith in his edition of *Wealth of Nations*, which Rae used as a source for his own book.

38. Willaim Playfair, *An Inquiry into the Permanent Causes of the Decline and Fall of Powerful and Wealthy Nations, Designed to Shew How the Prosperity of the British Empire May Be Prolonged*, 1st ed. (London: Greenland and Norris, 1805). Robert W. Jones created an electronic copy , which is available online at the Project Gutenberg website, www.gutenberg.org/etext/16575.

39. Ibid., xv–xvi.

40. In a communication, J. David Singer, cofounder of the Correlates of War Project, says that he was unaware of the *Statistical Breviary*. Because the Correlates of War database is the most comprehensive collection of its kind, it would seem that Playfair slipped between the cracks when quantitative international studies developed in the early 1960s.

41. See William Playfair, *Statistical Account of the United States of America* (London: Greenland and Norris, 1805). As an aside on the development of the national statistics, it is interesting to note that Thomas Jefferson gave a copy of one of Playfair's atlases to the German explorer Alexander von Humboldt, who later went on to invent the modern discipline of geography. See the letter from Humboldt to Jefferson of June 12, 1809, in which Humboldt writes, "You made me a gift of your copy of Playfair's but your inscription is lacking and this fact, you will admit, may cause me some embarrassment later on"; reproduced by Helmut de Terra, "Alexander von Humboldt's Correspondence with Jefferson, Madison, and Gallatin," *Proceedings of the American Philosophical Society* (Studies of Historical Documents in the Library of the American Philosophical Society) 103, no. 6 (December 15, 1959): 790. It is not clear whether Humboldt was referring to the *Statistical Breviary* or to the *Statistical Account of the United States of America*, which Playfair translated and dedicated to Jefferson. Playfair notes in the dedication that he gave Jefferson twenty-five copies, and included blank pages so that Jefferson could add material if he wished.

42. David Ricardo, *On the Principles of Political Economy and Taxation*, 3rd ed. (London: John Murray, 1821), chap. 7; available online at the Library of Economics and Liberty, www.econlib.org/LIBRARY/Ricardo/ricP.html. Robert Torrens is also credited with contributing to the concept of comparative advantage in his discussions of the Corn Laws and free trade; see Robert Torrens, *An Essay on the External Corn Trade* (London: J. Hatchard, 1815).

43. Playfair, *Inquiry into the Permanent Causes*, 290.

44. Letter from Jeremy Bentham to George Wilson, May 4/15, 1787, quoted in the Glasgow Edition of *The Works and Correspondence of Adam Smith* (1981–

1987), *Volume VI: The Correspondence of Adam Smith* (Oxford: Oxford University Press, 1876), appendix C, "Jeremy Bentham's Letters to Smith on the Defence of Usury (1787, 1790)"; http://oll.libertyfund.org/Texts/LFBooks/Smith0232/GlasgowEdition/Correspondence/HTMLs/0141–07_Pt03c_AppendixC.html.

45. John 19:23, *New American Standard Bible*: "Then the soldiers, when they had crucified Jesus, took His outer garments and made four parts, a part to every soldier and also the tunic; now the tunic was seamless, woven in one piece. So they said to one another, 'Let us not tear it, but cast lots for it, to decide whose it shall be.'"

46. See Ian Hacking, *The Emergence of Probability* (Cambridge: Cambridge University Press, 1975); and the excellent study by David G. Schwartz, *Roll the Bones: The History of Gambling* (New York: Gotham Books, 2006), 73–91.

47. Playfair, *Increase of Manufactures*, 109–10.

48. See John von Neumann and Oskar Morgenstern, *The Theory of Games and Economic Behavior* (Princeton, NJ: Princeton University Press, 1944); Bruce Bueno de Mesquita, *The War Trap* (New Haven, CT: Yale University Press, 1981); Bruce Bueno de Mesquita and David Lalman, *War and Reason: Domestic and International Imperatives* (New Haven, CT: Yale University Press, 1992); and Bruce Bueno de Mesquita, Alastair Smith, Randolph M. Siverson, and James D. Morrow, *The Logic of Political Survival* (Cambridge, MA: MIT Press, 2003).

49. See Mancur Olson, *The Logic of Collective Action: Public Goods and the Theory of Groups* (Cambridge, MA.: Harvard University Press; and Mancur Olson, *The Rise and Decline of Nations: Economic Growth, Stagflation, and Social Rigidities* (New Haven, CT: Yale University Press, 1982).

50. Playfair, *Inquiry into the Permanent Causes*, 121.

51. Ibid., 291.

52. William Playfair, *Outline of a Plan for a New and Solid Balance of Power in Europe* (London: John Stockdale, 1813). Quincy Wright, who published from the late 1920s until his passing in 1970, is generally accepted as the originator of modern international studies combining theoretical models and statistics. See the abridged reprint of his *A Study of War* (Chicago: University of Chicago Press, 1983). Louis Fry Richardson, whose work Wright rediscovered, is also given credit for his statistical analyses of arms races; see his *Statistics of Deadly Quarrels* (Pittsburgh: Boxwood Press, 1959) and his *Arms and Insecurity: The Theory of Arms Races* (Pittsburgh: Boxwood Press, 1959).

53. David Hume, *Essays: Moral, Political, and Literary*. Hume published this book in 1758. A version edited by Eugene F. Miller is available online as part

of the Library of Economics and Liberty at www.econlib.org/library/LFBooks/ Hume/hmMPL30.html.

54. Hans Morgethau, *Politics among Nations: The Struggle for Power and Peace* (New York: Alfred A. Knopf, 1948).

55. For a critical analysis of the balance of power theory, see Emerson M. S. Niou, Peter C. Ordeshook, and Gregory F. Rose, *The Balance of Power: Stability in International Systems* (Cambridge: Cambridge University Press, 1989); and Bruce Bueno de Mesquita, "Neorealism's Logic and Evidence: When Is a Theory Falsified?" in *Realism and the Balancing of Power: A New Debate*, ed. Colin Elman and John Vasquez (Englewood Cliffs, NJ: Prentice-Hall, 2003), 166–97.

56. See A. F. K. Organski, *World Politics* (New York: Alfred A. Knopf, 1958). Also see A. F. K. Organski, Jacek Kugler, J. Timothy Johnson, and Youssef Cohen, *Births, Deaths and Taxes: The Demographic and Political Transitions* (Chicago: University of Chicago Press, 1984).

57. See William H. Riker, *The Theory of Political Coalitions* (New Haven, CT: Yale University Press, 1962).

58. The Correlates of War capabilities index, though based on actual data, uses an arbitrary metric. In this case, the maximum value for the United Kingdom and the United States is about 2.0, and the charts for the other nations are drawn to the same scale.

59. Organski, *World Politics*, 486–87.

60. Ibid., 490.

Chapter Three

1. Walter Russell Mead, "The Jacksonian Tradition," *The National Interest*, Winter 1999, 5–29.

2. The most complete reference seems to be James Graham Leyburn, *The Scotch-Irish: A Social History* (Chapel Hill: University of North Carolina Press, 1962). Though, strictly speaking, "Scots" are a people and "Scotch" is a beverage, the name of the group is sometimes rendered as "Scots-Irish," and other times "Scotch-Irish." Even members of the group use both terms.

3. Alexander Hamilton ("Publius"), *Federalist No. 23*, "The Necessity of a Government as Energetic as the One Proposed to the Preservation of the Union," *New York Packet*, December 18, 1787.

4. Thomas Jefferson, *First Inaugural Address*, March 4, 1801, www.yale.edu/ lawweb/avalon/presiden/inaug/jefinau1.htm.

5. Andrew Jackson, *First Inaugural Address*, March 4, 1829, www.yale.edu/ lawweb/avalon/presiden/inaug/jackson1.htm.

6. Tourism statistics are from the United Nations World Tourism Organization's annual report, *Tourism Highlights*. Tourism trade fell after the September 11, 2001, terrorist attacks, and coincident with the SARS epidemic and the war in Iraq, the dollar volume fell partly as a result of the decline of the dollar against the euro. But neither of these changes the basic fact that Europeans travel abroad much more than Americans. There does not seem to be an official estimate of "active" passports, accounting for people who die, emigrate, etc. The State Department does report how many passports it issues each fiscal year, and passports are good for ten years; see www.travel.state.gov/passport/services/stats/stats_890.html. Between 1996 and 2005, the State Department issued 72,767,429 passports, which works out to be about 25 percent of the U.S. population.

7. See Michael Delli Carpini and Scott Keeter, *What Americans Know about Politics and Why It Matters* (New Haven, CT: Yale University Press, 1997).

8. Two relatively recent polls that reconfirm these trends are the *Pew Survey of American Foreign Policy Attitudes*, 2004 edition, conducted by the Pew Research Center for the People and the Press and the Council on Foreign Relations; and *Global Views 2004: American Public Opinion and Foreign Policy*, published by the Chicago Council on Foreign Relations.

9. Military pay scales are available at http://defenselink.mil, the Defense Department's official website. By comparison, the starting annual salary for a police officer in a typical Sunbelt city like Jacksonville—home to two large Navy installations—is $33,000 to $35,000. Applicants must have a college degree or an associate's degree and four years of military service—meaning that they would be the approximate age and have the experience of a sergeant or Navy petty officer, and would earn about the same salary. Top salaries for Jacksonville police officers reach $61,000 after seventeen years. Officers can retire after twenty years and receive 60 percent of their salary. Similarly, an experienced office administrator in the same region working for the federal government with no college education would be a GS-7 and earn $35,000 to $45,000 a year.

10. Officer promotion rates and time required in service for promotion, along with ceilings for the number of persons holding each grade, are established by statute and implemented under Department of Defense Instruction 1320.13, "Commissioned Officer Promotion Reports (COPRs) and Procedures," June 21, 1996. An "O-6"—which is a salary level, not a rank—requires twenty-two years in service and three years as an O-5. So, assuming an officer entered the service at the age of twenty-two, he or she could be a colonel at the age of forty-four. The services try to maintain the promotion rate from O-1 to O-2 and from

O-2 to O-3 at 100 percent; from O-3 to O-4 at 80 percent; from O-4 to O-5 at 70 percent; and from O-5 to O-6 at about 50 percent. Thus, the joint probability of a second lieutenant eventually making colonel is about one out of four.

11. An example of the coverage was the Associated Press report, "Lower Standards Help Army Meet Recruiting Goal," *USA Today*, October 9, 2006; and Thom Shanker, "U.S. Military Meets '06 Recruiting Goals," *New York Times*, October 10, 2006. For statistics from the Defense Department, see Donna Miles, "Official Debunks Myths about Military Recruits," Armed Forces Press Service, December 5, 2005.

12. Wallace is quoted by Gina Cavallaro, "Most Youth Ineligible for Army, Survey Says," *Military Times*, March 8, 2007.

13. See Michael R. Pakko and Patricia S. Pollard, "Burgernomics: A Big Mac™ Guide to Purchasing Power Parity," *Federal Reserve Bank of St. Louis Review*, November–December 2003, 9–28. Because McDonald's sells Big Macs worldwide, it is straightforward to calculate how many hours of work is required to buy one, and, from that, calculate purchasing power parity ratios or at least, as the authors report, give economists food for thought.

14. Of the twenty-four U.S. aircraft carriers, eleven are "large" carriers with catapults and arresting gear for conventional aircraft; the others operate helicopters and vertical or short takeoff and landing (V/STOL) aircraft. Four of the non-U.S. carriers operate conventional aircraft, the rest are for helicopters and V/STOL aircraft.

15. See "Air Force Alamanac," published annually by the U.S. Air Force Association in the May issue of *Air Force Magazine*. The fifty-odd non-U.S. long-range bombers are older Tu-95s and Tu-160s belonging to the Russian Air Force; the exact number that are operational is unclear, and probably depends on a combination of available parts, fuel, and the courage of the Russian pilots.

16. See "U.S. Nuclear Forces," *Bulletin of the Atomic Scientists*, January–February 2007; and Shannon N. Kile, Vitaly Fedchenko, and Hans M. Kristensen, "World Nuclear Forces, 2006," in *SIPRI Yearbook 2006* (Stockholm: Stockholm International Peace Research Institute, 2006). The Stockholm International Peace Research Institute estimates that China, France, Russia, Britain, and the United States together have 12,300 weapons. For estimates of weapons held by the announced and presumed nuclear powers that are not "recognized" by the Nuclear Nonproliferation Treaty (India, Israel, Pakistan, and North Korea), see Jeffery Lewis, "The Ambiguous Arsenal," *Bulletin of the Atomic Scientists*, May–June 2005; Robert S. Norris and Hans M. Kristensen. "India's Nuclear Forces, 2005," *Bulletin of the Atomic Scientists*, September–October 2005; Robert S. Norris and Hans M. Kristensen, "Pakistan's Nuclear Forces,

2001," *Bulletin of the Atomic Scientists*, January–February 2002; and Robert S. Norris and Hans M. Kristensen, "North Korea's Nuclear Program, 2005," *Bulletin of the Atomic Scientists*, May–June 2005.

17. See David Albright, Frans Berkhout, and William Walker, *Plutonium and Highly Enriched Uranium 1996: World Inventories, Capabilities, and Policies* (Oxford: Stockholm International Peace Research Institute and Oxford University Press, 1997); and the update provided in the Institute for Science and International Security monograph, "Global Stocks of Nuclear Explosive Materials: Summary Tables and Charts," September 7, 2005.

18. See Stephen Saunders, ed., *Jane's Fighting Ships*, 2005–6 (Alexandria, VA: Jane's Information Group, 2005). The Naval Registry lists U.S. Navy nuclear submarines in the following homeports: Bangor (eleven), Bremerton (one), Groton (eighteen), King's Bay (seven), Norfolk (thirteen), Pearl Harbor (fifteen), and San Diego (four).

19. See National Center for Education Statistics, *Comparative Indicators of Education in the United States and Other G8 Countries: 2004*, NCES 2005–021 (Washington, DC: Institute of Education Sciences, U.S. Department of Education, 2005). Among industrial nations, the United States comes out on top, spending $7,877 for each primary and secondary student; France, Germany, Japan, Britain, and Canada are in the $5,900 to $6,000 range. As a share of their economies, France is most generous, spending 4.3 percent of GDP on primary and secondary education. Japan is lowest at 3.0 percent, and the United States is in the middle at 3.9 percent. In spending on higher education, the competition is not even close; the United States spends about twice as much per student and double the percentage of its GDP.

20. E.g., see Katrin Bennhold, "A French Call for the EU to Raise Military Outlays," *International Herald Tribune*, June 10, 2005.

21. Ronald O'Rourke, *China Naval Modernization: Implications for U.S. Navy Capabilities* (Washington, DC: Congressional Research Service, 2007).

22. Statistics on illegal drugs are, of course, inherently difficult to gather, but these estimates seem to be generally accepted. Illegal drug sales statistics are from the UN Office on Drugs and Crime, *World Drug Report 2007* (Vienna: UN Office on Drugs and Crime, 2007), www.unodc.org/documents/data-and-analysis/WDR-2007.pdf. For a general discussion of the underground economy by a correspondent for *The Atlantic*, see Eric Schlosser, *Reefer Madness: Sex, Drugs, and Cheap Labor in the American Black Market* (New York: Houghton Mifflin, 2003).

23. A technical note: Currency exchange rates complicate comparing the GDP between countries. We measure our economy in dollars; Britain uses

pounds, Switzerland francs, Japan yen, most of Europe euros, and so on. The market today mainly determines the values of major currencies, but governments can still influence them by issuing more currency or regulating interest rates. U.S. officials have complained for years that China undervalues its currency, making Chinese goods unnaturally cheap in the United States. Chinese exporters and American consumers like this, American manufacturers and unions do not. This issue also affects comparisons of military spending; partly because of exchange rates, the price of a Chinese jet fighter on the world market is less than that of its American counterpart, just as Chinese cars are priced lower than American-made cars. To get around this problem, economists sometimes adjust GDP to reflect what they call "purchasing power parity," or the price of the goods and services produced in, say, China as if they were produced in the United States. But this creates other issues. Any advantage China gains by undervaluing the renminbi (literally, "people's money"; the basic unit is the yuan) is really a hidden tax that it imposes on Chinese citizens by making U.S. goods more expensive. This tax is hard to estimate precisely, but you can see the results as when, say, a Chinese graduate student decides to remain in America, where he or she can both buy low-cost Chinese goods and enjoy the benefits of American residence or citizenship. Then we gain, and China loses. I will refer to this adjustment when it is important, but unless otherwise noted, all figures are given in U.S. dollars at official or market exchange rates.

24. "The *Fortune* Global 500," *Fortune*, July 24, 2006.

25. "The World's Billionaires," *Forbes*, March 8, 2008.

26. See Stephen R. Mosley, *The Chimney of the World: A History of Smoke Pollution in Victorian and Edwardian Manchester* (Cambridge: White Horse Press, 2001).

27. See William R. Kerr, *The Ethnic Composition of U.S. Inventors*, Harvard Business School Working Paper 08–006 (Cambridge, MA: Harvard Business School, 2007); and Anna Lee Saxenian, "Silicon Valley's New Immigrant High-Growth Entrepreneurs," *Economic Development Quarterly*, Winter 2002, 20–31.

28. These statistics on research and development trends are from the National Science Foundation. E.g., see National Science Board, *Science and Engineering Indicators 2006* (Washington, DC: National Science Foundation, 2007). Also see "The State of Global R&D," *R&D Magazine*, September 2005.

29. See Vivek Wadhwa, Guillermina Jasso, Ben Rissing, Gary Gereffi, and Richard Freeman, *Intellectual Property, the Immigration Backlog, and a Reverse Brain-Drain: America's New Immigrant Entrepreneurs*, parts I–III (Kansas City: Ewing Marion Kauffman Foundation, 2007).

30. See Andrew Kohut, Roberto Suro, Scott Keeter, Carroll Doherty, and Gabriel Escobar, *America's Immigration Quandary: No Consensus on Immmigration Problem or Proposed Fixes* (Washington, DC: Pew Research Center for the People and the Press and Pew Hispanic Center, 2006).

31. Unemployment rates are readily available from the Bureau of Labor Statistics website, http://bls.gov. Precise time series for legal and illegal immigration are problematic, but for an estimate, see Steven A. Camarota, *Immigrants at Mid-Decade: A Snapshot of America's Foreign-Born Population in 2005* (Washington, DC: Center for Immigration Studies, 2005).

32. Statistical studies report that immigrants commit no more or less crime than native-born Americans; e.g., see Kristin F. Butcher and Anne Morrison Piehl, "Cross-City Evidence on the Relationship between Immigration and Crime," *Journal of Policy Analysis and Management*, January 1999; Kristin F. Butcher and Anne Morrison Piehl, *Recent Immigrants: Unexpected Implications for Crime and Incarceration*, NBER Working Paper 6067 (Cambridge, MA: National Bureau of Economic Research, 1997); and, more recently, Rubén G. Rumbaut, Roberto G. Gonzales, Golnaz Komaie, and Charlie V. Morgan, *Debunking the Myth of Immigrant Criminality: Imprisonment among First- and Second-Generation Young Men* (Washington, DC: Migration Policy Institute, 2006). Critics claim that immigrant crime is underreported, or more serious than crime committed by natives. E.g., see Carl F. Horowitz, *An Examination of U.S. Immigration Policy and Serious Crime* (Washington, DC: Center for Immigration Studies, 2001).

33. See Shirin Hakimzadeh and D'Vera Cohn, *English Usage among Hispanics in the United States* (Washington, DC: Pew Hispanic Center, 2007).

34. James Webb, *Born Fighting: How the Scots-Irish Shaped America* (New York: Broadway Books, 2004), 124. Webb, himself descended from Irish stock, traced the origins and evolution of the Scots-Irish and their culture in his book.

35. Mead, "Jacksonian Tradition," 11–12.

36. See Joseph S. Nye, *Bound to Lead: The Changing Nature of American Power* (New York: Basic Books, 1990). Also see his later books: Joseph S. Nye, *The Paradox of American Power* (New York: Oxford University Press, 2002); and Joseph S. Nye, *Soft Power: The Means to Success in World Politics* (New York: PublicAffairs, 2004).

37. Nye, *Paradox of American Power*, 9.

38. Arthur Hugh Clough, ed., *Plutarch's Lives: Cimon*, text 674, available at www.gutenberg.org. Also see W. R. Connor, "Two Notes on Cimon," *Transactions and Proceedings of the American Philological Association* 98 (1967): 67–75.

39. Cimon was such a Spartaphile that he once employed what we might today call the "Lacedaemonian Defense" to beat a treason charge. When

Cimon failed to pursue a Persian army he had cornered in Macedonia, his opponents accused him of taking a bribe. At his trial, he testified that every Athenian knew he modeled himself on the Lacedaemonians, admiring "the plainness of their habits, their temperance, and simplicity of living," which he "preferred to any sort of riches." So, Cimon argued, it was impossible to bribe him. When the verdict came in, Cimon walked.

40. See Andrew Kohut, Jodie Allen, Carrill Doherty, and Carolyn Funk, *American Character Gets Mixed Reviews: U.S. Image Up Slightly, but Still Negative*, Report of Pew Global Attitudes Project (Washington, DC: Pew Research Center, 2005), 1.

41. Andrew Kohut and Bruce Stokes, *America against the World: How We Are Different and Why We Are Disliked* (New York: Times Books, 2006).

42. See Tim Kane, Kim R. Holmes, and Mary Anastasia O'Grady, *2007 Index of Economic Freedom* (Washington, DC: Heritage Foundation, 2007); and James Gwartney and Robert Lawson, *Economic Freedom of the World: 2006 Annual Report* (Vancouver: Fraser Institute, 2007). A comparison of these surveys is provided by Steve H. Hanke and Stephen J. K. Walters, "Economic Freedom, Prosperity, and Equality: A Survey," *Cato Journal* 17, no. 2 (Fall 1997): 117–46. Hanke and Walters found that surveys focusing exclusively on eonomic freedom are highly correlated, whereas those that also focus on political freedoms and civil liberties have a somewhat lower correlation. They conclude that most economic freedom surveys are measuring the same thing, and that there is general agreeement about who has economic freedom and who does not.

43. See Report of the Secretary-General, *International Migration and Development* (New York: United Nations, 2006). Also see James Rogers, "Moscow 'to Cut Migrant Workers,'" BBC News Report, June 7, 2007.

44. Statistics are taken from *Atlas of Student Mobility* (New York: Institute of International Education, 2005).

45. Debra S. Van Ostal, Chad Evans, Rnadal Kempner, Dadid Attis, and Sam Leiken, *Where America Stands: Entrepreneurship Competitiveness Index* (Washington, DC: Council on Competitiveness, 2007).

46. *Income Mobility in the U.S. from 1996 to 2005* (Washington, DC: Department of the Treasury, 2007).

47. E.g., see Daniel Kimmage and Kathleen Ridolfo, *The War of Images and Ideas: How Sunni Insurgents in Iraq and the Supporters Worldwide Are Using the Media* (Washington, DC: Radio Free Europe / Radio Liberty, 2007); and Philip Kennicott, "Insurgents Muster Their Forces Online: Radio Free Europe Report Describes Iraq Fighters' New Media Versatility," *Washington Post*, June 26, 2007.

48. George S. Low and Ronald A. Fullerton provide a scholarly history of brand management in "Brands, Brand Management, and the Brand Manager System: A Critical-Historical Evaluation," *Journal of Marketing Research*, May 1994, 173–90. Also see David A. Aaker, *Managing Brand Equity* (New York: Free Press, 1991).

49. See the biography by Barry M. Horstman, "Neil McElroy: He Served at P&G, Pentagon," *Cincinnati Post*, July, 6, 1999.

50. Another P&G contribution to American culture under McElroy was, naturally enough, the soap opera, first on radio and later on television. Soap operas were sufficiently engaging to capture a listener's attention but not so complex that one had to follow them continuously. In short, it was the perfect entertainment for a homemaker doing housework—and listening to commercials designed to sell more soap. The soap opera has been translated into almost every culture, and is another example of American influence, which is to say soft power.

51. Griff Witte, "Branded for Life," *Washington Post*, January 23, 2005.

52. See Simon Anholt, "Nation-Brands of the Twenty-First Century," *Journal of Brand Management*, June 1998, 395–406, in which Anholt introduced the term "nation branding." Also see Lee Hudson Teslik, "Nation Branding Explained," Council on Foreign Relations Backgrounder, November 9, 2007, www.cfr.org/publication/14776/.

53. "The Best D-Schools for Creative Talent," *Business Week*, October 9, 2006.

54. See John Tagliabue, "In Europe, Going Global Means, Alas, English," *New York Times*, May 18, 2002; Joyce Howard Price, "World Speaks Our Language and Attends Our Colleges," *Washington Times*, December 29, 2004; and "Statement by Mr. Jose Antonio Ocampo, Under-Secretary-General of the United Nations for Economic and Social Affairs to the Electronic Media Forum," held in Tunis, November 15, 2005.

55. The predominance of any language also exerts influence by determining who can take part in public transactions and who cannot. But that is a mixed bag as far as power is concerned. E.g., because most websites are in English, almost all Americans can use them, and many foreigners cannot. Foreign English speakers are gently channeled to sites in which Americans can take part. But because Americans have fewer incentives to learn foreign languages, foreigners can more easily cut out Americans from transactions that have a limited audience but that can be very important; few than 1 percent of all websites use Arabic, but a disproportionate number of them are used to recruit and mobilize terrorists.

56. Richard Rose makes this argument; see his *Language, Soft Power, and Assymetrical Internet Commuication,* Research Report 7 (Oxford: Oxford Internet Institute, 2005).

57. Motion Picture Association of America, *U.S. Theatrical Market* (Washington, DC: Motion Picture Association of America, 2005).

58. Adjusted for inflation; the film was released in 1993, and, according to the Internet Moivie Database, cost at the time $110 million and grossed $250 million.

Chapter Four

1. These statistics were taken from U.S. Commerce Department, *Historical Statistics of the United States* (Washington, DC: U.S. Government Printing Office, 1975). The spikes in the data for the Civil War and Spanish-American War were taken from Al Nofi, "Statistical Summary: America's Major Wars," www.cwc.lsu.edu/ cwc/other/stats/warcost.htm. Nofi is cited and discussed at greater length by Carl Kaysen, Steven Miller, Martin Malin, William Nordhaus, and John Steinbruner, *War with Iraq: Costs, Consequences, and Alternatives* (Cambridge, MA: American Academy of Arts and Sciences, 2002).

2. See Scott Keeler, *Trends in Public Opinion about the War in Iraq 2003–2007* (Washington, DC: Pew Research Center for the People and the Press, 2007); and Jodie T. Allen, Nilanthi Samaranayake, and James Albrittain Jr., *Iraq and Vietnam: A Crucial Difference in Opinion* (Washington, DC: Pew Research Center for the People and the Press, 2007).

3. Notice the spike in resistance to defense spending in May 1999; Gallup happened to take its survey during NATO air strikes against Serbia, including the day a U.S. aircraft accidentally bombed the Chinese embassy in Belgrade. Also note that between 1961 and 1969, Gallup changed the question to ask whether its respondents supported U.S. participation in the Vietnam War. Gallup found roughly the same proportion of Americans in the late 1960s and early 1970s believed the "war in Vietnam was a mistake" (about 60 percent) as believed in early 2007 that using U.S. military force in Iraq was the "wrong decision" (about 54 percent).

4. E.g., see *Americans Favor Force in Iraq, Somalia, Sudan and . . .* (Washington, DC: Pew Research Center, 2002); and Gallup International Poll press release, www.gallup-international.com/download/GIA%20press%20release%20 Iraq% 20Survey%202003.pdf.

5. Eric Schmitt, "Pentagon Contradicts General on Iraq Occupation Force's Size," *New York Times,* February 28, 2003.

6. Donald H. Rumsfeld, Defense Department transcript of "Secretary Rumsfeld Media Availability with Afghan President Karzai," February 27, 2003.

7. See Bob Davis, "Bush Economic Aid Says the Cost of Iraq War May Top $100 Billion," *Wall Street Journal*, September 16, 2002.

8. Six months later, soon after Lindsey resigned, a reporter at a White House briefing asked Press Secretary Ari Fleisher to give an estimate of the war's costs. The reporter said, "The recently departed Larry Lindsey put forward an estimate back in December based on a percentage of GDP, which was in line with the spending on . . ." Fleischer quickly shot back, "Are you asking me to follow the example and be recently departed?" See "Press Briefing by Ari Fleischer," Office of the White House Press Secretary, Washington, February 26, 2003, www.whitehouse.gov/news/releases/2003/02/20030226–7.html.

9. Schmitt, "Pentagon Contradicts General."

10. James Fallows, "Blind into Baghdad," *The Atlantic*, January/February 2004.

11. Transcript of *The Newshour with Jim Lehrer*, broadcast April 16, 2006, www.pbs.org/newshour/bb/military/jan-june06/iraq_4–13.html.

12. The comments here from Brent Scowcroft are quoted from a 1996 interview he gave for the PBS series *Frontline*, www.pbs.org/wgbh/pages/frontline/gulf/oral/decision.html.

13. Vernon Loeb and Thomas E. Ricks, "Questions Raised about Invasion Force; Some Ex-Gulf War Commanders Say U.S. Needs More Troops, Another Armored Division," *Washington Post*, March 25, 2003.

14. Barry R. McCaffrey, "A Time to Fight," *Wall Street Journal*, April 1, 2003.

15. See Benjamin S. Lambeth, "Task Force Hawk," *Air Force Magazine*, February 2002, 78–83; and *Kosovo Air Operations: Army Resolving Lessons Learned Regarding the Apache Helicopter*, GAO-01–401 (Washington, D.C. U.S. General Accounting Office, 2001).

16. General Tommy Franks with Malcolm McConnell, *American Soldier* (New York: ReganBooks, 2004).

17. Michael Dobbs, "Old Strategy on Iraq Sparks New Debate," *Washington Post*, December 27, 2001; and Editorial, "Battle Plans for Iraq," *New York Times*, July 6, 2002.

18. Libby Quaid, "Powell Forces Rice to Defend Iraq Planning," AP News Report, April 30, 2006.

19. "Gen. William S. Wallace Reflects on Invasion of Iraq," TRADOC News Service (Fort Monroe, VA), March 14, 2006.

20. Michael R. Gordon and Bernard E. Trainor, *Cobra II: The Inside Story of the Invasion and Occupation of Iraq* (New York: Pantheon Books, 2006), 74–94.

21. Kevin M. Woods, with Michael R. Pease, Mark E. Stout, Williamson Murray, and James G. Lacey, *Iraqi Perspectives Project: A View of Operation Iraqi Freedom from Saddam's Senior Leadership*, Study by the Joint Center for Operational Analysis (Alexandria, VA: Institute for Defense Analysis, 2006), 149.

22. Several documents pertaining to the establishment of the Future of Iraq Project are available at the National Security Archive's website at www.gwu.edu/%7Ensarchiv/NSAEBB/NSAEBB163/. The project report, obtained under the Freedom of Information Act, is posted at the Memory Hole website at www.thememoryhole.org/state/future_of_iraq/.

23. Conrad C. Crane and W. Andrew Terrill, *Reconstructing Iraq: Insights, Challenges, and Missions for Military Forces in a Post-Conflict Scenario* (Carlyle, PA: U.S. Army War College Strategic Studies Institute, 2003).

24. It should also be noted that the planning assumptions included "Iraqi regime has WMD capability." U.S. military commanders, along with almost everyone else, believed Iraq did in fact have nuclear, chemical, or biological weapons, and planned their operation around this assumption.

25. The primary source for this section is briefing slides prepared by U.S. Central Command in August 2002 and obtained in declassified form by the National Security Archive under the Freedom of Information Act. A complete set and discussion is available from the archive's website at www.gwu.edu/~nsarchiv/NSAEBB/NSAEBB214/ index.htm#docs. Also see Michael R. Gordon, "The Struggle for Iraq; A Prewar Slide Show Cast Iraq in Rosy Hues," *New York Times*, February 15, 2007.

26. Crane and Terrill, *Reconstructing Iraq*, 33.

27. Philip H. Gordon and Michael E. O'Hanlon, "No Easy Victory," *Washington Post*, April 12, 2003.

28. See "Prepared Statement of Colonel Scott R. Feil (Ret.)," Senate Foreign Relations Committee, February 11, 2003. For an account of the Army History Center study, see Vernon Loeb, "100,000 Soldiers Needed to Rebuild Iraq after Invasion," *Washington Post*, September 23, 2002. For the Center for Strategic and Budgetary Assessments analysis, see Steven M. Kosiak, "Potential Cost of a War with Iraq and Its Post-War Occupation" (Washington, DC: Center for Strategic and Budgetary Assessments, 2003).

29. James Dobbins, John G. McGinn, Keith Crane, Seth G. Jones, Rollie Lal, Andrew Rathmell, Rachel M. Swanger, and Anga Timilsina, *America's Role in Nation Building: From Germany to Iraq* (Santa Monica, CA: RAND Corporation, 2003).

30. Gordon and Trainor, *Cobra II*.

31. Woods et al., *Iraqi Perspectives Project*, 97.

32. See the interviews with L. Paul Bremer III conducted on June 26 and August 18, 2006 for *Frontline*, www.pbs.org/wgbh/pages/frontline/yeariniraq/inter views/bremer.html#3.

33. See the Central Command briefing previously cited, www.gwu.edu/ ~nsarchiv/NSAEBB/NSAEBB214/index.htm#docs.

34. See L. Paul Bremer III, "How I Didn't Dismantle Iraq's Army," *New York Times*, September 6, 2007.

35. E.g., see Gordon and Trainor, *Cobra II*, chap. 8.

36. The Army is currently reorganizing itself into brigades, smaller units that can deploy more rapidly and flexibly than its traditional armored and mechanized infantry divisions. This is yielding a somewhat larger number of combat-ready soldiers. Also note that U.S. troops posted abroad in Europe and South Korea are not "deployed" but rather "stationed" at permanent bases that offer most of the support units would have in the United States. Finally, of the approximately 130,000 personnel deployed to Iraq, about 25,000 are Marines. None of these details affect the point being made here.

37. Statement of Douglas Holtz-Eakin before the House Armed Services Committee, "The Ability of the U.S. Military to Sustain an Occupation in Iraq," Congressional Budget Office, Washington, November 5, 2003.

38. To be precise, there were 15,286,197 in 2006. The data are from *Fiscal Year 2006 Annual Report to the Congress of the United States* (Arlington, VA: Selective Service System, 2006).

39. For a history of conscription, see George Q. Flynn, *Conscription and Democracy: The Draft in France, Great Britain, and the United States* (Westport, CT: Greenwood Press, 2001). For a history of the development of the All-Volunteer Force, see Bernard D. Rostker, *I Want You! The Evolution of the All-Volunteer Force*, RAND Monograph MG-265 (Santa Monica, CA: RAND Corporation, 2006).

40. See Merritt Roe Smith, *Harpers Ferry Armory and the New Technology* (Ithaca, NY: Cornell University Press, 1977); and David A. Hounshell, *From the American System to Mass Production, 1800–1932* (Baltimore: Johns Hopkins University Press, 1984). As in the case of many—if not most—inventions and inventors of the time, historians dispute Whitney's claim to inventing both the cotton gin and the so-called "American system" of mass production with standardized parts. Whitney's success may have mainly been in convincing Army officials to agree to the process and award him a contract, but that is often the hardest part of any military "invention."

41. For a comprehensive analysis of the experience the United States and other countries have had with a draft, see Bernard D. Rostker, *I Want You! The*

Evolution of the All-Volunteer Force (Santa Monica, CA: RAND Corporation, 2006).

42. HR 393, "Universal National Service Act of 2007," 110th Congress, 1st Session, introduced January 10, 2007.

43. See Max Boot, *The Savage Wars of Peace: Smal Wars and the Rise of American Power* (New York: Basic Books, 2003).

44. John Hackett, *The Third World War: August 1985* (New York: Macmillan, 1978); also see his sequel, *The Third World War: The Untold Story* (New York: Macmillan, 1982). For an example of the modeling used to assess force ratios on the Central Front, see Nora Slatkin, *Army Ground Force Modernization for the 1980s* (Washington, DC: Congressional Budget Office, 1982).

45. James T. Quinlivan, "Force Requirements in Stability Operations," *Parameters*, Winter 1995, 59–69.

46. Interview with Fox News, June 17, 2007.

47. See Charles Wolf, "Shareholders Don't Shoot Each Other," *Wall Street Journal*, November 23, 2005.

48. Department of Defense Directive 3000.05, "Military Support for Stability, Security, Transition, and Reconstruction (SSTR) Operations," November 28, 2005.

49. See Office of the Director of Central Intelligence, *Comprehensive Report of the Special Advisor to the DCI on Iraq's WMD* (Washington, DC: Office of the Director of Central Intelligence, 2004), "Key Findings."

50. Hashim Khan and Richard E. Randall, *Squash Racquets: The Khan Game* (Detroit: Wayne State University Press, 1967), 61.

51. The "cakewalk" comment is generally attributed to Kenneth Adelman; see his "Cakewalk in Iraq," *Washington Post*, February 13, 2002. For my views on the difficulty of a land invasion, see my piece, "Gulf War II? There's a Better Way," *Wall Street Journal*, February 5, 1998.

Chapter Five

1. For details of the planning by al-Qaeda leading up to the attacks on New York City and Washington, see 9/11 Commission, *The 9/11 Commission Report* (Washington, DC: U.S. Government Printing Office, 2004), chap. 5.

2. *Report of the Official Account of the Bombings in London on 7th July 2005* (London: Her Majesty's Stationery Office, 2006), 20–21.

3. See Grant T. Hammond, *The Mind of War: John Boyd and American Security* (Washington, DC: Smithsonian Books, 2001); Robert Coram, *Boyd:*

The Fighter Pilot Who Changed the Art of War (Boston: Little, Brown, 2002); and Bruce Berkowitz, *The New Face of War: How War Will Be Fought in the Twenty-First Century* (New York: Free Press, 2003).

4. 9/11 Commission, *The 9/11 Commission Report*, describes deliberations over how to attack bin Laden on pp. 189–91, and 210–14, including the considerations over the Predator that follow.

5. Kevin Woods, with Michael R. Pease, Mark E. Stout, Williamson Murray, and James G. Lacey, *Iraqi Perspective Project: A View of Operation Iraqi Freedom from Saddam's Senior Leadership: Study by the Joint Center for Operational Analysis* (Alexandria, VA: Institute for Defense Analysis, 2006).

6. For a study of Groves and his management style in the Manhatten Project, see Robert S. Norris, *Racing for the Bomb: General Leslie R. Groves and the Manhattan Project's Indispensible Man* (South Royalton, VT: Steerforth Press, 2002. Also see Leslie R. Groves, *Now It Can Be Told: The Story of the Manhattan Project* (New York: Harper, 1962).

7. Michael Warner, *The Office of Strategic Services: America's First Intelligence Agency* (Washington, DC: Central Intelligence Agency, 2000).

8. See, e.g., the text of Tenet's testimony to the 9/11 Commission, April 14, 2004.

9. See, e.g., John J. Hamre, "Reconstruction and Rehabilitation In Iraq," testimony before the Committee on Armed Services, U.S. House of Representatives, October 8, 2003. Hamre, who had been Deputy Secretary of Defense during Clinton's second term, had been part of a team sent by Rumsfeld to report on conditions.

10. "Toyota Trimming Auto-Development Time to 12 Months," Bloomberg News Service, September 17, 2005. Toyota is often cited as the model of speed; see the Massachusetts Institute of Technology study described by James P. Womak, Daniel Jones, and Daniel Roos, *The Machine That Changed the World* (New York: Rawson Associates, 1990).

11. See *DOD Personnel Clearances: Additional OMB Actions Are Needed to Improve the Security Clearance Process*, Report GAO 06–1070 (Washington, DC: U.S. Government Accountability Office, 2006).

12. C. Northcote Parkinson, *Parkinson's Law: The Pursuit of Progress* (London: John Murray, 1958).

13. The authoritative source on the U-2 project, on which this and subsequent sections are based, is Gregory W. Pedlow and Donald E. Welzenbach, *The CIA and the U-2 Program 1954–1974* (Washington, DC: History Staff, Center for the Study of Intelligence, Central Intelligence Agency, 1998). Also see Jonathan E. Lewis, *Spy Capitalism: Itek and the CIA* (New Haven, CT: Yale University Press, 2002).

14. For this and the sections about CIA operations in Afghanistan after September 11 that follow, see Gary C. Schroen, *First In: An Insider's Account of How the CIA Spearheaded the War on Terror in Afghanistan* (Novato, CA: Presidio Press, 2005); and Gary Berntsen and Ralph Pezzullo, *JAWBREAKER: The Attack on Bin Laden and al-Qaeda—A Personal Account by the CIA's Key Field Commander* (New York: Crown, 2005).

15. See Pedlow and Welzenbach, *CIA and the U-2 Program*, 15–16. For a scholarly account of how these authorities were established, see David M. Barrett, *The CIA and Congress: The Untold Story from Truman to Kennedy* (Lawrence: University Press of Kansas, 2005).

16. For the Explorer 1 program, see "They Shine in a Rocket's Bright Glare," *Time*, February 10, 1958; and Gordon Harris, *A New Command* (Plainfield, NJ: Logos International, 1976). Both are somewhat hyped accounts but give the basic outline of the story. The Explorer 1 satellite was simply an additional rocket stage mated to a Redstone and was such an obvious step that it could have been launched in 1956. According to some accounts, the Eisenhower administration wanted the Soviet Union to orbit the first satellite to establish the principle that one country could fly a satellite over another country's territory. To avoid reaching orbit, the Army thus tested the Explorer 1 configuration using a dummy upper stage. Some of these writers contrast the "military" Army program with the Navy's "scientific" Vanguard program, but this is a misreading of rocket geneology. The Vanguard was derived from the Viking research rocket, which the Naval Resarch Laboratory had developed as a replacement for the V-2 rockets it had obtained from Germany. The Viking set the form for all U.S. rockets—military and scientific—that followed, in that it had a separable payload, a cylindrical shape, tanks that were part of the rocket's structure, and a steerable engine. The Viking's contractor, Martin, went on to build the Titan intercontinental ballistic missile for the Air Force, and von Braun's Army team used many of the innovations of the Viking in its Redstone missile and, later, the Saturn family of launch vehicles. All these programs were interrelated, and led by aggressive, risk-taking, entrepreneurial project managers.

17. Grant Hammond provided materials on the Air Force ballistic missile program, which he has used in courses at the Air War University. Also see Stephen B. Johnson, *The United States Air Force and the Culture of Innovation 1945–1965* (Washington, DC: Air Force History and Museums Program, 2002); and Jacob Neufeld, *The Development of Ballistic Missiles in the United States Air Force 1945–1960* (Washington, DC: Office of Air Force History, 1990).

18. See Donald M. Horan and Bruce Berkowitz, "The Clementine Lunar Mission," in *Reducing Space Mission Cost*, ed. J. Wertz and W. J. Larson (Torrance, CA: Space Technology Library, 1996); and Bruce Berkowitz, "The

Clementine Mission," *Technology Review*, April 1995, 24–31. To be sure, some of the space missions planned under the rubric "faster, cheaper, better" did not turn out well. For example, NASA's Lewis satellite failed in 1997 because the program did not fund enough staff to monitor the spacecraft continuously when it first entered orbit—which experienced space operators know is the trickiest, riskiest phase of most missions. When the satellite began spinning, no one was available to correct the problem. Lewis's solar cells had not charged the satellite's batteries. By the time the crew returned, the satellite had died, unable to receive commands. The moral is that simple-minded risk taking can be as costly as trying to eliminate all risks.

19. See Henry A. Crumpton, "Intelligence and War; Afghanistan 2001–2002," in *Transforming U.S. Intelligence*, ed. Jennifer E. Sims and Burton Gerber (Washington, DC: Georgetown University Press, 2005), 162–79; the quotation is on 163. Also see Schroen's references to "Hank C" in *First In*; 93–94. Bernsten and Pezzullo also refer to "Hank" and his willingness to take risks; see *JAWBREAKER*, 63, and elsewhere in their book. George Tenet and Bill Harlow cite Crumpton as the head of the Counterterrorism Center's Special Operations Branch, established for the campaign to fight al-Qaeda in Afghanistan; see their *At the Center of the Storm: My Years at the CIA* (New York: HarperCollins, 2007), 211–21.

20. Bernsten and Pezzullo, *JAWBREAKER*, 124.

21. Whether King actually said this is in dispute. It was widely reported during World War II; see, e.g., the review of his memoirs, "Old Crustacean," *Time*, November 24, 1952. According to other sources, King once said that he did not coin the phrase but would have if he thought of it. It is more significant that people automatically associate the comment with King, who was universally known as an SOB and relished the reputation.

22. Albert Weimorts died in December 2005. For the highlights of his career, see the obituary by Douglas Martin, "Albert Weimorts: Designer of 'Bunker Buster,'" *New York Times*, December 25, 2005. Parts of this section are based on a paper by Carlo Kopp, "The GBU-28 Bunker Buster," January 24, 2002, which, in turn, was based mainly on a paper disseminated by Barry Barlow, "The GBU-28 February 1991," May 1996. Additional material was provided by the Public Affairs Office at Eglin Air Force Base.

23. For details of Wallis's remarkable career, see J. E. Morpurgo, *Barnes Wallis: A Biography* (New York: St. Martin's Press, 1972).

24. The quotations are from Bill Kaczor, "'Bunker-bustrers' Also Like Caves, Says Eglin Bomb Expert," Associated Press, November 23, 2001.

25. "How TTR Helped the Air Force Ready a New Bomb," *Sandia Lab News*, July 26, 1991.

26. Anthony Downs, *Inside Bureaucracy* (New York: Scott Foresman, 1967).

27. Giles K. Smith, Hyman L. Schulman, and Robert S. Leonard, *Application of F-117 Acquisition Strategy to Other Program in the New Acquisition Environment* (Santa Monica, CA: RAND Corporation, 1996). For a comprehensive history of the F-117 program and its management, see David C. Aronstein and Albert C. Piccirillo, *Have Blue and the F-117A: Evolution of the "Stealth Fighter"* (Reston, VA: American Institute of Aeronautics and Astronautics, 1997).

28. See Smith, Schulman, and Leonard, *Application of F-117 Acquisition Strategy*, and Aronstein and Piccirillo, *Have Blue and the F-117A*, for a discussion of the impact of security regulations on the F-117A delivery schedule. For a discussion of how the specialized nature of the F-117A isolated it from mainstream Air Force planning, see Bill Sweetman, "Unconventional Weapon," *Air & Space / Smithsonian*, December 2007–January 2008, 42–51.

Chapter Six

1. For a history of the executive branch offices and the Eisenhower Building, see Elsa M. Santoyo, Paula Mohr, and Mary. F. Bellor, eds., *Creating an American Masterpiece: Architectural Drawings of the Old Executive Office Building, 1871–1888* (Washington, DC: American Architectural Foundation, 1988). Also see the official histories provide at the White House web site, www.white house.gov/history/eeobtour/. Drawings of the first Executive Offices do not provide dimensions, but they generally resemble gentry houses of the Virginia-Maryland region, like Gunston Hall, which provided 2,000 to 4,000 square feet. See Mark R. Wenger, "The Central Passage in Virginia: Evolution of an Eighteenth-Century Living Space," *Perspectives in Vernacular Architecture* 2 (1986): 137–49.

2. See Tom Wheeler, *Mr. Lincoln's T-Mails: The Untold Story of How Abraham Lincoln Used the Telegraph to Win the Civil War* (New York: Collins, 2006).

3. Main Navy and its neighbor, the Munitions Building, were temporary in the sense that they stood for only fifty-two years. After outlasting nine administrations, President Nixon gave the Navy a direct order to vacate, and the structure was finally reduced to rubble in 1970. William Safire recounted the epic struggle in *Before the Fall: An Inside View of the Pre-Watergate White House* (New York: Doubleday, 1975), 250–62.

4. See Steve Vogel, *The Pentagon: A History* (New York: Random House, 2007).

5. See Siobhan Gorman, "Nation's Spy Chief Loads the Moving Van . . . Again," *Baltimore Sun*, November 19, 2007. An Office of the Director of National Intelligence spokesperson later provided part of an official announcement, which stated that the move would consolidate activities then being carried out in CIA and Defense Intelligence Agency facilities, and suggested that the organization might be relocated after a review of available office space. See Shaun Waterman, "DNI Moves Again to Liberty Crossing in '08," UPI, November 21, 2007.

6. See Bob Woodward, *State of Denial: Bush at War, Part III* (New York: Simon & Schuster, 2006). Also see Woodward's account in "Should He Stay?" *Washington Post*, October 2, 2006.

7. U.S.C. 402, Sec. 101, National Security Act of 1947, as amended.

8. Cabinet officers, by tradition, because the Senate confirms them, and because they are, as noted, the chief executive officers of large organizations, have enjoyed a special status in protocol. Certainly Cabinet officers themselves seem to think they deserve special status. But keep in mind that this is just tradition and custom, not law. The Constitution as drafted only said the Senate had the prerogative of "advise and consent" on key appointments, without specifying what those might be. The Cabinet itself was not even mentioned in the Constitution until 1967, with the passage of the Twenty-Fifth Amendment, and that amendment was only intended to clarify the order of Presidential succession. Even then, the Twenty-Fifth Amendment refers to "principal officers," not the Cabinet per se.

9. It is important to note that Scowcroft was deputy to Henry Kissinger when Kissinger was National Security Adviser under Presidents Nixon and Ford, and many of the basic procedures that the Tower Commission used as a reference point were established then. Most studies of the National Security Council and its operation begin with the 1987 report of the President's Special Review Board, better known as the Tower Commission, the first official examination of the NSC and its operation since its establishment. See *Report of the President's Special Review Board* (Washington, DC: U.S. Government Printing Office, 1987). Since then, two scholars have published books on the subject: John Prados, *Keepers of the Keys: A History of the National Security Council from Truman to Bush* (New York: William Morrow, 1991); and David Rothkopf, *Running the World: The Inside Story of the National Security Council and the Architects of American Power* (New York: PublicAffairs, 2005). In addition, the independent counsel investigating the Iran-Contra affair published his report. It did not analyze the operation of the NSC, but it documents and supplements many of the events in the Tower Commission report. See Lawrence E. Walsh, *Final Report*

of the Independent Counsel for Iran/Contra Matters (Washington, DC: U.S. Court of Appeals for the District of Columbia Circuit, 1993).

10. See *The Tower Commission Report: The Full Text of the President's Special Review Board* (New York: Times Books, 1987), 62–79; the quotation is on 62.

11. George Bush and Brent Scowcroft, *A World Transformed* (New York: Alfred A. Knopf, 1998), 30–31.

12. Barton Gellman and Jo Becker, "A Different Understanding with the President," *Washington Post*, June 24, 2007.

13. Bob Woodward, "The World According to Rummy," *Washington Post*, October 8, 2006. After leaving office, Rumsfeld put his views on the record; e.g., in one op-ed he wrote: "But with the passage of more than half a century, the end of the Cold War, the attacks of 9/11 and the rise of an Islamic extremist movement that hopes to use terrorism and weapons of mass destruction to alter the course of humankind, it has become obvious that the national security institutions of the industrial age urgently need to be adapted to meet the challenges of this century and the information age. . . . At home, the entrenched bureaucracies and diffuse legislative processes of the U.S. government make it hard to creatively, swiftly and proactively handle security threats. Turf-conscious subcommittees in Congress inhibit the country's ability to mobilize government agencies to tackle new challenges. For example, U.S. efforts to build up the police and military capacity of partner nations such as Afghanistan, Iraq and Pakistan to fight al-Qaeda and other extremists have been thwarted over the past six-plus years by compartmentalized budgets, outdated restrictions and budget cycles that force a nation at war to spend three years to develop, approve and execute a program." See Donald Rumsfeld, "The Smart Way to Beat Tyrants Like Chavez," *Washington Post*, December 2, 2007.

14. See the report to the Joint Chiefs by the Special Operations Review Group, August 23, 1980, also known as the "Holloway Report," after its chairman, retired admiral James Holloway.

15. See Gordon Lederman, *Reorganizing the Joint Chiefs of Staff: The Goldwater-Nichols Act of 1986* (Westport, CT: Greenwood Press, 1999); and James R. Locher III, *Victory on the Potomac: The Goldwater-Nichols Act Unifies the Pentagon* (College Station: Texas A&M University Press, 2002). For recent assessments of the effectiveness of Goldwater-Nichols, and how it might be improved and applied in other contexts, see Clark A. Murdock, Michèle A. Flournoy, Christopher A. Williams, and Kurt M. Campbell, *Beyond Goldwater-Nichols: Defense Reform for a New Strategic Era*, Phase 1 Report (Washington, DC: Center for Strategic and International Studies, 2004). Also see Clark A. Murdock and Richard W. Weitz, "Beyond Goldwater-Nichols: New Proposals

for Defense Reform," *Joint Forces Quarterly*, issue 38 (Third Quarter, 2005): 34–41.

16. See, e.g., the report by the Investigations Subcommittee of the Committee on Armed Services, U.S. House of Representatives, *Adequacy of U.S. Marine Corps Security in Beirut* (Washington, DC: U.S. Government Printing Office, 1983), 43.

17. The other set of reforms under Goldwater-Nichols, which were aimed at improving military acquisition, were less effective, partly because they created too much bureaucracy and paperwork. Also, where competition in the chain of command is usually bad, competition in the development of weapons is often good. Trying to eliminate what looks like waste often creates more problems than it solves. Conversely, Goldwater-Nichols also included reforms that ensured the services' systems could all work together — "interoperability" — and this was a significant improvement.

18. See Martin J. Gorman and Alexander Krongard, "A Goldwater-Nichols Act for the U.S. Government: Institutionalizing the Interagency Process," *Joint Force Quarterly*, issue 39 (Fourth Quarter, 2005): 51–58; and Bruce Berkowitz and Kori Schake, "National Security: A Better Approach," *Hoover Digest*, Winter 2005–6, 58–65.

INDEX

Abu Ghraib prison images, 20–21, 235*n*8
Achenwald, Gottfried, 61
Adams, Charles, 241*n*2
Adams, Eddie, 21
Adelman, Kenneth, 260*n*51
adversaries with staying power, 4–14
Afghanistan: allies in, 161, 175–76; and al-Qaeda, 175–76, 227; CIA role in, 193, 196–97, 262*n*14, 263*n*19; direct action raids by special operations forces in, 227; occupation troops in, 155; removal of troops from to fight in Iraq, 175–76; and suicide bombers, 28
Africa: and climate change, 51; demographic changes in, 16; and WTO farm subsidies, 229. *See also specific countries*
age of population in fastest-growing countries, 52
agility, 179–205; of al-Qaeda's planning of September 11, 2001 attacks, 179–80; and decision cycle, 181; in earlier U.S. history, 183–88; examples of, 191–203; need for, 4, 15, 225; and reasons for slow response, 190–91; and size of staff, 204; and

staffing up, 188–90; as valued trait, 205; ways to increase, 203–5
Airbus, 187
Air Force, U.S.: development time for aircraft, 184, 185*f*, 186–87, 192; development time for GBU-28 bomb, 192, 197–200; Predator aircraft, 181–82; on Russian long-range bombers, 250*n*15
Albright, David, 236*n*14
Algeria, 33
al-Jazeera, 8
al-Qaeda: in Afghanistan, 175–76, 227; agility of, 179–80; brand recognition of, 122–24; compared to Soviets in Cold War, 7–8, 225; in Iraq, 123–24; London terrorist bombings (2005), 180–81; morale and public support for, 7–8; strength and capability of, 107; telecommunications methods of, 8, 23, 234*n*6, 236*n*10
America Against the World: How We Are Different and Why We Are Disliked (Kohut & Stokes), 119
American edge, 93–132; brands as measure of power, 122–32; cultural dimension of, 95, 118–22;

269

Eisenhower, Dwight, 126, 138, 184, 212, 262*n*16
elections and defense spending, 138–39
The End of the American Era (Kupchan), 69
endurance, need for, 15. *See also* pacing and constraints
energy, 13, 112, 173–74, 228. *See also* greenhouse gases (GHGs)
English language and cultural influence, 129–30, 255*n*55
enlargement doctrine of Clinton administration, 173
entrepreneurship, 83, 85
environmentalist causes, 3
Espinasse, Isaac, 245*n*36
ethics of choices facing the U.S., 230
ethnic conflicts, 3, 170, 172
Europe: attitude toward Muslims in, 8, 34; breakup of colonial empires, 35, 38; commuting distance in, 48; demographic changes in, 16; design schools in, 129; and nuclear development, 25; and travel to other countries, 98, 249*n*6. *See also* European Union
European Union: carbon emission shares produced by, 45*f*, 47*f*, 48, 240*n*30; and climate change, 41–42; constitution, 36; economic share of, 109*f*, 110; military expenditures of, 104, 104*f*, 105; population decline in, 48*t*, 49; and population growth, 49; reduction of greenhouse gases in, 51–52; in WTO, 229
executive offices in D.C., 207–9, 264*n*1

expected value, 81–83
Explorer I satellite, 192, 194, 195, 262*n*16

F-117A, 192, 201, 202–3, 205, 264*n*28
Fadayyen Saddam, 150
failed states, 2
fall of Soviet Union, 3, 12, 35, 36, 38–39, 91
farm subsidies, 229
Feil, Scott, 153
Feith, Douglas, 188
Fermat, Pierre de, 81
Field, George, 238*n*23
Finland, 114
Fleisher, Ari, 257*n*8
foreign direct investment in U.S., 119
former Soviet Union: carbon emission shares produced by, 45*f*, 46, 47*f*. *See also specific states*
France: alliance of Britain and Russia proposed to contain France (1813), 85–86; attitude toward U.S., 127; comparative advantage of, 78; counterfeit French currency produced by Playfair, 72–73, 245*n*36; educational expenditures in, 251*n*19; index of national power (1816–2001), 90, 92*f*; Jacobinism after French Revolution, 72; military budget of, 104, 104*f*, 106–7; military capability of, 106, 107; military draft in, 163–64, 165; Muslim subcultures in, 34; as naval threat to Britain in 1600s, 58–60; reduction of greenhouse gases in, 51–52; rejection of EU proposed constitution (May 2005), 36; students from abroad in, 121. *See also* European Union

92f; military expenditures of, 104,
104f; military strength of, 100;
movie making in, 128; political
policy of, 228; population growth
in, 48t, 95, 228
Indonesia, 112, 227, 228
Industrial Revolution, 164
influence. *See* soft power
information technology (IT), evolution of, 16, 17–22, 231; ease of
reproduction and distribution,
20–22; and military trends, 22–23
*An Inquiry into the Permanent Causes
of the Decline and Fall of Powerful
and Wealthy Nations* (Playfair), 73,
74f, 75, 76, 78, 84, 85, 90
insular nature of Americans, 98
Intel, 20, 187, 235n4
intellectual property issues in China,
229
Intelligence Reform and Terrorism
Prevention Act of 2004, 180, 209,
221
Interbrand Corp., 126
intercontinental ballistic missiles
(ICBMs), development of, 192
International Climate Change Panel
(ICCP), 239nn27–28
international crime, 3
International Institute for Strategic
Studies (IISS), 100, 101f
international relations: scholars'
failure to focus on demographics,
87–88; studies combining theoretical models and statistics, 85–86,
247n52
Internet: al-Qaeda use of websites and
e-mail, 8, 234n6, 236n10; conveying
different message than official one

over, 130–31; global connectivity
of, 19; and military planning, 23
inventions by immigrants to U.S., 114
investment and business environment,
worldwide comparison, 119–20
Iran: as arm's-length ally of U.S.
against al-Qaeda, 176; and
Hezbollah, 175; and nuclear development, 25; population size as
making occupation unreasonable,
168
Iran-Contra affair (1980s), 212–13,
265n9
Iranian hostage crisis (1979–1981),
216
Iraq: Clinton policy toward, 173; as
major threat to U.S. (1997 to
present), 4, 5f; no-fly zones over,
173, 227; Oil for Food Program in,
173–74; oil rights in, 171; reconstruction and unclear U.S. chain of
command, 219; sanctions against,
174; sectarian divisions and
violence in, 35, 38–39, 171, 177;
and terrorists, 123–24; tribal organizations in, 33; and weapons of
mass destruction, 25, 26, 176, 177,
236nn13–14, 258n24. *See also*
Desert Storm; Saddam Hussein
Iraqi Perspectives Project, 150, 156
Iraqi Survey Group report after war,
174
Iraq War: and Abu Ghraib prison
images, 20–21, 235n8; bombs to
destroy deep command bunkers,
192, 197–98; compared to Gulf
War (1991), 156, 160; comparison
of occupation to WWII occupations, 156–57; cost of, 138, 143–46,